Sven Danø

Nonlinear and Dynamic Programming

An Introduction

Springer-Verlag
Wien New York

Prof. Dr. Sven Danø
Professor of Managerial Economics
University of Copenhagen

With 36 Figures

Library of Congress Cataloging in Publication Data. Danø, Sven. Nonlinear and dynamic programming. Bibliography: p. 1. Nonlinear programming. 2. Dynamic programming. I. Title. T57.8.D36. 519.7'6. 75-6503

ISBN 978-3-211-81289-1 ISBN 978-3-7091-8394-6 (eBook)
DOI 10.1007/978-3-7091-8394-6

Preface

This book is intended to provide an introductory text of Nonlinear and Dynamic Programming for students of managerial economics and operations research. The author also hopes that engineers, business executives, managers, and others responsible for planning of industrial operations may find it useful as a guide to the problems and methods treated, with a view to practical applications.

The book may be considered as a sequel to the author's *Linear Programming in Industry* (1960, 4th revised and enlarged edition 1974), but it can be used independently by readers familiar with the elements of linear programming models and techniques. The two volumes constitute an introduction to the methods of mathematical programming and their application to industrial optimization problems. The author feels that the vast and ever-increasing literature on mathematical programming has not rendered an introductory exposition superfluous. The general student often tends to feel somewhat lost if he goes straight to the special literature; he will be better equipped for tackling real problems and using computer systems if he has acquired some previous training in constructing small-scale programming models and applying standard algorithms for solving them by hand. The book is intended to provide this kind of training, keeping the mathematics at the necessary minimum.

The text contains numerous exercises. The reader should work out these problems for himself and check with the answers given at the end of the book.

The text is based on lectures given at the University of Copenhagen. Students who have been exposed to earlier mimeographed versions have suggested improvements for which I am grateful. Chapter IV on quadratic programming is a revised version of an article in *Erhvervsøkonomisk Tidsskrift*, 1966.

Copenhagen, January, 1975

Sven Danø

Contents

I. Linear and Nonlinear Programming

1. Any problem of *linear programming* can be formulated as the maximization of a linear function subject to side conditions in the form of linear inequalities and to sign restrictions (nonnegativity requirements),

$$\begin{aligned} f = c_1 x_1 + c_2 x_2 + \ldots + c_n x_n &= \text{maximum} \\ a_{i1} x_1 + a_{i2} x_2 + \ldots + a_{in} x_n &\leqslant b_i \qquad (i = 1, 2, \ldots, m) \\ x_j &\geqslant 0 \qquad (j = 1, 2, \ldots, n). \end{aligned} \tag{1}$$

If the linear preference function (objective function) f is to be minimized, this is equivalent to maximizing $g = -f$. Similarly, inequalities of the type $\geqslant$ can be written in the standard form (1) by multiplying by -1; and a side condition in equality form ($=$) is equivalent to a pair of inequalities, $\geqslant$ and $\leqslant$. Conversely, the side conditions of (1) can be transformed into equations by introducing nonnegative slack variables x_i',

$$a_{i1} x_1 + a_{i2} x_2 + \ldots + a_{in} x_n + x_i' = b_i, \qquad x_i' \geqslant 0,$$

as we do when the problem is to be solved numerically, e.g. by the simplex method.

As an example, consider the following problem of production planning. A manufacturing plant produces two commodities in quantities x_1 and x_2 units per period, using two machine inputs and two current (or variable) inputs, labour and raw material. Input requirements per unit of output, a_{ij}, are given in the following table together with input prices q_i and the selling prices of the two products, p_1 and p_2.

a_{ij}		Product no. $j =$ 1	2	Price (q_i)	Capacity (b_i)	
Input	1	1.0	1.0	—	≤ 5	(machine A)
no.	2	1.0	2.0	—	≤ 8	(machine B)
$i =$	3	0.3	0.1	10	—	(labour)
	4	1.0	2.0	1	—	(raw material)
Price (p_j)		8	9			

Machine inputs are measured in machine hours and so are the capacities, the two machines being available up to 5 and 8 hours per period. Since the costs of using the machines are independent of the degree of capacity utilization, no prices are associated with machine hours used.

With these data, gross profit per unit of each product (selling price minus costs of current inputs) will be a constant,

$$c_1 = p_1 - q_3 a_{31} - q_4 a_{41} = 4$$
$$c_2 = p_2 - q_3 a_{32} - q_4 a_{42} = 6,$$

and total profit f is a linear function which is to be maximized subject to two linear capacity restrictions and to nonnegativity requirements:

$$\begin{aligned} f = 4x_1 + 6x_2 &= \max \\ 1x_1 + 1x_2 &\leqslant 5 \\ 1x_1 + 2x_2 &\leqslant 8 \\ x_1, x_2 &\geqslant 0. \end{aligned} \tag{2}$$

This linear programming problem is shown geometrically in Fig. 1 a[1].

2. Clearly the linearity of the optimization problem depends on the constancy of the prices p_j and q_i and of the technological input-output coefficients a_{ij}.

If the structure of the market is such that the selling prices p_j depend on the quantities to be sold,

$$p_j = p_j(x_j) \quad (j = 1,2) \text{ or, more generally,}$$
$$p_j = p_j(x_1, x_2),$$

the c_j will be functions of the x_j and the preference function f will no longer be linear. Input prices depending on the quantities v_i of labour or raw material to be purchased,

$$q_i = q_i(v_i) \text{ where } v_i = a_{i1}x_1 + a_{i2}x_2 \quad (i = 3,4),$$

will have a similar effect.

Nonlinearities in the technology will destroy the linearity of the preference function if the labour and material coefficients are functions of the level of output,

$$a_{ij} = a_{ij}(x_j) \qquad (i = 3,4);$$

and if the machine time coefficients a_{ij} $(i = 1, 2)$ are no longer constant the linearity of the capacity restrictions goes by the board too[2].

[1] The optimal solution is $x_1 = 2$, $x_2 = 3$; $f = 26$.

[2] A linear technology requires the a_{ij} to be independent of x_j ("homogeneity") as well as of x_k, $k \neq j$ (additivity).

Assume, for example, that instead of $p_1 = 8$, $p_2 = 9$ we have

$$p_1 = 12 - 1x_1, \qquad p_2 = 13 - 2x_2,$$

everything else being as shown in the table above. This leads to unit profits which are functions of the amount produced,

$$c_1(x_1) = 12 - 1x_1 - 4 = 8 - 1x_1$$
$$c_2(x_2) = 13 - 2x_2 - 3 = 10 - 2x_2,$$

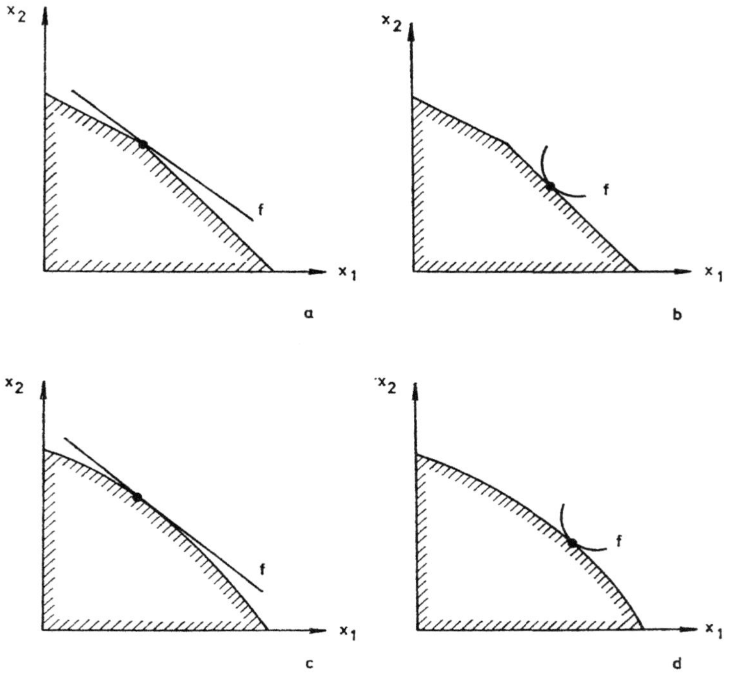

Fig. 1a—d

so that we have a *nonlinear programming* problem[1]

$$\begin{aligned} f = 8x_1 - 1x_1^2 + 10x_2 - 2x_2^2 &= \max \\ 1x_1 + 1x_2 &\leqslant 5 \\ 1x_1 + 2x_2 &\leqslant 8 \\ x_1, x_2 &\geqslant 0. \end{aligned} \tag{3}$$

As another example of nonlinear programming, let all prices p_j

[1] More particularly, a problem of "quadratic programming"; cf. Ch. IV.

and q_i as well as the a_{ij} for $i = 3, 4$ take the values given in the table, but replace the linear capacity restrictions by a nonlinear (quadratic) inequality:

$$\begin{aligned} f = 4x_1 + 6x_2 &= \max \\ x_2 &\leqslant 4 - 0.3x_1 - 0.1x_1^2 \\ x_1, x_2 &\geqslant 0. \end{aligned} \tag{4}$$

Problems (3)–(4) are illustrated in Fig. 1 b–c. Fig. 1 d shows a problem combining the nonlinear preference function of (3) with the nonlinear side condition of (4).

The four problems are examples of *mathematical programming.* Any problem of mathematical programming (MP) can be written in the form

$$\begin{aligned} f = f(x_1, x_2, \ldots, x_n) &= \text{maximum} \\ g_i(x_1, x_2, \ldots, x_n) &\geqslant 0 \qquad (i = 1, 2, \ldots, m) \\ x_j &\geqslant 0 \qquad (j = 1, 2, \ldots, n), \end{aligned} \tag{5}$$

that is, as the maximization of some function subject to inequality restrictions and nonnegativity requirements. When all of the functions f and g_i are linear, we have the special case of linear programming (LP), cf. Fig. 1 a and (1)[1]; when f and/or some or all of the g_i are nonlinear, we have a problem of nonlinear programming (NLP), cf. Fig. 1 b–d.

---

[1] With $g_i = b_i - a_{i1}x_1 - a_{i2}x_2 - \ldots - a_{in}x_n$.

II. Elements of the Mathematical Theory of Nonlinear Programming

A. Constrained Optimization

1. In general terms, an *optimization* problem consists in selecting from among a set of feasible alternatives one which is optimal according to a given criterion of optimality. Economic problems are typically of this nature since economics—theory as well as practical applications e.g. to industrial planning problems—is largely about optimal allocation of given or scarce resources. The first stage of a rational procedure for solving a problem of economic optimization is to determine the set of alternatives to choose from, *the feasible region*; the next stage is to establish a criterion of economic optimality in the form of a *preference function* (objective function). The optimal allocation can then be determined by comparing the values of the preference function associated with the feasible alternatives, the optimal allocation being that alternative for which the preference function is a *maximum* (or minimum).

When the number of alternatives constituting the feasible region is *finite*, the optimal solution can in principle be determined by *enumeration*, i.e., by listing the alternatives and comparing them on the basis of the optimality criterion. This may be a workable procedure when it is clear what the alternatives are. For example, if a company is to choose between a number of mutually exclusive investment projects, using maximum net present value as a criterion, the obvious procedure is to estimate the net present value C_j of each project ($j = 1, 2, \ldots$) and select the project with the largest C_j. Similarly, the problem of determining the shortest route from a point P to another point Q through a network of roads can be solved by enumerating the various feasible routes (chains of road segments) and comparing their lengths.

In cases where the number of feasible alternatives is large (though still finite), solution by enumeration may be impracticable because it is difficult to enumerate the set of alternatives. This will be the case if the feasible region is generated by some combinatorial mechanism. In the shortest-route problem, for example, the network may be too complex for complete enumeration of all possible chains of road segments. Another example is the "scheduling" problem of determining the order in which a number of jobs are to be processed on each of a number of machines such that total flow time is minimized[1]; even for comparatively small numbers of jobs and machines the number of combinations will be enormous. In such cases special methods will have to be resorted to, such as dynamic programming (for solution of the shortest-route problem)[2] or the various algorithms developed for solving scheduling problems.

A wide variety of optimization problems, however, are characterized by an *infinite* number of alternatives to choose from, because the feasible region is defined by a number of constraints (equations and/or inequalities) imposed on the variables of the problem. Each alternative is represented by a particular solution to the system of constraints and the optimization problem can be formulated as *the maximization* (or minimization) *of the preference function subject to the constraints.* Linear and nonlinear programming problems belong to this class of optimization problems (*"constrained maximization"*).

2. Consider first the following problem

$$\left.\begin{array}{l} f = f(x_1, x_2, \ldots, x_n) = \max \\ \text{subject to} \\ g_i(x_1, x_2, \ldots, x_n) = 0 \qquad (i = 1, 2, \ldots, m;\ m < n) \end{array}\right\} \quad (1)$$

where the system of side conditions—the constraints $g_i = 0$—define the feasible region. The functions f and g_i are assumed to be differentiable.

In principle, (1) can always be reduced to the maximization of a function of $n—m$ independent variables, *eliminating m dependent variables* from the preference function by means of the side conditions and setting the partial derivatives equal to zero. The resulting $n—m$ optimality conditions determine the $n—m$ independent variables; substituting into the side conditions we have m equations which can be solved for the m dependent variables. The same procedure applies to minimization problems.

Example 1:

$$c = 2v_1 + 3v_2 = \min$$

$$v_1 \cdot v_2 = 6,$$

which can be interpreted as a cost minimization problem: the side condition states that 6 units of some product can be produced with any

[1] Cf. S. Danø (1974), pp. 51ff.

[2] Cf. below, Ch. VI. A.

combination of two inputs (v_1 and v_2) satisfying the equation; 2 and 3 are the prices per unit of the inputs. We choose to eliminate v_2:

$$v_2 = 6/v_1, \quad c = 2v_1 + 18/v_1 = \min$$

$$\frac{dc}{dv_1} = 2 - 18/v_1^2 = 0 \Rightarrow v_1 = 3, \quad v_2 = 2; \quad c = 12.$$

In the more general case where the number of variables is large the procedure of elimination is less easy to handle, particularly when the functions g_i do not immediately give m variables as explicit functions of the other $n-m$ variables, and some other method must be resorted to. A simple procedure is provided by the classical *method of undetermined multipliers*, due to *Lagrange*.

Form the *Lagrangian* expression

$$L = f(x_1, x_2, \ldots, x_n) + \sum_{i=1}^{m} u_i \cdot g_i(x_1, x_2, \ldots, x_n) \tag{2}$$

where the multipliers u_i are provisionally undetermined constants. Then the constrained maximization problem (1) can be shown to be equivalent to that of finding an unconstrained maximum of L, treating $x_1, x_2, \ldots, x_n$ as independent variables. Necessary conditions for a maximum of L with respect to the x_j are

$$\frac{\partial L}{\partial x_j} = \frac{\partial f}{\partial x_j} + \sum_{i=1}^{m} u_i \cdot \frac{\partial g_i}{\partial x_j} = 0 \qquad (j = 1, 2, \ldots, n)$$

which together with the side conditions

$$\left(\frac{\partial L}{\partial u_i} =\right) \; g_i(x_1, x_2, \ldots, x_n) = 0 \qquad (i = 1, 2, \ldots, m)$$

determine the x_j and the u_i. If we are not interested in the values of the u_i we can eliminate them so that we are left with n equations in the x_j; the latter system of equations is easily shown to be identical with the set of necessary maximum conditions obtained if f is reduced to a function of $n-m$ independent variables[1]. The Lagrangian procedure applies equally to minimization problems.

Applying the method to *example 1* above, write the constraint

$$g(v_1, v_2) = 6 - v_1 v_2 = 0$$

to get the Lagrangian

$$L = 2v_1 + 3v_2 + u \cdot (6 - v_1 v_2).$$

[1] Note that since the solution satisfies $g_i = 0$, we have $L = f^{\max}$ in the optimum.

The minimum conditions are

$$\left.\begin{aligned} 2 - u\,v_2 &= 0 \\ 3 - u\,v_1 &= 0 \end{aligned}\right\} \Rightarrow u = 2/v_2 = 3/v_1$$

which with the side condition give the solution $v_1 = 3$, $v_2 = 2$, $u = 1$; $c = 12$.

3. The applicability of these "classical" methods of constrained optimization is subject to the limitation that they fail to deal with *inequalities*. This is serious because most economic optimization problems contain restrictions in inequality form.

In the first place, economic variables are generally defined over the nonnegative region because negative values of the variables do not make sense (e.g. negative production of a commodity). This means that *nonnegativity requirements* will have to be imposed on the variables, $x_j \geqslant 0$. There is nothing in the methods to guarantee that these requirements are automatically satisfied. Of course we can always try to apply the classical methods, provisionally disregarding the sign restrictions, and hope for the best. If the solution happens to respect them, all is well; if it does not, the maximum solution is not feasible, being devoid of economic meaning, and some other method has to be resorted to.

In the second place, some or all of the side conditions may have the form of *structural inequalities* rather than equations, so that we have $g_i\,(x_1, x_2, \ldots, x_n) \geqslant 0$. For example, capacity restrictions will generally be inequalities. Again, we can always solve the problem without paying explicit attention to the inequalities; but if it turns out that the solution does not respect them we are back again where we started. Another approach is to transform the inequalities into equations by introducing slack variables x_i' so that we get equality constraints of the form $g_i\,(x_1, x_2, \ldots, x_n) - x_i' = 0$; however, in order to ensure that the inequality $g_i' \geqslant 0$ is not reversed, x_i' must be required to be nonnegative so that one inequality has been replaced by another.

Optimization problems of this nature—maximization or minimization of a preference function subject to inequality restrictions—are called *mathematical programming* (MP) problems. The general MP problem can be written as follows:

$$\left.\begin{aligned} f = \; & f\,(x_1, x_2, \ldots, x_n) = \max \\ \text{subject to} \\ & g_i\,(x_1, x_2, \ldots, x_n) \geqslant 0 \qquad (i = 1, 2, \ldots, m) \\ & g_h\,(x_1, x_2, \ldots, x_n) = 0 \qquad (h = m + 1, m + 2, \ldots) \\ & x_j \geqslant 0 \qquad (j = 1, 2, \ldots, n) \end{aligned}\right\} \quad (3)$$

where the feasible region is defined by the side conditions $g_h = 0$,

$g_i \geqslant 0$ and the nonnegativity requirements $x_j \geqslant 0$. The inequalities $g_i \geqslant 0$ may be transformed into equations by introducing nonnegative slack variables; conversely, an equality constraint $g_h = 0$ can be replaced by the equivalent pair of inequalities, $g_h \geqslant 0$ and $-g_h \geqslant 0$.

If the functions f, g_h, and g_i are all linear we have the special case of *linear programming* (LP). Otherwise (3) is a problem of *nonlinear programming* (NLP).

As mentioned above, we can always try to solve an NLP problem by provisionally disregarding the inequalities $g_i \geqslant 0$ and/or $x_j \geqslant 0$ and applying classical procedures (elimination, Lagrange's method, or—in the absence of side equations $g_h = 0$—simple unconstrained maximization, setting the $\partial f/\partial x_j = 0$)[1]. If the resulting solution is feasible, we have solved the problem; otherwise some other method must be resorted to.

Example 2: Let the variables of example 1 be required to be nonnegative, $v_j \geqslant 0$. Solving without regard to these inequalities we have (as in example 1) $v_1 = 3$, $v_2 = 2$. Since this solution is positive and is the best solution with no sign requirements imposed, it is clearly also the best solution in the nonnegative region and the problem has been solved.

Example 3:

$$c = 2v_1 + 3v_2 = \min$$

$$v_1 \cdot (v_2 + 3) = 6$$

$$v_1, v_2 \geqslant 0$$

(with a similar interpretation as example 1, only the side condition has a different form). Leaving out the nonnegativity requirements and solving by the Lagrange method, using the Lagrangian

$$L = 2v_1 + 3v_2 + u \cdot \{6 - v_1 (v_2 + 3)\},$$

we get the solution[2]

$$v_1 = 3, \quad v_2 = -1, \quad u = 1$$

which violates $v_2 \geqslant 0$ so that classical methods have failed to produce a feasible optimal solution.

Example 4: A commodity is produced subject to a capacity restriction $x \leqslant 3$, and sold at a price depending on the quantity to be sold,

---

[1] In LP problems this procedure does not work because the partial derivatives never become equal to zero.

[2] The necessary optimum conditions are also satisfied by $v_1 = -3$, $v_2 = -5$, which represents a local *maximum*.

$p = 10 - x$. Variable unit cost is 2. Total profit then becomes $f = (10 - x) \cdot x - 2x$ and we have the optimization problem

$$f = 8x - x^2 = \max$$

$$x \leqslant 3 \quad (\text{i.e., } g(x) = 3 - x \geqslant 0)$$

$$x \geqslant 0.$$

Provisionally disregarding the inequalities we have an unconstrained maximization problem whose solution, $x = 4$, violates the capacity restriction. Alternatively, turning the capacity restriction into an equation

$$x + x' = 3 \quad \text{or} \quad 3 - x - x' = 0$$

and maximizing f subject to this equality constraint, we get $x = 4$, $x' = -1$, which does not respect the requirement $x' \geqslant 0$.

Thus, when we try to solve an optimization problem involving inequality constraints by disregarding the inequalities and applying classical procedures, we may come out with a solution which violates one or more of the inequalities which set limits to the region of feasible solutions. This indicates that the optimum cannot be an interior solution but will be a boundary (or "corner") solution, that is, a point on the boundary of the feasible region where one or more of the inequalities is "*binding*" (or effective), i.e., satisfied in *equality* form. In example 3 we found a solution which violated the nonnegativity requirement $v_2 \geqslant 0$; this would suggest that $v_2 \geqslant 0$ is a binding inequality so that we have $v_2 = 0$ in the optimal solution[1]. Similarly, in example 4 we would expect $x = 3$ to be the maximum solution so that $x \leqslant 3$ is a binding constraint, whereas $x \geqslant 0$ is not binding so that it might have been left out.

If we knew beforehand which of the inequality constraints are binding and which are not, the classical methods would be immediately applicable to any problem of this type. All we had to do was to maximize the preference function subject to the binding side conditions in equality form and with those variables whose nonnegativity requirements are binding set $= 0$ beforehand, whereas nonbinding inequalities could be disregarded because they are not effective constraints. However, the trouble is that we do not possess such advance information. Except in very simple cases we cannot be sure that the binding restrictions are precisely those which are violated by the solution we get when all inequalities are disregarded.

This means that if we want to solve the problem by classical methods,

---

[1] In fact $v_1 = 2$, $v_2 = 0$ is the optimal solution.

we have to examine separately all possible combinations of (hypothetically) binding and nonbinding inequalities. The procedure starts with assuming that no inequalities are binding, maximizing without paying any attention to these restrictions. If the solution turns out to respect all of them, the problem is solved; if it violates one or more of them, we proceed to maximize subject to one restriction in equality form, and so on. Among the feasible solutions to all these maximization problems we pick the one which gives the maximum value of the preference function.

Applying this combinatorial procedure to *example 4* above, we have to maximize $f = 8x - x^2$ subject to 0, 1, and 2 hypothetically binding inequalities. The combinations are:

(i) no binding inequalities, i.e., the unconstrained maximum: $x = 4$, which is not feasible because it violates $x \leqslant 3$;

(ii) $x \leqslant 3$ binding, i.e., $x = 3$, which respects $x \geqslant 0$ and gives $f = 15$;

(iii) $x \geqslant 0$ binding, leading to the feasible solution $x = 0$, $f = 0$;

(iv) both inequalities binding, which is inconsistent: no solution.

The optimal solution is $x = 3$, $f = 15$ [case (ii)][1].

In the special case of *linear programming* problems, a combinatorial procedure is simplified by the fact that we know something about the *number* of binding inequalities. The Fundamental Theorem of linear programming[2] tells us that, if an LP problem with m structural inequality constraints has an optimal solution, then there exists such a solution in which at most m of the variables (including slack variables) are positive. This means that only combinations which represent basic solutions have to be examined. Moreover, the *simplex method* provides a systematic procedure for exploring the set of basic feasible solutions without having to compute all of them: starting from an arbitrary basic feasible solution, the simplex criterion will tell whether it pays to shift to a neighbouring basis, and so on, until a basic solution is attained which satisfies the simplex criterion of optimality. The simplex method is essentially an iterative elimination procedure: at each step, m of the variables are singled out as dependent (basic) variables to be eliminated from the preference function by means of the side conditions so that f becomes a function of the independent (nonbasic) variables; the signs of the coefficients in this function will tell whether the nonbasic variables should all be set $= 0$ or the solution can be improved by making some of them positive, thereby changing the basis.

---

[1] **Exercise 1:** Apply a similar procedure to example 4 after replacing $x \leq 3$ by the equivalent formulation $x + x' = 3$, $x' \geq 0$.

[2] Cf. S. Danø (1974), p. 10.

Example 5 (optimal capacity utilization):

$$f = 2x_1 + 3x_2 = \max$$
$$x_1 + x_2 \leqslant 12, \text{ i.e., } x_1 + x_2 + x' = 12$$
$$x_1, x_2, x' \geqslant 0.$$

By the Fundamental Theorem, at most one variable will be positive ($m = 1$), i.e., at least two of the nonnegativity requirements will be binding. The combinatorial procedure points out three basic solutions, each having two zero variables:

$$x_1 = 12,\ f = 24;\ x_2 = 12,\ f = 36;\ x' = 12,\ f = 0,$$

which are all feasible; the second is the best.—Solving instead by the simplex method, we start by picking a basis of one (dependent) variable, say x_1, to be eliminated:

$$x_1 = 12 - x_2 - x',\ f = 24 + x_2 - 2x'.$$

The corresponding basic solution $x_1 = 12$, $x_2 = 0$, $x' = 0$, $f = 24$ is feasible but not optimal since f is an increasing function of x_2. With x_2 as the basic variable to be eliminated we have

$$x_2 = 12 - x_1 - x',\ f = 36 - x_1 - 3x',$$

which satisfies the simplex criterion: f is a maximum for $x_1 = x' = 0$.

In *nonlinear* cases, the combinatorial procedure is in general an extremely inefficient method of solution if only because the problem has to be stated and solved separately for each combination. Clearly a method is called for which can deal with all of the inequalities simultaneously and in a symmetrical manner. Such a procedure is provided by the generalized Lagrange method, due to *Kuhn* and *Tucker*[1].

B. Kuhn-Tucker Optimization

1. Assume first that all of the side conditions of the general MP problem (3) are *inequalities*,

$$\begin{aligned} f = f(x_1, x_2, \ldots, x_n) &= \max \\ g_i(x_1, x_2, \ldots, x_n) &\geqslant 0 \qquad (i = 1, 2, \ldots, m) \\ x_j &\geqslant 0 \qquad (j = 1, 2, \ldots, n), \end{aligned} \tag{4}$$

[1] Cf. H. W. Kuhn and A. W. Tucker (1951).

and write the Lagrangian function[1]

$$L = f(x_1, x_2, \ldots, x_n) + \sum_{i=1}^{m} u_i \cdot g_i(x_1, x_2, \ldots, x_n). \tag{5}$$

Then the problem (4) of maximizing f subject to $g_i \geqslant 0$ and $x_j \geqslant 0$ can be shown to be equivalent to that of determining a *saddle point* for L—i.e., a point which represents a maximum with respect to the x_j and a minimum with respect to the u_i—subject to $x_j \geqslant 0$ and $u_i \geqslant 0$.

For any differentiable function $L(x_1, \ldots, x_n, u_1, \ldots, u_m)$ where the variables are not confined to the nonnegative region, a saddle point is characterized by

$$\partial L/\partial x_j = 0, \quad \partial L/\partial u_i = 0.$$

When the x_j and the u_i are required to be nonnegative, these necessary conditions must be modified. If some x_j happens to be zero at the saddle

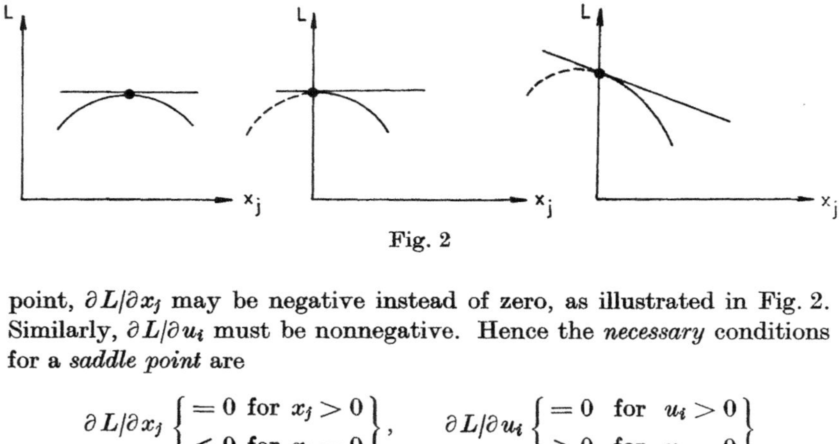

Fig. 2

point, $\partial L/\partial x_j$ may be negative instead of zero, as illustrated in Fig. 2. Similarly, $\partial L/\partial u_i$ must be nonnegative. Hence the *necessary* conditions for a *saddle point* are

$$\partial L/\partial x_j \begin{Bmatrix} = 0 \text{ for } x_j > 0 \\ \leqslant 0 \text{ for } x_j = 0 \end{Bmatrix}, \qquad \partial L/\partial u_i \begin{Bmatrix} = 0 \text{ for } u_i > 0 \\ \geqslant 0 \text{ for } u_i = 0 \end{Bmatrix}$$

which may be written in the form

$$\partial L/\partial x_j \leqslant 0, \quad x_j \geqslant 0, \quad x_j \cdot (\partial L/\partial x_j) = 0 \quad (j = 1, 2, \ldots, n) \tag{6a–c}$$

$$\partial L/\partial u_i \geqslant 0, \quad u_i \geqslant 0, \quad u_i \cdot (\partial L/\partial u_i) = 0 \quad (i = 1, 2, \ldots, m), \tag{7a–c}$$

where

$$\partial L/\partial x_j = \partial f/\partial x_j + \sum_{i=1}^{m} u_i \cdot (\partial g_i/\partial x_j) \quad \text{and} \quad \partial L/\partial u_i = g_i.$$

[1] Note that the side conditions must be written in the form $g_i \geq 0$ so that the u_i are coefficients of nonnegative expressions. A side condition of the form $G_i(x) \leq b_i$, for example, will have to be rewritten $g_i = b_i - G_i \geq 0$.

It can be shown that, subject to certain mild qualifications as to the functions g_i, conditions (6)–(7) are also *necessary for a maximum of f subject to $g_i \geqslant 0$ and $x_j \geqslant 0$*, or in other words: in order for a point $(x_1^\circ, \ldots, x_n^\circ)$ to be an optimal solution to (4) there must exist nonnegative multipliers u_i° which, with the x_j°, satisfy the saddle point conditions (6)–(7), known as the *Kuhn-Tucker conditions.*

The inequalities $x_j \geqslant 0$ and $\partial L/\partial u_i \geqslant 0$, of which the latter represent the side conditions $g_i \geqslant 0$, are the feasibility conditions of the problem. The other conditions in (6)–(7) characterize an optimal solution; observe that Lagrange multipliers associated with nonbinding side conditions ($g_i > 0$ in the optimum) are $= 0$, just as $\partial L/\partial x_j = 0$ if the corresponding sign restriction is not binding ($x_j > 0$).

Sufficient conditions for a point (x°, u°) satisfying the necessary conditions (6)–(7) to be a *saddle point* are

$$L(x, u^\circ) \leqslant L(x^\circ, u^\circ) + \sum_{j=1}^{n} (\partial L/\partial x_j)^\circ \cdot (x_j - x_j^\circ) \tag{8}$$

$$L(x^\circ, u) \geqslant L(x^\circ, u^\circ) + \sum_{i=1}^{m} (\partial L/\partial u_i)^\circ \cdot (u_i - u_i^\circ) \tag{9}$$

for all $x_j \geqslant 0$, $u_i \geqslant 0$. It can be proved that (6), (7), and (8) are *sufficient* conditions for a *global maximum of f subject to $g_i \geqslant 0$ and $x_j \geqslant 0$.*

Moreover, if the functions f and g_i are all *concave*[1] for $x_j \geqslant 0$, conditions (8)–(9) are automatically satisfied so that in this case the Kuhn-Tucker conditions (6)–(7) are *necessary and sufficient for a global maximum of f subject to $g_i \geqslant 0$ and $x_j \geqslant 0$* (as well as for a saddle point of L)[2].

The Kuhn-Tucker conditions (6)–(7) do not immediately provide an

---

[1] A function $F(x)$ is said to be *concave* if linear interpolation between any two points never overestimates the actual value of the function at the point of interpolation. This is illustrated below for a one-variable case, where for all x and x° in the region of definition we have

$$(1 - \vartheta)\, F(x^\circ) + \vartheta F(x) \leq F\{(1 - \vartheta)\, x^\circ + \vartheta x\} \quad (0 \leq \vartheta \leq 1).$$

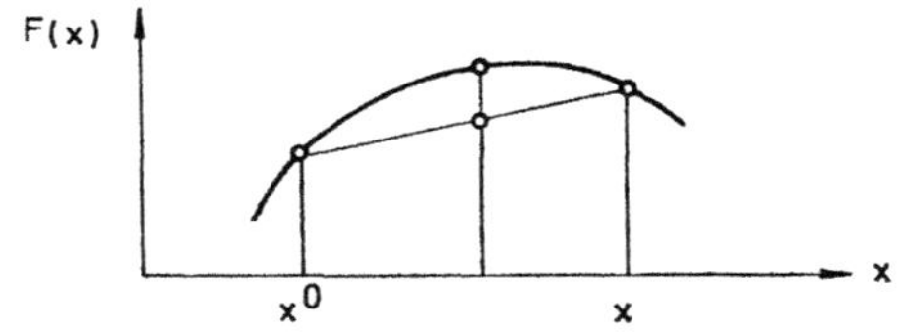

Convexity is defined as the reverse (linear interpolation never underestimates the value of the function).

[2] Note that, since by (7) we have $u_i^\circ \cdot (g_i)^\circ = 0$ for all i, we have in the optimum $L = f_{\max}$.

algorithm for numerical solution of mathematical programming problems. While the classical Lagrange conditions constitute a system of equations to be solved for the x_j and the u_i, the Kuhn-Tucker conditions are essentially inequalities; the equations in (6)–(7) merely represent the *combinatorial* nature of the conditions. For certain classes of nonlinear programming problems computational techniques have been developed to find solutions satisfying the Kuhn-Tucker conditions[1], but in the general case (6)–(7) only provide a *criterion* for testing whether a solution which has been found by other methods is in fact an optimal solution. In simpler cases with a small number of variables, however, such a solution may be found by systematically exploring the combinations which satisfy the equations, or by making use of intuition or intelligent guessing as to which of the variables we may expect to be positive in the optimum.

In *example 4* above we have the Lagrangian

$$L = 8x - x^2 + u \cdot (3 - x)$$

from which we obtain the Kuhn-Tucker conditions

$$8 - 2x - u \leqslant 0, \quad x \geqslant 0, \quad x \cdot (8 - 2x - u) = 0 \tag{6'}$$

$$3 - x \geqslant 0, \quad u \geqslant 0, \quad u \cdot (3 - x) = 0. \tag{7'}$$

By the combinatorial nature of the equations, (at least) one of the inequalities in (6′) must be satisfied in equality form, and similarly for (7′). Hence there are four possible combinations:

1. $8 - 2x - u = 0$, $3 - x = 0$; that is, $x = 3$, $u = 2$. This solution satisfies $x \geqslant 0$ and $u \geqslant 0$.
2. $8 - 2x - u = 0$, $u = 0$; i.e., $x = 4$, which violates $3 - x \geqslant 0$.
3. $x = 0$, $3 - x = 0$: inconsistent.
4. $x = 0$, $u = 0$: this solution violates $8 - 2x - u \leqslant 0$.

These cases correspond to combinations (ii), (i), (iv), and (iii) on p. 11 above. Only the first combination gives a solution to the Kuhn-Tucker conditions; since the functions $f = 8x - x^2$ and $g = 3 - x$ are both concave[2], the solution $x = 3$, $u = 2$ represents a global maximum of f subject to $g \geqslant 0$, $x \geqslant 0$. — In this simple case it would be natural to start by guessing $x > 0$, which — by (6′) — would imply $8 - 2x - u = 0$. By (7′), we should then have either $3 - x = 0$ or $u = 0$, of which the first (i.e., case 1) is seen to satisfy all of the conditions contained in (6′)–(7′) so that we have solved the problem.

---

[1] Some of the algorithms for quadratic programming are based directly on the conditions (6)–(7); cf. Ch. IV.

[2] The function $-x^2$ is easily shown to be concave; a linear function is both concave and convex; and a linear combination (with positive coefficients) of concave functions is concave.

A problem of constrained *minimization*,

$$
\begin{aligned}
F = F(x_1, x_2, \ldots, x_n) &= \min \\
g_i(x_1, x_2, \ldots, x_n) &\geqslant 0 \qquad (i = 1, 2, \ldots, m) \qquad (10) \\
x_i &\geqslant 0 \qquad (j = 1, 2, \ldots, n),
\end{aligned}
$$

is equivalent to the maximization of $f = -F$ subject to $g_i \geqslant 0$ and $x_j \geqslant 0$. Hence the Kuhn-Tucker conditions must in this case be derived from the Lagrangian

$$L = -F + \sum_{i=1}^{m} u_i \cdot g_i.$$

The conditions are also *sufficient* for a *global minimum* if the function F is *convex* (i.e., f concave) and the g_i are *concave.*

Example 6: For production of a commodity, two plants are available, with cost functions

$$c_1 = 5x_1 + 0.10x_1^2 \quad \text{and} \quad c_2 = 7x_2 + 0.20x_2^2$$

where x_1 and x_2 denote the numbers of units produced per day. A total production of at least 37 units per day is required. Determine the allocation of production to plants which minimizes total cost, $c = c_1 + c_2$. Then we have the Lagrangian

$$L = -(5x_1 + 0.10x_1^2 + 7x_2 + 0.20x_2^2) + u \cdot (x_1 + x_2 - 37)$$

and the Kuhn-Tucker conditions are

$$
\begin{aligned}
&-5 - 0.20x_1 + u \leqslant 0, \quad x_1 \geqslant 0, \quad x_1 \cdot (-5 - 0.20x_1 + u) = 0 \\
&-7 - 0.40x_2 + u \leqslant 0, \quad x_2 \geqslant 0, \quad x_2 \cdot (-7 - 0.40x_2 + u) = 0 \\
&x_1 + x_2 - 37 \geqslant 0, \quad u \geqslant 0, \quad u \cdot (x_1 + x_2 - 37) = 0.
\end{aligned}
$$

Try $x_1, x_2 > 0$, which implies $\partial L/\partial x_1 = \partial L/\partial x_2 = 0$, i.e.,

$$\text{(i)} \quad u = 5 + 0.20x_1 = 7 + 0.40x_2.$$

Then either $u = 0$, which would give $x_1, x_2 < 0$, or $\partial L/\partial u = 0$, i.e.,

$$\text{(ii)} \quad x_1 + x_2 - 37 = 0.$$

Solving (i)–(ii) we have $x_1 = 28$, $x_2 = 9$, $u = 10.6$, which satisfies all of the conditions. Since c_1 and c_2 are convex (so that $-c$ is concave), the solution is a global minimum and we have $c^{\min} = 297.60$.

Mathematical programming problems of the type (4) or (10) are said to be problems of *convex programming* if the functions have the convexity or concavity properties required for the solution to the Kuhn-

Tucker conditions to represent a global maximum or minimum, i.e., if f is concave or F convex and the g_i concave[1].

It is sometimes convenient[2] to transform the inequalities of the Kuhn-Tucker conditions into equations by introducing nonnegative slack variables v_j and y_i. Then (6)–(7) are replaced by

$$\partial f/\partial x_j + \sum_{i=1}^{m} u_i \cdot (\partial g_i/\partial x_j) + v_j = 0 \tag{11}$$

$$g_i - y_i = 0 \tag{12}$$

$$x_j, v_j, u_i, y_i \geqslant 0 \tag{13}$$

$$x_j v_j = u_i y_i = 0 \qquad (j = 1, 2, \ldots, n; \quad i = 1, 2, \ldots, m) \tag{14}$$

where $v_j = -\partial L/\partial x_j$ and $y_i = g_i$. The problem of finding a solution to the Kuhn-Tucker conditions is equivalent to *finding a solution to a system of equations*, (11)–(12)—$n + m$ equations in the $2n + 2m$ variables x_j, v_j, u_i, y_i—which is *nonnegative* in all of the variables and which is *in "standard form"*, i.e., satisfies (14): if a variable x_j or u_i is positive, its "corresponding" slack variable v_j or y_i respectively must be equal to zero.

2. In the general MP problem (3) we have "*mixed*" side conditions, i.e., *equations* $g_h = 0$ as well as *inequalities* $g_i \geqslant 0$. Kuhn-Tucker conditions for this type of problem can be established if the problem is reformulated in the form (4), replacing each of the equations $g_h = 0$ by the equivalent pair of inequalities $g_h \geqslant 0$, $-g_h \geqslant 0$. Then the Lagrangian, with multipliers u_i, λ_h, and μ_h, becomes

$$L = f + \sum_i u_i g_i + \sum_h \lambda_h g_h - \sum_h \mu_h g_h.$$

The Kuhn-Tucker conditions derived from this Lagrangian[3] are readily seen to imply the following conditions:

$$(\partial L/\partial x_j =)\ \partial f/\partial x_j + \sum_i u_i \cdot (\partial g_i/\partial x_j) + \sum_h u_h \cdot (\partial g_h/\partial x_j) \leqslant 0,$$

$$x_j \geqslant 0, \quad x_j \cdot (\partial L/\partial x_j) = 0 \tag{15}$$

[1] The term *convex* programming refers to the following equivalent standard formulation of (4) or (10),

$$F = \min \text{ subject to } G_i \leq 0 \text{ (or } \widehat{G}_i \leq b_i,\ b_i \text{ constant) and } x_j \geq 0$$

where $F = -f$ and $G_i = -g_i$ (or $\widehat{G}_i - b_i = -g_i$). The Kuhn-Tucker conditions (6)—(7) are necessary and sufficient for a global minimum of F if the functions F and G_i (or $\widehat{G}_i$) are all convex.

[2] For example, in certain quadratic programming algorithms (cf. Ch. IV).

[3] **Exercise 2:** Write down the conditions.

$$(\partial L/\partial u_i =) \quad g_i \geqslant 0, \qquad u_i \geqslant 0, \quad u_i \cdot g_i = 0 \tag{16}$$

$$(\partial L/\partial u_h =) \quad g_h = 0 \tag{17}$$

where $u_h = \lambda_h - \mu_h$ so that

$$L = f + \sum_i u_i g_i + \sum_h u_h g_h. \tag{18}$$

The multipliers λ_h and μ_h are required to be nonnegative, but the Kuhn-Tucker conditions impose no such restriction on their difference, u_h[1]. Hence, for each of the equality constraints we write $\partial L/\partial u_h = g_h = 0$ in the Kuhn-Tucker conditions as derived from the Lagrangian (18); all other conditions are the same as in the pure inequality case.

If all of the side conditions are equations and the x_j are not required to be nonnegative, the Kuhn-Tucker conditions reduce to the classical Lagrange conditions $\partial L/\partial x_j = 0$, $\partial L/\partial u_h = g_h = 0$.

Applying this procedure to the minimization problem of *example 3*, write the Lagrangian

$$L = -(2v_1 + 3v_2) + u \cdot \{6 - v_1(v_2 + 3)\}.$$

The Kuhn-Tucker conditions are

$$\begin{aligned} -2 - u(v_2 + 3) &\leqslant 0, \quad v_1 \geqslant 0, \quad v_1 \cdot \{-2 - u(v_2 + 3)\} = 0 \\ -3 - uv_1 &\leqslant 0, \quad v_2 \geqslant 0, \quad v_2 \cdot (-3 - uv_1) = 0 \\ 6 - v_1(v_2 + 3) &= 0. \end{aligned}$$

Try the guess $v_1, v_2 > 0$; this implies $v_1 = 3, v_2 = -1$, $u = -1$, which violates $v_2 \geqslant 0$. Try instead $v_2 = 0$, which by the side condition implies $v_1 = 2$ and, by the first combinatorial equation, $u = -2/3$. This solution is seen to satisfy all of the conditions[2].

3. *A linear programming problem* with side conditions in inequality form is a special case of the MP problem (4):

$$\begin{aligned} f = \sum_{j=1}^{n} c_j x_j &= \max \\ \sum_{j=1}^{n} a_{ij} x_j &\leqslant b_i \qquad (i = 1, 2, \ldots, m) \\ x_j &\geqslant 0 \qquad (j = 1, 2, \ldots, n). \end{aligned} \tag{19}$$

---

[1] (17) is derived from $g_h \geq 0$, $-g_h \geq 0$. The corresponding equations $\lambda_h g_h = 0$, $-\mu_h g_h = 0$ are automatically satisfied for $g_h = 0$. The sign restrictions $\lambda_h \geq 0$, $\mu_h \geq 0$ can be left out since it is always possible to find nonnegative λ_h, μ_h such that $\lambda_h - \mu_h = u_h$ regardless of the sign of u_h.

[2] **Exercise 3:** Add a capacity restriction $v_1 \leq 2$ and nonnegativity requirements $v_1, v_2 \geq 0$ to example 1 above, and solve the problem.

With the Lagrangian

$$L_I = \sum_{j=1}^{n} c_j x_j + \sum_{i=1}^{m} u_i \cdot \left(b_i - \sum_{j=1}^{n} a_{ij} x_j\right) = \max_{x_j} \min_{u_i} \tag{20}$$

the Kuhn-Tucker conditions become

$$\left(\frac{\partial L_I}{\partial x_j} = \right) c_j - \sum_{i=1}^{m} a_{ij} u_i \leqslant 0, \quad x_j \geqslant 0, \quad x_j \cdot \frac{\partial L_I}{\partial x_j} = 0 \tag{21}$$

$$\left(\frac{\partial L_I}{\partial u_i} = \right) b_i - \sum_{j=1}^{n} a_{ij} x_j \geqslant 0, \quad u_i \geqslant 0, \quad u_i \cdot \frac{\partial L_I}{\partial u_i} = 0. \tag{22}$$

(21) and (22) are *necessary and sufficient* conditions for a global maximum since all functions involved are linear, i.e., concave as well as convex.

The Lagrange multipliers u_i can be identified with the *dual variables* y_i in the optimum [which can be interpreted as shadow prices associated with the scarce resources represented by the constraints in (19)][1]. The *dual problem* corresponding to (19) is

$$\begin{aligned} F = \sum_{i=1}^{m} b_i y_i &= \min \\ \sum_{i=1}^{m} a_{ij} y_i &\geqslant c_j \\ y_i &\geqslant 0\,; \end{aligned} \tag{23}$$

with multipliers v_j [and recalling that min F = max $(-F)$] the Lagrangian is

$$L_{II} = -\sum_{i=1}^{m} b_i y_i + \sum_{j=1}^{n} v_j \cdot \left(\sum_{i=1}^{m} a_{ij} y_i - c_j\right) = \max_{y_i} \min_{v_j},$$

which is seen to be equivalent to

$$-L_{II} = \sum_{j=1}^{n} c_j v_j + \sum_{i=1}^{m} y_i \cdot \left(b_i - \sum_{j=1}^{n} a_{ij} v_j\right) = \max_{v_j} \min_{y_i}. \tag{24}$$

(24) is seen to be identical with (20) for $u_i = y_i$ and $v_j = x_j$ so that it is formally the same problem we solve in deriving Kuhn-Tucker conditions from (20) and (24); the structural variables of the primal problem (19) are Lagrange multipliers of the dual (23) and *vice versa*. Writing the common Lagrangian

$$L = \sum_{j=1}^{n} c_j x_j + \sum_{i=1}^{m} y_i \cdot \left(b_i - \sum_{j=1}^{n} a_{ij} x_j\right) = \max_{x_j} \min_{y_i}$$

[1] Cf. S. Danø (1974), Ch. VI.

the corresponding Kuhn-Tucker conditions for both problems will be (21)–(22) with u_i replaced by y_i.

With slack variables x_i' and y_j' in the side conditions of (19) and (23), the Kuhn-Tucker conditions can be rewritten in the form[1]

$$\sum_{i=1}^{m} a_{ij} y_i - y_j' = c_j \tag{25}$$

$$\sum_{j=1}^{n} a_{ij} x_j + x_i' = b_i \tag{26}$$

$$x_j, y_i, x_i', y_j' \geqslant 0 \tag{27}$$

$$x_j \cdot y_j' = y_i \cdot x_i' = 0; \tag{28}$$

that is, the solutions to the problem and its dual must be feasible—cf. (25)–(27)—and at least one from each pair of "corresponding" variables (x_j, y_j') and (y_i, x_i') must be equal to zero. The simplex method provides a procedure for finding a solution satisfying these requirements. We know from the Duality Theorem for linear programming[2] that if we can find a (nondegenerate) basic feasible solution $(x_j^\circ, x_i'^\circ)$ to (19) which satisfies the simplex criterion, then there exists a basic feasible solution $(y_i^\circ, y_j'^\circ)$ to the dual which also satisfies the simplex criterion and such that the value of any basic variable in (19) is numerically equal to the simplex coefficient of the corresponding variable in (23) and *vice versa*, which implies that the corresponding variable is nonbasic and therefore equal to zero. Hence a solution satisfying the simplex criterion represents a global maximum of f and a global minimum of F.

4. Another special case is a *quadratic programming problem*, where the side conditions are linear as in the LP case while the preference function contains quadratic as well as linear terms:

$$\begin{aligned} f = \sum_{j=1}^{n} c_j x_j + \sum_{k=1}^{n} \sum_{j=1}^{n} c_{kj} x_k x_j &= \max \\ \sum_{j=1}^{n} a_{ij} x_j \leqslant b_i \qquad & (i = 1, 2, \ldots, m) \\ x_j \geqslant 0 \qquad & (j = 1, 2, \ldots, n) \end{aligned} \tag{29}$$

where the matrix of coefficients c_{kj} is square and symmetric[3]. Writing

[1] Corresponding to (11)–(14) above. In the linear case we have $\partial L / \partial x_j = c_j - \sum_i a_{ij} y_i = -y_j'$ and $\partial L / \partial y_i = b_i - \sum_j a_{ij} x_j = x_i'$.

[2] Cf. S. Danø (1974), p. 105.

[3] The sum of quadratic terms can always be written in this form by splitting the coefficient of each cross product term into two equal parts, c_{kj} and c_{jk}. See below Ch. IV, p. 33.

out the preference function term by term it is readily seen that

$$\partial f / \partial x_j = c_j + 2 \sum_{k=1}^{n} c_{kj} x_k .$$

If the preference function is concave, the Kuhn-Tucker conditions as derived from the Lagrangian

$$L_{\mathrm{I}} = \sum_{j=1}^{n} c_j x_j + \sum_{k=1}^{n} \sum_{j=1}^{n} c_{kj} x_k x_j + \sum_{i=1}^{m} u_i \cdot \left(b_i - \sum_{j=1}^{n} a_{ij} x_j \right)$$

are necessary and sufficient for a global maximum subject to the constraints.

To any quadratic maximization problem corresponds a *dual problem* which is a quadratic minimization problem. The dual of (29) is

$$\begin{aligned} & g = \sum_{i=1}^{m} b_i y_i - \sum_{k=1}^{n} \sum_{j=1}^{n} c_{kj} x_k x_j = \min \\ & \sum_{i=1}^{m} a_{ij} y_i \geqslant c_j + 2 \sum_{k=1}^{n} c_{kj} x_k \quad (= \partial f / \partial x_j) \\ & x_j, y_i \geqslant 0 \quad (j = 1, 2, \ldots, n; \; i = 1, 2, \ldots, m) \end{aligned} \tag{30}$$

where the y_i are dual variables. In contradistinction to the linear case, the dual also contains the structural variables of the primal problem, x_j. Rewriting (30) as a maximization problem $\{\max(-g) = \min g\}$, the Lagrangian for (30) with multipliers w_j becomes

$$L_{\mathrm{II}} = - \sum_{i=1}^{m} b_i y_i + \sum_{k=1}^{n} \sum_{j=1}^{n} c_{kj} x_k x_j + \sum_{j=1}^{n} w_j \cdot \left(\sum_{i=1}^{m} a_{ij} y_i - c_j - 2 \sum_{k=1}^{n} c_{kj} x_k \right).$$

Deriving the Kuhn-Tucker conditions for the two problems from L_{I} and L_{II} respectively, it is readily seen that the two sets of conditions are identical if the y_i are identified with the u_i and the w_j with the x_j. If the Kuhn-Tucker conditions for (29) have a solution x_j°, u_i°, then the conditions for the dual (30) will be satisfied for $x_j = x_j^\circ$, $y_i = u_i^\circ$, and $w_j = x_j^\circ$. —The proof is left to the reader.

III. Linearization of Nonlinear Programming Problems

A. Linear Approximations and Linear Programming

In the absence of general algorithms for nonlinear programming problems, it lies near at hand to explore the possibilities of approximate solution by linearization. If the nonlinear functions of an MP problem can be replaced by piecewise linear functions, these approximations may be expressed in such a way that the whole problem is turned into a case of linear programming. Applying the simplex method we get a solution which—assuming that all functions involved have the concavity or

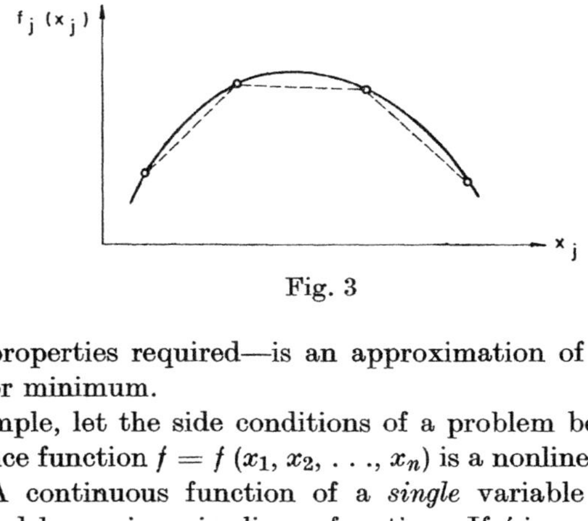

Fig. 3

convexity properties required—is an approximation of the true global maximum or minimum.

For example, let the side conditions of a problem be linear whereas the preference function $f = f\ (x_1, x_2, \ldots, x_n)$ is a nonlinear differentiable function. A continuous function of a *single* variable can always be approximated by a piecewise linear function. If f is *separable*, i.e., if it can be written in the form

$$f = f_1\ (x_1) + f_2\ (x_2) + \ldots + f_n\ (x_n),$$

this procedure can be applied to each of the terms $f_j\ (x_j)$ as shown in Fig. 3. The closer the points of interpolation are placed, the better the approximation.

The next step is to reformulate the problem as an LP problem, making use of the fact that f is now linear within each of the successive intervals of the x_j. This can be done in several ways. In the following we shall deal with two such procedures, the method of *partitioning the variables* and the method known as *separable programming*[1]. Either method is equally applicable to problems where the piecewise linear function is not an approximation but represents the true preference function; in such a case the simplex solution to the linearized problem is the true solution, not an approximation.

B. Partitioning of Variables

1. Consider the following problem of *optimal utilization of machine capacities*: A company manufactures two products which have to be processed on the same two machines whose capacities set limits to production. x_1 and x_2 units are produced per period and sold at prices which depend on the quantities to be sold, $p_1 = 12 - x_1$ and $p_2 = 13 - 2x_2$ (\$ per unit); the variable costs of labour, raw materials, and other current inputs are 4 and 3 respectively per unit of product. Hence total gross profit is

$$f = (12 - x_1)\, x_1 + (13 - 2x_2)\, x_2 - 4x_1 - 3x_2$$

which is to be maximized subject to the capacity restrictions, one for each machine:

$$\begin{aligned} f = 8x_1 - x_1^2 + 10x_2 - 2x_2^2 &= \max \\ x_1 + x_2 &\leqslant 5 \\ x_1 + 2x_2 &\leqslant 8 \\ x_1, x_2 &\geqslant 0 \end{aligned} \tag{1}$$

where the coefficients of x_1 and x_2 in the capacity restrictions represent machine hours required per unit of product and the right-hand sides are machine hours available per period.

Since the linear functions in the side conditions, $g_1 = 5 - x_1 - x_2$ and $g_2 = 8 - x_1 - 2x_2$, are concave and each term in the function to be maximized is also concave, the Kuhn-Tucker conditions are necessary and sufficient for a global maximum of f subject to the inequality constraints.

To find an approximate solution, we first *separate* the preference function into $f_1(x_1) = 8x_1 - x_1^2$ and $f_2(x_2) = 10x_2 - 2x_2^2$, and next *approximate* each of these by piecewise linear functions. Starting with $f_1(x_1)$, it is clear from the capacity restrictions that the nonnegative variable x_1 cannot be greater than 5, so we must interpolate between

---

[1] See e.g. E. M. L. Beale (1968), Ch. 14; G. B. Dantzig (1963), Ch. 24; S. Vajda (1961), Ch. 12; and R. Henn and H. P. Künzi (1968), Vol. II, Ch. 6.

the points (0, 0) and (5, 15) on $f_1(x_1)$. With (3, 15) as an intermediate point we get the piecewise linear approximation $f_1^*(x_1)$ shown as OAB in Fig. 4a.

The slopes of the linear segments OA and AB are 5 for $0 \leqslant x_1 \leqslant 3$ and 0 for $3 \leqslant x_1 \leqslant 5$.

To express this approximation in terms of an LP model, we partition

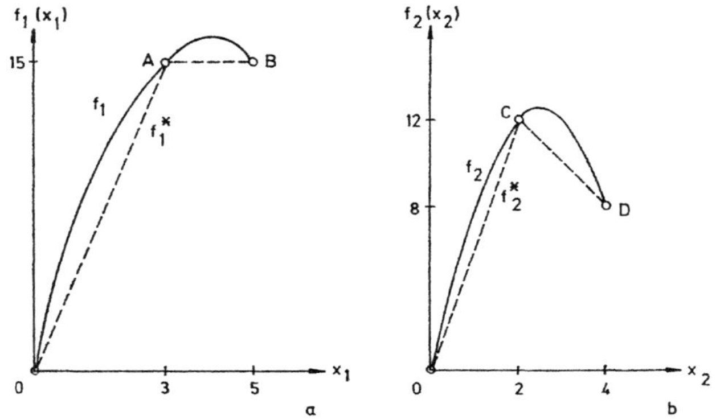

Fig. 4 a–b

x_1 into nonnegative *auxiliary variables* u_1 and u_2 *associated with the two linear segments*, and express f_1^* accordingly:

$$\begin{aligned} x_1 &= u_1 + u_2 \\ 0 &\leqslant u_1 \leqslant 3 \\ 0 &\leqslant u_2 \leqslant 2 \qquad (= 5 - 3) \\ f_1^* &= 5u_1 + 0u_2. \end{aligned} \tag{2}$$

Similarly, for f_2 we construct the approximation shown in Fig. 4b, based on the points (0, 0), (2, 12), and (4, 8); x_2 cannot be greater than 4. With auxiliary variables v_1 and v_2 this leads to

$$\begin{aligned} x_2 &= v_1 + v_2 \\ 0 &\leqslant v_1 \leqslant 2 \\ 0 &\leqslant v_2 \leqslant 2 \qquad (= 4 - 2) \\ f_2^* &= 6v_1 - 2v_2, \end{aligned} \tag{3}$$

the slopes of the linear segments being 6 and − 2. All we have to do now is to transform the problem (1) by means of (2)–(3). Substitute the expressions for x_1 and x_2 in the side conditions, adding the upper and lower bounds on the auxiliary variables to the list of inequalities (and deleting $x_1, x_2 \geqslant 0$ as being how redundant), and replace f_1 and f_2 by the approximations $f_1{}^*$ and $f_2{}^*$ so that the preference function becomes $f^* = f_1{}^* + f_2{}^*$. Then we have

$$\begin{aligned} f^* = 5u_1 + 0u_2 + 6v_1 - 2v_2 &= \max \\ u_1 + u_2 + v_1 + v_2 &\leqslant 5 \\ u_1 + u_2 + 2v_1 + 2v_2 &\leqslant 8 \\ u_1 &\leqslant 3 \\ u_2 &\leqslant 2 \\ v_1 &\leqslant 2 \\ v_2 &\leqslant 2 \\ u_1, u_2, v_1, v_2 &\geqslant 0. \end{aligned} \tag{4}$$

This is an LP problem in the auxiliary variables which can be solved by the simplex method. The optimal solution is[1]

$$u_1 = 3, \quad u_2 = 0, \quad v_1 = 2, \quad v_2 = 0; \quad f^* = 27$$

or in terms of x_1 ($= u_1 + u_2$) and x_2 ($= v_1 + v_2$)

$$x_1 = 3, \quad x_2 = 2; \quad f^* = 27,$$

which is an approximate solution to the nonlinear problem (1)[2].

In general, the approximation can be improved by increasing the number of points of interpolation, but against this we have to weigh the cost of extra computational labour (computer time). The number of auxiliary variables and restrictions increases in proportion to the number of points chosen.

In order for $f_1{}^* = 5u_1 + 0u_2$ to represent the approximation shown in Fig. 4a, u_2 must not be allowed to be positive before u_1 is "used up": a solution in which $u_1 < 3$ and $u_2 > 0$ would not be a point on the piecewise linear function. This requirement,

$$(u_1, u_2) = \begin{cases} (x_1, 0) & \text{for } 0 \leqslant x_1 \leqslant 3 \\ (3, x_1 - 3) & \text{for } 3 \leqslant x_1 \leqslant 5, \end{cases} \tag{5}$$

[1] **Exercise 4:** Show this by solving (4), using simplex tableaux.

[2] Actually this happens to be the exact solution to (1) because the points of interpolation which we picked ($x_1 = 3$ and $x_2 = 2$) coincide with the correct solution. **Exercise 5:** Solve the problem as indicated but with $x_1 = 2$ instead of $x_1 = 3$ as a point of interpolation in Fig. 4a.

and the analogous restriction on (v_1, v_2) were not included in (2) and (3) because they do not fit into an LP model.

This would seem to indicate that the method of linearization by partitioning of variables is of limited applicability because there is apparently no guarantee that the LP solution respects these requirements. However, if the function to be maximized is *concave*, as it is in the example (1), we do have such a guarantee. Because f_1 is concave, the slopes of the successive linear segments will be decreasing for increasing x_1; in the example, the coefficient of u_1 in $f_1{}^*$ is greater than that of u_2. Therefore, since u_1 and u_2 are technically equivalent in the capacity restrictions, the simplex procedure will automatically prefer the more profitable variable u_1 to u_2 in the basis so that u_2 will never be positive as long as u_1 is less than its upper bound. Similarly, v_1 will be preferred to v_2 as far as possible. This result clearly holds for any number of auxiliary variables we may choose to approximate the functions.

In other words, the method applies without qualification to problems of maximizing a separable concave function subject to linear constraints. Problems of this type belong to the class of MP problems known as *convex programming* problems[1].

2. As another example, consider the following *inventory problem*. A tobacco factory is planning its production of a particular cigar brand for a period of one year (four quarters). Estimated sales are as follows:

Quarter no.	Expected sales, thousands	Cumulated sales, thousands
1	712	712
2	578	1,290
3	547	1,837
4	1,216	3,053

The factory operates in two shifts with capacity limits 550.5 and 453.0 (in thousands of cigars per quarter) so that total production in each quarter, x_t ($t = 1, 2, 3, 4$), cannot exceed 1,003.5. Initial inventory is assumed to be zero, and inventory at the and of each quarter, h_t—i.e., accumulated production minus accumulated sales—is required to be nonnegative for the first three quarters and zero at the end of the year. The problem is to determine the x_t in such a way as to minimize total

[1] Cf. the definition in Ch. II, pp. 16 f.

costs of production and storage, $c = c_1 + c_2$, subject to these requirements:

$$\begin{aligned} c = c_1 + c_2 &= \min \\ x_1 &\geqslant 712 \\ x_1 + x_2 &\geqslant 1{,}290 \\ x_1 + x_2 + x_3 &\geqslant 1{,}837 \\ x_1 + x_2 + x_3 + x_4 &= 3{,}053 \\ x_t &\leqslant 1{,}003.5 \qquad (t = 1, 2, 3, 4) \\ x_t &\geqslant 0 \qquad (t = 1, 2, 3, 4). \end{aligned} \tag{6}$$

where the slack variables of the first three restrictions can be identified with the terminal inventories h_1, h_2, and h_3 (whereas $h_4 = 0$).

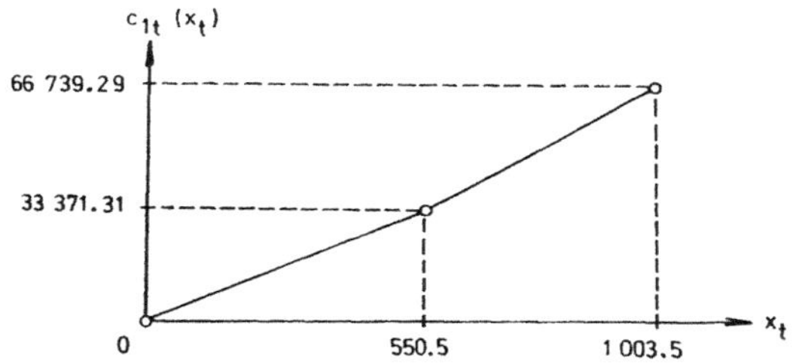

Fig. 5

The cost of producing 1,000 cigars is 60.62 Danish crowns in shift 1 and 73.66 D. cr. in shift 2. Hence total cost of production for the year can be written as a sum of (identical) convex functions,

$$c_1 = c_{11}(x_1) + c_{12}(x_2) + c_{13}(x_3) + c_{14}(x_4) \tag{7}$$

where $c_{1t}(x_t)$ is a piecewise linear function of x_t with slopes 60.62 for $0 \leqslant x_t \leqslant 550.5$ and 73.66 for $550.5 \leqslant x_t \leqslant 1{,}003.5$ as shown in Fig. 5. The cost of storing 1,000 cigars for a quarter is 1.01 D. cr. so that storage cost in each quarter is 1.01 times the average number of units (thousands) held in inventory during the quarter, as approximated by the mean of initial and terminal inventories. For the whole year we have

$$c_2 = 1.01 \cdot \left(\frac{0 + h_1}{2} + \ldots + \frac{h_3 + 0}{2}\right) = 1.01 \cdot (h_1 + h_2 + h_3)$$

where the h_t, to be identified with the slack variables in the three first inequalities of (6), can be expressed in terms of the x_t so that we get

$$c_2 = 3.03 x_1 + 2.02 x_2 + 1.01 x_3 - 3{,}877.39. \tag{8}$$

Thus the total preference function $c = c_1 + c_2$ is nonlinear, the components of c_1 being only piecewise linear, but c is separable in the x_t. Therefore, we can apply the procedure of partitioning the variables to this problem as well; the case differs from the previous example (1) in that the piecewise linear functions are not approximations but the "true" functions.

The partitioning simply consists in the introduction of a particular variable for each shift,

$$x_t = x_{1t} + x_{2t} \qquad (t = 1, 2, 3, 4); \tag{9}$$

each term $c_{1t}(x_t)$ in (7) can now be written

$$c_{1t}(x_t) = 60.62x_{1t} + 73.66x_{2t} \qquad (t = 1, 2, 3, 4).$$

Substituting (9) in the inventory cost function (8) and in the side conditions, and adding the further constraints

$$x_{1t} \leqslant 550.5, \qquad x_{2t} \leqslant 453.0, \qquad (t = 1, 2, 3, 4),$$

we get an LP problem in the nonnegativity variables x_{1t} and x_{2t}. The optimal solution[1],

$$x_{11} = x_{12} = x_{13} = x_{14} = 550.5, \quad x_{21} = 161.5,$$
$$x_{22} = 27.5, \quad x_{23} = 209.0, \quad x_{24} = 453.0; \quad c = 196{,}385,$$

is an *exact* solution to the nonlinear problem (6)–(8) because no approximations were made; the LP model is a mere reformulation of (6)–(8).

Like the previous example, (6)–(8) is a *convex programming* problem: the side conditions are linear and the function to be *minimized* is *convex*. The convexity of the cost function c ensures that we can never get an LP solution in which some x_{2t} is positive while $x_{1t} < 550.5$ (i.e., shift 2 is used before the capacity of the first shift is exhausted). The simplex method will automatically see to it that the first shift, which has a smaller coefficient in the cost function, is preferred up to its capacity.

C. Separable Programming

1. We shall now proceed to demonstrate an alternative method of linearization, known as *separable programming*. Like the method of partitioning variables, separable programming starts by *separating* the nonlinear preference function and *approximating* each term over the relevant range of the variable x_j by a piecewise linear function (unless the problem is already in this form); but the way in which the approximation is expressed in LP terms is different.

---

[1] Cf. S. Danø (1974), pp. 56—59, where the problem is presented in its linearized form and solved by inspection.

To solve problem (1) by separable programming, we can use the same approximations $f_1^*(x_1)$ and $f_2^*(x_2)$, based on the points

x_1	0	3	5
$f_1(x_1)$	0	15	15

and

x_2	0	2	4
$f_2(x_2)$	0	12	8

(cf. Fig. 4a–b). Any point on the piecewise linear function $f_1^*(x_1)$ can now be expressed as a *convex combination* (a weighted average) of the three points,

$$x_1 = 0z_1 + 3z_2 + 5z_3 \tag{10}$$

$$f_1^* = 0z_1 + 15z_2 + 15z_3 \tag{11}$$

$$z_1 + z_2 + z_3 = 1 \tag{12}$$

where (12) expresses the requirement that the weights shall add up to unity. For example, the midpoint on the first linear segment is represented by $z_1 = z_2 = 0.5$, $z_3 = 0$. The "*special variables*" z_i are of course required to be nonnegative.

For f_2^* we have similarly, with further nonnegative special variables,

$$x_2 = 0z_4 + 2z_5 + 4z_6 \tag{13}$$

$$f_2^* = 0z_4 + 12z_5 + 8z_6 \tag{14}$$

$$z_4 + z_5 + z_6 = 1. \tag{15}$$

Substituting the expressions (10) and (13) for x_1 and x_2 in the side conditions, and replacing the preference function by the approximation $f^* = f_1^* + f_2^*$ as given by (11) and (14), we get the following LP problem in the six special variables,

$$\begin{aligned} f^* = 0z_1 + 15z_2 + 15z_3 + 0z_4 + 12z_5 + 8z_6 &= \max \\ 0z_1 + 3z_2 + 5z_3 + 0z_4 + 2z_5 + 4z_6 &\leqslant 5 \\ 0z_1 + 3z_2 + 5z_3 + 0z_4 + 4z_5 + 8z_6 &\leqslant 8 \\ z_1 + z_2 + z_3 \qquad\qquad\qquad &= 1 \\ z_4 + z_5 + z_6 &= 1 \\ z_i \geqslant 0 \qquad (i = 1, 2, \ldots, 6)& \end{aligned} \tag{16}$$

after adding the "*convexity constraints*" (12) and (15). The optimal solution is[1]

$$z_2 = 1, \quad z_5 = 1; \quad f^* = 27$$

or, translated by means of (10) and (13),

$$x_1 = 3, \quad x_2 = 2; \quad f^* = 27,$$

corresponding to the solution we found above by the method of partitioning.

[1] **Exercise 6:** Solve problem (16) by the simplex method, using simplex tableaux.

Now, just as the approximations (2) and (3) were incomplete because they did not rule out solutions involving $u_1 < 3$ and $u_2 > 0$, or $v_1 < 2$ and $v_2 > 0$, so are (10)–(12) and (13)–(15) incomplete. A solution in which z_1, z_2, and z_3 were all positive would represent an interior point of the triangle OAB in Fig. 4a; $z_1 > 0$, $z_2 = 0$, and $z_3 > 0$ would correspond to a point on OB. In order for a solution to the LP problem to represent a point on the approximation f_1^* (OAB) it must consist of either a single positive variable or two positive variables which are "*neighbours*" (in this case, z_1 and z_2, or z_2 and z_3), and similarly for f_2^*.

However, when the function to be maximized is *concave*, these requirements will automatically be satisfied by the LP solution. The simplex procedure will see to it that no point below OAB stays in the basis, because there is always a better point on OAB. Hence the method of separable programming as demonstrated above can be applied without modification to a convex programming problem with linear constraints. If the preference function is not concave the simplex procedure will have to be modified such as to rule out the occurrence of non-neighbouring special variables in the basis[1]. If there is only one special variable from a particular group (cf. (12) and (15) respectively) in the basis, only its neighbours are considered as possible new basic variables; if two special variables are present in the basis a third is not allowed to enter[2].

2. To solve the inventory problem (6)–(8) by separable programming, the nonlinear (in this case, piecewise linear) functions $c_{1t}(x_t)$, cf. Fig. 5, are expressed as follows:

$$x_t = 0z_{t1} + 550.5z_{t2} + 1{,}003.5z_{t3} \tag{17}$$

$$c_{1t}(x_t) = 0z_{t1} + 33{,}371.31z_{t2} + 66{,}739.29z_{t3} \tag{18}$$

$$z_{t1} + z_{t2} + z_{t3} = 1 \qquad (t = 1, 2, 3, 4). \tag{19}$$

Substituting (17)–(18) in (6)–(8) and adding the convexity constraints (19) we get an LP problem in the 12 nonnegative special variables z_{ti}[3]. Since the function to be minimized is convex the simplex procedure will automatically prefer the first shift to the second up to its capacity.

---

[1] Cf. E. M. L. Beale (1968), p. 125.

[2] When f is not concave the solution is a *local* maximum but not necessarily a global optimum.

[3] In this case separable programming will be much less efficient than partitioning of variables as a method of solving the problem.

3. Separable programming can also be used to solve problems in which nonlinear functions occur in the constraints. A simple example is the following.

Two commodities are produced subject to the nonlinear capacity restriction

$$x_2 \leqslant -0.1x_1^2 - 0.3x_1 + 4, \tag{20}$$

cf. Fig. 6. Total profit, which is to be maximized, is a linear function of the quantities produced per period,

$$z = 6x_1 + 9x_2 = \max. \tag{21}$$

Since the function $g = -0.1x_1^2 - 0.3x_1 + 4 - x_2 \ (\geqslant 0)$ is concave, (20)–(21) is a problem in convex programming.

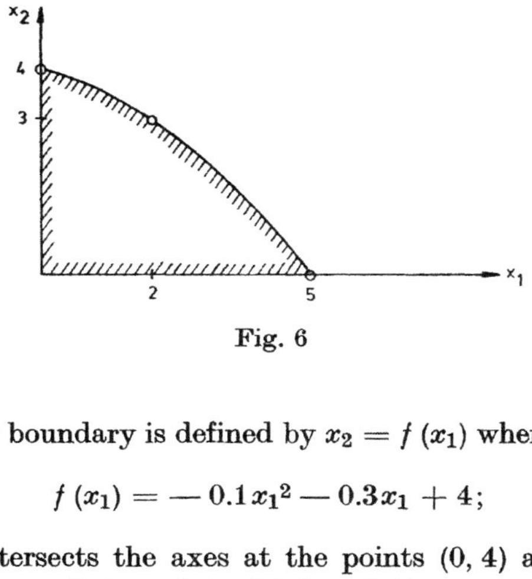

Fig. 6

The capacity boundary is defined by $x_2 = f(x_1)$ where

$$f(x_1) = -0.1x_1^2 - 0.3x_1 + 4;$$

this function intersects the axes at the points (0, 4) and (5, 0). With (2, 3) as an intermediate point of interpolation we get the piecewise linear approximation over the range $0 \leqslant x_1 \leqslant 5$:

$$x_1 = 0z_1 + 2z_2 + 5z_3$$
$$f^*(x_1) = 4z_1 + 3z_2 + 0z_3$$

where the z_i are nonnegative special variables adding up to unity. Then the capacity constraint (20) as approximated by $x_2 \leqslant f^*(x_1)$ becomes

$$4z_1 + 3z_2 + 0z_3 - x_2 \geqslant 0 \tag{22}$$

where

$$z_1 + z_2 + z_3 = 1. \tag{23}$$

Maximizing the linear preference function, which now becomes

$$z = 0z_1 + 12z_2 + 30z_3 + 9x_2,$$

subject to (22)–(23) with $x_2, z_i \geqslant 0$, we get the LP solution $z_2 = 1$, $x_2 = 3$, i.e.,

$$x_1 = 2, \quad x_2 = 3; \quad z = 39.$$

4. Special facilities for computer solution of nonlinear problems by separable programming are provided by some LP systems such as MPS-360 or LP/90/94.

IV. Quadratic Programming

A. Linear and Quadratic Programming

1. *Quadratic programming* (QP) is the maximization (or minimization) of a quadratic function subject to linear side conditions (equations or inequalities) and to nonnegativity requirements.

Any QP problem can be written in the following form:

$$\begin{aligned} f &= \sum_{j=1}^{n} c_j x_j + Q(x_1, x_2, \ldots, x_n) = \max \\ &\sum_{j=1}^{n} a_{ij} x_j \leqslant b_i \qquad (i = 1, 2, \ldots, m) \\ &x_j \geqslant 0 \qquad\qquad (j = 1, 2, \ldots, n) \end{aligned} \tag{1}$$

where Q is a *quadratic form* in the variables x_j, i.e., a sum of n square terms $c_{jj}x_j^2$ and $n(n-1)/2$ terms with cross products $x_k x_j$ $(k \neq j)$. Splitting the coefficient of each cross product term into two equal parts c_{kj} and c_{jk} so that the term can be written

$$(c_{kj} + c_{jk}) x_k x_j = c_{kj} x_k x_j + c_{jk} x_j x_k \qquad (c_{kj} = c_{jk},\ k \neq j),$$

the quadratic form can be written as a sum of n^2 terms,

$$Q(x_1, x_2, \ldots, x_n) = \sum_{k=1}^{n} \sum_{j=1}^{n} c_{kj} x_k x_j \tag{2}$$

where the matrix of coefficients c_{kj} is square and symmetric[1].

(1) differs from an LP problem only in that these quadratic terms have been added in the preference function.

2. By way of example, consider the following problem of optimal capacity utilization. Two commodities are produced on the same two machines, available up to 5 and 8 hours per period respectively. Then,

[1] For example, $Q = 4x_1^2 + 16x_2^2 + 6x_1x_2$ can be written

$$\begin{aligned} Q &= 4x_1x_1 + 3x_1x_2 \\ &\quad + 3x_2x_1 + 16x_2x_2. \end{aligned}$$

with x_1 and x_2 denoting numbers of units produced per period, the feasible region is defined by $x_1, x_2 \geqslant 0$ and the capacity constraints

$$x_1 + x_2 \leqslant 5 \tag{3}$$

$$x_1 + 2x_2 \leqslant 8 \tag{4}$$

where the coefficients on the left-hand sides are machine times required per unit of product. Let p_1 and p_2 be the prices at which the products can be sold, and let $c_1(x_1)$ and $c_2(x_2)$ be total (variable) costs of producing the respective commodities. With maximum profit per period as the company's objective, optimal production can now be determined by maximizing

$$f = p_1 x_1 + p_2 x_2 - c_1(x_1) - c_2(x_2) \tag{5}$$

subject to (3)–(4) and to $x_1, x_2 \geqslant 0$.

Now if the selling prices and unit costs can be taken to be constant, (5) is a *linear* function and we have an LP problem. For example, let $p_1 = 10$, $p_2 = 9$, $c_1 = 4x_1$, and $c_2 = 3x_2$; then (5) becomes

$$f = 6x_1 + 6x_2. \tag{5a}$$

But if the prices depend on the quantities to be sold and the dependencies can be represented—at least approximately—by linear functions, or if the cost functions $c_1(x_1)$ and $c_2(x_2)$ are quadratic, (3)–(5) becomes a problem in *quadratic* programming.

For example, let the demand functions for the firm's product be

$$p_1 = 12 - x_1, \qquad p_2 = 13 - 2x_2$$

while unit costs are 4 and 3 respectively; then (5) becomes

$$\begin{aligned} f &= (12 - x_1)\,x_1 + (13 - 2x_2)\,x_2 - 4x_1 - 3x_2 \\ &= 8x_1 + 10x_2 - x_1^2 - 2x_2^2. \end{aligned} \tag{5b}$$

[More generally, x_1 as well as x_2 might depend linearly on both prices, in which case there would also be a cross product term with x_1x_2 in the quadratic part of (5b)].

Whatever the shape of the preference function, the *feasible region* as defined by (3)–(4) and $x_1, x_2 \geqslant 0$ will be the convex polygon OCPB in Fig. 7. The *preference function* is represented by a family of straight lines in the linear case (5a). In the quadratic case (5b), the geometric picture of f will be a family of concentric similar ellipses, each corresponding to a particular value of the profit f. Writing (5b) in the form

$$x_1^2 - 8x_1 + 2x_2^2 - 10x_2 = -f$$

we get

$$(x_1 - 4)^2 + 2 \cdot (x_2 - 2.5)^2 = 28.5 - f$$

or, treating the right-hand side as a parameter k,

$$\frac{(x_1 - 4)^2}{(\sqrt{k})^2} + \frac{(x_2 - 2.5)^2}{(\sqrt{k/2})^2} = 1,$$

which represents an ellipse with centre (4, 2.5)—point Q in Fig. 7—and with axes $2\sqrt{k}$ and $2\sqrt{k/2} = \sqrt{2k}$. For $f = 0$, i.e., $k = 28.5$, we have an ellipse passing through the origin (no production, no profit). A larger

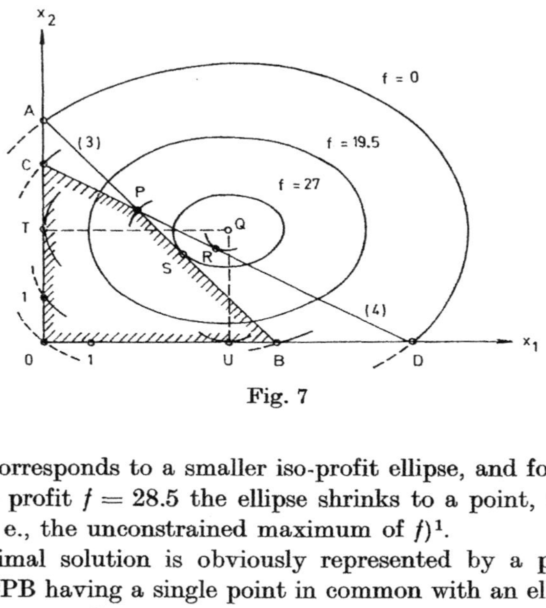

Fig. 7

value of f corresponds to a smaller iso-profit ellipse, and for the largest conceivable profit $f = 28.5$ the ellipse shrinks to a point, the common centre Q (i. e., the unconstrained maximum of f)[1].

The optimal solution is obviously represented by a point on the boundary CPB having a single point in common with an ellipse—in the present case point $S = (3, 2)$ where PB is tangent to the ellipse corresponding to $f = 27$ ($k = 1.5$). If the unconstrained maximum (Q) had been a point of the feasible region, this point would of course have been the optimal solution; the constraints (3)–(4) would then have been redundant (non-binding).

It was shown in Ch. III above how this QP problem could be solved approximately by linearization. In the present chapter we shall indicate some procedures for finding an exact numerical solution.

[1] If there had been a cross product term in the preference function, the axes of the ellipses would not have been parallel to the co-ordinate axes.

B. The Kuhn-Tucker Conditions

1. A solution to the general QP problem (1) must satisfy the Kuhn-Tucker conditions. With the side conditions written

$$(g_i =)\ \ b_i - \sum_{j=1}^{n} a_{ij} x_j \geqslant 0 \qquad (i = 1, 2, \ldots, m),$$

the Lagrangian $L = f + \sum_i u_i g_i$ leads to the Kuhn-Tucker conditions for problem (1):

$$c_j + \partial Q/\partial x_j - \sum_i a_{ij} u_i \leqslant 0, \quad x_j \geqslant 0, \quad x_j \cdot (c_j + \partial Q/\partial x_j - \sum_i a_{ij} u_i) = 0 \qquad \text{(6a–c)}$$

$$b_i - \sum_j a_{ij} x_j \geqslant 0, \quad u_i \geqslant 0, \quad u_i \cdot (b_i - \sum_j a_{ij} x_j) = 0 \qquad \text{(7a–c)}$$

which are *necessary* conditions for a maximum of f subject to the linear side conditions $g_i \geqslant 0$ and to $x_j \geqslant 0$. (6)–(7) are *necessary and sufficient* for a *global* maximum is f is *concave*.

A problem of *minimizing* a quadratic function g can be treated as the maximization of $f = -g$, where f is concave if the function to be minimized is *convex*.

Since the quadratic form (2) is a sum of square terms $c_{jj} x_j^2$ and cross product terms $c_{kj} x_k x_j$ $(k \neq j)$, with derivatives $2 c_{jj} x_j$ and $c_{kj} x_k$ respectively, $\partial Q/\partial x_j$ is a linear expression in the x_j so that (6a) is a linear inequality in the variables x_j and u_i:

$$(\partial L/\partial x_j =)\ \ c_j + 2 \sum_k c_{kj} x_k - \sum_i a_{ij} u_i \leqslant 0.$$

Therefore, solving the QP problem (1) is equivalent to finding a nonnegative solution (x_j°, u_i°) to the linear inequalities (6a) and (7a) which also satisfies the combinatorial equations (6c) and (7c), that is, either x_j or $\partial L/\partial x_j$ (or both) must be zero and similarly for u_i and $\partial L/\partial u_i$[1]. As we shall see, some of the algorithms for QP are based upon this linearity of the Kuhn-Tucker conditions.

2. Applying this to the example above—(3)–(4) with (5b)—the Lagrangian is

$$L = 8x_1 + 10x_2 - x_1^2 - 2x_2^2 + u_1 (5 - x_1 - x_2) + u_2 (8 - x_1 - 2x_2)$$

---

[1] If some or all of the side conditions are *equations* $(g_h = 0)$, the multipliers u_h are not required to be nonnegative and the corresponding conditions (7a–c) must be replaced by $(\partial Q/\partial u_h =)\ g_h = 0$. See Ch. II, pp. 17 f.

from which we derive the Kuhn-Tucker conditions

$$8 - 2x_1 - u_1 - u_2 \leqslant 0, \quad x_1 \geqslant 0, \quad x_1 \cdot (8 - 2x_1 - u_1 - u_2) = 0 \qquad \text{(8a–c)}$$

$$10 - 4x_2 - u_1 - 2u_2 \leqslant 0, \quad x_2 \geqslant 0, \quad x_2 \cdot (10 - 4x_2 - u_1 - 2u_2) = 0 \qquad \text{(9a–c)}$$

$$5 - x_1 - x_2 \geqslant 0, \quad u_1 \geqslant 0, \quad u_1 \cdot (5 - x_1 - x_2) = 0 \qquad \text{(10a–c)}$$

$$8 - x_1 - 2x_2 \geqslant 0, \quad u_2 \geqslant 0, \quad u_2 \cdot (8 - x_1 - 2x_2) = 0. \qquad \text{(11a–c)}$$

The geometric solution $(x_1, x_2) = (3, 2)$—point S in Fig. 7—is seen to satisfy these conditions with $(u_1, u_2) = (2, 0)$. It represents a global maximum since the preference function is concave term by term.

3. More generally, the quadratic form Q in the preference function will also have cross product terms, $c_{kj} x_k x_j$ $(k \neq j)$. In such cases it is not obvious whether Q is concave or convex over the region of definition, or neither concave nor convex.

It can be proved[1] that if the quadratic form is *positive semidefinite*, i.e., $Q \geqslant 0$ for all values of $x_1, x_2, \ldots, x_n$, the form—and thus also f—will be *convex*; if it is *negative semidefinite*, i. e., $Q \leqslant 0$, the quadratic form is *concave*. If, furthermore, Q $(\geqslant 0)$ vanishes only for all $x_j = 0$ so that it is *positive definite*, the quadratic form is *strictly convex*, that is, linear interpolation will always overestimate the value of Q. A *negative definite* quadratic form ($Q \leqslant 0$, $Q = 0$ only for all $x_j = 0$) is *strictly concave*[2].

To examine whether a given quadratic form is definite, the method of "completing the square" can be applied. Consider the form

$$Q = 5x_1^2 + 10x_2^2 - 10x_1x_2 \qquad (12)$$

and reduce it to a sum of squares

$$Q = (ax_1 + bx_2)^2 + (cx_1 + dx_2)^2 = (x_1 - 3x_2)^2 + (2x_1 - x_2)^2$$

where a, b, c, and d are determined by rearranging terms and equating the coefficients of like terms[3]. The reduced expression is nonnegative for all values of x_1 and x_2 and vanishes only for $x_1 = x_2 = 0$, hence Q

[1] See e.g. S. Vajda (1961), p. 223.

[2] **Exercise 7:** Show geometrically that the quadratic form in (5b) is negative definite and strictly concave in the nonnegative region.

[3] The reduction is not unique.

is positive definite. The procedure is readily generalized to cases of more than two variables.

Equivalent necessary and sufficient conditions for a quadratic form (2) to be *positive definite* are[1]

$$c_{11} > 0, \quad \begin{vmatrix} c_{11} & c_{12} \\ c_{21} & c_{22} \end{vmatrix} > 0, \quad \begin{vmatrix} c_{11} & c_{12} & c_{13} \\ c_{21} & c_{22} & c_{23} \\ c_{31} & c_{32} & c_{33} \end{vmatrix} > 0, \quad \ldots$$

that is, the determinant of the (symmetric) matrix of coefficients c_{kj} and its principal minors must all be positive. Q is *negative definite* if and only if the determinants are alternatively negative and positive ($c_{11} < 0$, etc.). Applying these conditions to (12) we have

$$5 > 0, \quad \begin{vmatrix} 5 & -5 \\ -5 & 10 \end{vmatrix} = 25 > 0$$

so that the form is positive definite. The quadratic form in (5b) is negative definite because

$$-1 < 0, \quad \begin{vmatrix} -1 & 0 \\ 0 & -2 \end{vmatrix} = 2 > 0^2.$$

C. Combinatorial Solution

1. The Kuhn-Tucker conditions provide a criterion by which a feasible solution to a QP problem can be tested for optimality, but they give no instructions as to how an optimal solution is to be found[3].

In simple cases a *guessing* procedure can be used to solve the problem by hand, making use of the *combinatorial* nature of conditions (6c) and (7c): either x_j or $\partial L/\partial x_j$ (or both) must vanish and similarly for u_i and $\partial L/\partial u_i$. Making a guess as to which of the variables x_j and u_i are positive, we can solve the corresponding linear equations $\partial L/\partial x_j = 0$ and $\partial L/\partial u_i = 0$ and see if the solution satisfies all of the conditions; if it does not, the guess is revised, and so on.

---

[1] See, for example, R. G. D. Allen (1938), pp. 485ff.

[2] **Exercise 8:** Examine the following quadratic forms for definiteness:

$$Q_1 = 26x_1^2 + 8x_2^2 - 24x_1x_2,$$
$$Q_2 = -26x_1^2 - 8x_2^2 + 24x_1x_2,$$
$$Q_3 = -26x_1^2 - 8x_2^2 + 30x_1x_2.$$

[3] Cp. the simplex criterion, which has to be supplemented with an algorithm (the simplex method) for LP problems.

Applying this procedure to the numerical example above,

$$\begin{aligned} f &= 8x_1 + 10x_2 - x_1^2 - 2x_2^2 \\ x_1 + x_2 &\leqslant 5 \\ x_1 + 2x_2 &\leqslant 8 \\ x_1, x_2 &\geqslant 0 \end{aligned} \tag{13}$$

with the Kuhn-Tucker conditions (8)–(11), let us guess

$$x_1 > 0, \quad x_2 > 0$$

which would require

$$\begin{aligned} (\partial L/\partial x_1 =) \quad 8 - 2x_1 - u_1 - u_2 &= 0 \\ (\partial L/\partial x_2 =) \quad 10 - 4x_2 - u_1 - 2u_2 &= 0. \end{aligned}$$

If we make the further guess

$$u_2 > 0 \quad (\text{but } u_1 = 0)$$

so that

$$(\partial L/\partial u_2 =) \quad 8 - x_1 - 2x_2 = 0,$$

we have 3 equations in 3 variables (with u_1 set $= 0$); the solution is

$$x_1 = 11/3, \quad x_2 = 13/6, \quad u_1 = 0, \quad u_2 = 2/3$$

which satisfies conditions (8), (9), (10b–c), and (11). It remains to see whether (10a) is also satisfied. We have

$$\partial L/\partial u_1 = 5 - x_1 - x_2 = -5/6 < 0$$

which violates (10a). The solution must therefore be rejected.

Now try instead $x_1, x_2 > 0$ combined with

$$u_1 > 0 \quad (\text{but } u_2 = 0)$$

so that $\partial L/\partial u_2 = 0$ is replaced by

$$(\partial L/\partial u_1 =) \quad 5 - x_1 - x_2 = 0.$$

Solving the three equations we get the solution

$$x_1 = 3, \quad x_2 = 2, \quad u_1 = 2, \quad u_2 = 0$$

which is seen to satisfy all of the conditions, including (11a):

$$\partial L/\partial u_2 = 8 - x_1 - 2x_2 = 1 > 0$$

so that the solution represents an optimum.

This procedure soon becomes inapplicable to problems of larger dimension because the number of combinations increases fast with the number of variables (x_j) and side conditions (i.e., u_i)—the more so as we do not know beforehand how many x's and u's will be positive in the optimal solution.

2. A more systematic procedure for exploring the possible combinations has been developed by Theil and van de Panne and made the basis of an algorithm for quadratic programming.

As we have seen above[1], a problem in nonlinear programming could be solved by "classical" methods if we knew in advance which of the inequalities (side conditions and nonnegativity requirements) are binding (i.e., satisfied in equality form) in the optimum and which are not. For each combination of (hypothetically) binding and non-binding inequalities the maximum solution is computed, applying the classical Lagrange method to the binding side conditions and ignoring those which are not assumed to be binding, and the resulting values of the preference function are compared. The solution which gives the largest value of f and satisfies the non-binding restrictions (in inequality form) represents the optimum solution.

In the example above—cf. also Fig. 7— the optimal solution may be an *interior* point of the feasible region OCPB, that is, none of the inequalities is binding, or else it must be a point on the *boundary* of the region where at least one restriction is satisfied in equality form. This exhausts the possibilities. All we have to do, therefore, is to examine all cases of 0, 1, or 2 binding inequalities[2].

Assuming that *no inequality is binding*, the solution will be the point at which f is an unconstrained maximum, determined by

$$\partial f/\partial x_1 = 8 - 2x_1 = 0, \quad \partial f/\partial x_2 = 10 - 4x_2 = 0$$

from which we have

$$x_1 = 4, \quad x_2 = 2.5; \quad f = 28.5 \tag{14}$$

corresponding to *point Q* in Fig. 7 (the centre of the ellipses). The solution violates both of the side conditions and must therefore be rejected.

With *one binding inequality* there are four possibilities since the problem has two side conditions and two nonnegativity requirements.

If the first side condition is binding, the corresponding solution is found by applying the Lagrangian $L = f + u_1 (5 - x_1 - x_2)$ in the classical fashion:

$$\begin{aligned} \partial L/\partial x_1 &= 8 - 2x_1 \qquad\qquad - u_1 = 0 \\ \partial L/\partial x_2 &= 10 \qquad\qquad - 4x_2 - u_1 = 0 \\ (\partial L/\partial u_1 &=)\ 5 - x_1 - x_2 \qquad\qquad = 0 \end{aligned}$$

[1] Cf. p. 10.

[2] There is no point in the feasible region OCPB at which more than two inequalities are satisfied exactly.

which gives the solution

$$x_1 = 3, \quad x_2 = 2, \quad u_1 = 2; \quad f = 27 \tag{15}$$

(*point S* in Fig. 7, where AB is tangent to the ellipse $f = 27$). This is a feasible solution, and therefore possibly an optimal one.

With the second side condition as the sole binding restriction we get similarly

$$x_1 = 11/3, \quad x_2 = 13/6, \quad u_2 = 2/3; \quad f = 169/6$$

which is *point R*. The solution violates the first capacity constraint.

If the nonnegativity requirement $x_1 \geqslant 0$ is binding, we set $x_1 = 0$ in the preference function and maximize f with respect to x_2. This leads to the feasible solution

$$x_1 = 0, \quad x_2 = 2.5; \quad f = 12.5$$

(*point T*, the best point on the vertical axis); similarly, with $x_2 \geqslant 0$ binding we get *point U*,

$$x_1 = 4, \quad x_2 = 0; \quad f = 16,$$

which is also a feasible solution.

Finally, assume that *two restrictions* are binding. There are six combinations in this group; each of the six solutions is uniquely determined by the corresponding two equations so that no maximization is involved.

The resulting $1 + 4 + 6 = 11$ solutions are shown in the following table, where f has been calculated for feasible solutions only. The best feasible solution is the one corresponding to point S in Fig. 7.

Number of binding inequalities	x_1	x_2	f	Point in Fig. 7
0	4	2.5	—	Q
1	3	2	27	S
	11/3	13/6	—	R
	0	2.5	12.5	T
	4	0	16	U
2	2	3	24	P
	0	5	—	A
	5	0	15	B
	0	4	8	C
	8	0	—	D
	0	0	0	O

3. Such a combinatorial procedure is clearly an inefficient method of solution, especially when the number of variables and side conditions is greater than in our example (13). However, it can be put to good use as the starting point of the *Theil-van de Panne algorithm* for QP[1].

Like the procedure above, the algorithm starts by determining the unconstrained maximum (no binding restrictions). If this is a feasible solution, the problem has been solved; if not, we proceed to maximize subject to one binding constraint, and so forth. However, it is not necessary to examine all of the combinations. The method indicates a criterion by which a feasible solution attained at some step of the procedure can be tested for optimality; this means that the procedure normally terminates before all of the combinations have been explored. Moreover, the algorithm indicates rules for steering clear of some of the combinations[2].

The optimality criterion can be formulated as follows. A solution corresponding to a given set of (hypothetically) binding inequalities is optimal if it is *feasible* (i.e., respects the nonbinding inequalities) and *if the Lagrange multipliers associated with the binding side conditions are positive.*

Solution (15) above is seen to satisfy this criterion; it is feasible and u_1 is positive. Since (15) was determined by setting the partial derivatives of $L = f + u_1(5 - x_1 - x_2)$ equal to zero, assuming $x_1 + x_2 = 5$, this means that the solution satisfies the Kuhn-Tucker conditions for a maximum of f subject to $x_1 + x_2 \leqslant 5$ $(x_1, x_2 \geqslant 0)$ because we have

$$\begin{aligned} 8 - 2x_1 - u_1 &= 0, & x_1 &> 0, & x_1 \cdot (8 - 2x_1 - u_1) &= 0 \\ 10 - 4x_2 - u_1 &= 0, & x_2 &> 0, & x_2 \cdot (10 - 4x_2 - u_1) &= 0 \\ 5 - x_1 - x_2 &= 0, & u_1 &> 0, & u_1 \cdot (5 - x_1 - x_2) &= 0. \end{aligned}$$

Moreover, since it is a feasible solution to the complete problem (13),

$$8 - x_1 - 2x_2 \geqslant 0.$$

It follows that the solution also satisfies the Kuhn-Tucker conditions for the complete problem, (8)–(11), for $u_2 = 0$. It is therefore an optimal solution to (13) and the procedure terminates with the second step; there is no need to calculate the remaining nine solutions in the table above.

---

[1] Cf. H. Theil and C. van de Panne (1960). See also J. C. G. Boot (1961), (1962), and (1963).

[2] Compare the simplex method, which also indicates rules for getting to an optimal solution without having to enumerate all of the combinations (corners) which are candidates for optimality.

The Theil-van de Panne algorithm requires the preference function to be strictly concave (in minimization problems, strictly convex). The procedure is obviously best suited for problems in which the optimal solution is "not too far from" the unconstrained maximum, i.e., cases in which only a few restrictions can be expected to be binding.

D. Wolfe's Method

1. As we have seen, finding a solution to the Kuhn-Tucker conditions for a quadratic problem is equivalent to finding a nonnegative solution to a system of linear inequalities (6a–b) and (7a–b) which also satisfies the combinatorial equations (6c) and (7c). We shall now demonstrate an algorithm—*Wolfe's method*[1]—which makes use of the linear simplex technique to find such a solution.

As in linear programming, the linear inequalities are first converted into linear equations, introducing nonnegative slack variables v_j into (6a) and y_i into (7a):

$$\partial L/\partial x_j + v_j = 0 \qquad (j = 1, 2, \ldots, n)$$

$$\partial L/\partial u_i - y_i = 0 \qquad (i = 1, 2, \ldots, m).$$

Since $v_j = -\partial L/\partial x_j$ and $y_i = \partial L/\partial u_i$, the combinatorial equations (6c) and (7c) can now be written

$$x_j v_j = 0, \qquad u_i y_i = 0.$$

Applying this to the numerical example (13), the corresponding Kuhn-Tucker conditions (8)–(11) can be written[2]

$$8 - 2x_1 \qquad - u_1 - u_2 + v_1 = 0 \qquad (16)$$

$$10 \qquad - 4x_2 - u_1 - 2u_2 \qquad + v_2 = 0 \qquad (17)$$

$$5 - x_1 - x_2 \qquad - y_1 = 0 \qquad (18)$$

$$8 - x_1 - 2x_2 \qquad - y_2 = 0, \qquad (19)$$

where

$$x_1, x_2, y_1, y_2, u_1, u_2, v_1, v_2 \geqslant 0 \qquad (20)$$

and

$$x_1 v_1 = 0, \quad x_2 v_2 = 0, \quad u_1 y_1 = 0, \quad u_2 y_2 = 0. \qquad (21)$$

If we can find a basic feasible solution to (16)–(19) which is in "*standard*

---

[1] Cf. P. Wolfe (1959). See also W. S. Dorn (1963), pp. 183—188, H. P. Künzi and W. Krelle (1962), Ch. 8, S. Vajda (1961), pp. 239—241, and S. Vajda (1962), pp. 108f.

[2] Cf. Ch. II, p. 17 [conditions (11)–(14)].

form", i.e., satisfies (21), we have solved the problem. In linear programming terms, (21) merely implies a restriction on the choice of basic variables: at most one from each pair of "corresponding variables" (x_j, v_j) or (u_i, y_i) is allowed to be basic. If x_j, say, is positive, i.e. basic, v_j must be nonbasic and therefore equal to zero in the basic solution.

2. The choice of an initial basis in Wolfe's algorithm proceeds as follows. As in linear programming, it is convenient to have as many *slack variables* as possible in the basis, but the solution obtained by setting all other variables (the x_j and the u_i) equal to zero will be negative in some of the slack variables v_j or y_i; the negative slack variables must therefore be replaced by *artificial variables* in the basis[1].

In a quadratic *maximization* problem such as (13), negative values will typically occur for some or all of the v_j. Setting $x_1 = x_2 = u_1 = u_2 = 0$ in (16)–(19) we have the basic solution

$$v_1 = -8, \quad v_2 = -10, \quad y_1 = 5, \quad y_2 = 8$$

which is in standard form but not feasible. We therefore introduce nonnegative artificial variables z_1 and z_2 with coefficients -1 in (16) and (17),

$$8 - 2x_1 \qquad - u_1 - u_2 + v_1 \qquad - z_1 \qquad = 0 \qquad (16\,a)$$

$$10 \qquad - 4x_2 - u_1 - 2u_2 \qquad + v_2 \qquad - z_2 = 0, \qquad (17\,a)$$

and select z_1, z_2, y_1, and y_2 as initial basic variables; the corresponding basic solution is

$$z_1 = 8, \quad z_2 = 10, \quad y_1 = 5, \quad y_2 = 8,$$

which is positive.

All we have to do now is to proceed to another basic feasible solution in which z_1 and z_2 have been thrown out of the basis (i. e., $z_1 = z_2 = 0$) so that (16)–(17) are satisfied in their original form along with (18)–(19). This can be done by *minimizing the linear function*

$$g = z_1 + z_2$$

subject to (16a), (17a), (18), and (19) and to the nonnegativity requirements (including $z_1, z_2 \geqslant 0$). This is a common LP problem which can be solved by the simplex method, with the slight modification that the restriction implied by (21) must be taken into account when the basis is changed. The minimum value of g ($g = 0$ for $z_1 = z_2 = 0$) will be

[1] Compare the use of artificial basic variables in LP problems with inequalities of the type $\geq$. (See S. Danø (1974), pp. 81ff.)

attained in a finite number of iterations[1]. In the present case the optimum solution comes out in the fourth simplex tableau:

				0	0	0	0	0	0	0	0	1	1
			x_0	x_1	x_2	y_1	y_2	u_1	u_2	v_1	v_2	z_1	z_2
	1	z_1	8	2				1	1	−1		1	
	1	z_2	10		**4**			1	2		−1		1
I	0	y_1	5	1	1	1							
	0	y_2	8	1	2		1						
		g	18	2	4	0	0	2	3	−1	−1	0	0
	1	z_1	8	2				1	1	−1		1	
	0	x_2	5/2		1			1/4	1/2		−1/4		1/4
II	0	y_1	5/2	**1**		1		−1/4	−1/2		1/4		−1/4
	0	y_2	3	1			1	−1/2	−1		1/2		−1/2
		g	8	2	0	0	0	1	1	−1	0	0	−1
	1	z_1	3			−2		**3/2**	2	−1	−1/2	1	1/2
	0	x_2	5/2		1			1/4	1/2		−1/4		1/4
III	0	x_1	5/2	1		1		−1/4	−1/2		1/4		−1/4
	0	y_2	1/2			−1	1	−1/4	−1/2		1/4		−1/4
		g	3	0	0	−2	0	3/2	2	−1	−1/2	0	−1/2
	0	u_1	2			−4/3		1	4/3	−2/3	−1/3	2/3	1/3
	0	x_2	2		1	1/3			1/6	1/6	−1/6	−1/6	1/6
IV	0	x_1	3	1		2/3			−1/6	−1/6	1/6	1/6	−1/6
	0	y_2	1			−4/3	1		−1/6	−1/6	1/6	1/6	−1/6
		g	0	0	0	0	0	0	0	0	0	−1	−1

Observe that, in the third tableau, u_1 is selected as the new variable to come into the basis although u_2 has a larger simplex coefficient ($2 > 3/2$). The introduction of u_2 would throw z_1 out of the basis, which would imply that u_2 and y_2 would both be in the next basis so that (21) would be violated.

The solution in Tableau IV satisfies the complete Kuhn-Tucker conditions (16)–(21) and therefore represents the optimal solution of the QP problem (13)[2].

[1] The point of the preference function $g = z_1 + z_2$ is that only those variables which we want to get rid of have positive coefficients; all other variables have the coefficient zero in g so that a basis of non-artificial variables will eventually be preferred. Cf. the way in which artificial variables are eliminated from the basis in linear minimization problems because they are given a large but unspecified coefficient M in the function to be minimized.

[2] The solution in Tableau IV is not a unique solution to the problem of minimizing g subject to (16a), (17a), (18), and (19); but the nonbasic

Wolfe's method is immediately applicable to problems in which the quadratic form in the preference function is definite. When the form is only semidefinite, a modified two-stage version of the algorithm must be used.

3. In *minimization* problems, where the side conditions are typically inequalities of the form $\geqslant$, the basic solution in the slack variables (v_j, y_i) will be negative in some or all of the y_i. To get a feasible initial basic solution these variables will have to be replaced in the basis by artificial variables in the side conditions.

Consider, for example, the following problem:

$$\begin{aligned} F = \; & 2x_1 + 8x_2 + x_1^2 + 2x_2^2 = \min \\ & 10x_1 + 16x_2 \geqslant 72 \\ & x_1, x_2 \geqslant 0. \end{aligned} \tag{22}$$

Rewriting it as a maximization problem (max f where $f = -F$) we have the Lagrangian

$$L = -2x_1 - 8x_2 - x_1^2 - 2x_2^2 + u \cdot (10x_1 + 16x_2 - 72)$$

which leads to the following Kuhn-Tucker conditions with slack variables v_1, v_2, and y:

$$-2 - 2x_1 + 10u + v_1 = 0 \tag{23}$$

$$-8 - 4x_2 + 16u + v_2 = 0 \tag{24}$$

$$-72 + 10x_1 + 16x_2 - y = 0 \tag{25}$$

$$x_1, x_2, y, u, v_1, v_2 \geqslant 0 \tag{26}$$

$$x_1 v_1 = 0, \quad x_2 v_2 = 0, \quad uy = 0. \tag{27}$$

Solving (23)–(25) for the slack variables we find that the v_j are now positive, whereas $y = -72 < 0$ so that an artificial variable z has to be added in (25) with the coefficient $+1$:

$$-72 + 10x_1 + 16x_2 - y + z = 0. \tag{25a}$$

A feasible initial basis is (v_1, v_2, z). Minimizing the function $g = z$ (more generally: $g = \sum z_i$) will solve the problem in four steps as shown in Tableaux I–IV below. The optimal solution to (22) is seen to be $x_1 = 4$, $x_2 = 2$, $u = 1$.

---

variables whose simplex coefficients are $= 0$ cannot be introduced into the basis without violating (21). **Exercise 9:** Show this for each of the variables y_1, u_2, v_1, and v_2.

				0	0	0	0	0	0	1
			x_0	x_1	x_2	y	v_1	v_2	u	z
I	0	v_1	2	-2			1		**10**	
	0	v_2	8		-4			1	16	
	1	z	72	10	16	-1				1
		g	72	10	16	-1	0	0	0	0
II	0	u	1/5	$-1/5$			1/10		1	
	0	v_2	24/5	**16/5**	-4		$-8/5$	1		
	1	z	72	10	16	-1				1
		g	72	10	16	-1	0	0	0	0
III	0	u	1/2		$-1/4$			1/16	1	
	0	x_1	3/2	1	$-5/4$		$-1/2$	5/16		
	1	z	57		**57/2**	-1	5	$-25/8$		1
		g	57	0	57/2	-1	5	$-25/8$	0	0
IV	0	u	1			$-1/114$	5/114	2/57	1	1/114
	0	x_1	4	1		$-5/114$	$-16/57$	10/57		5/114
	0	x_2	2		1	$-2/57$	10/57	$-25/228$		2/57
		g	0	0	0	0	0	0	0	-1

E. The Simplèx Method for Quadratic Programming

1. The next algorithm to be demostrated—*the simplex method for quadratic programming*, also known as *the Dantzig-van de Panne method*[1]—is related to Wolfe's method in that it is based directly on the Kuhn-Tucker conditions, written in equality form. No artificial variables are used, however; the initial basis is composed of slack variables only, negative values being permitted. Using a modified simplex procedure, the basis is changed in a sequence of simplex tableaux in such a manner that negative values are eventually got rid of in the x_0 column.

2. To solve the *maximization* problem (13) by the quadratic simplex method, write the Kuhn-Tucker conditions in the form (16)–(21) and select v_1, v_2, y_1, and y_2 as basic variables for the linear equations (16)–(19). Then v_1 and v_2 will be negative in the initial basic solution. The successive transformations of the tableaux proceed according to the rules of the simplex method for LP, except that the variable to be introduced and the variable to be replaced at each step are selected differently. Only the "dual variables" u_i and v_j are allowed to take

[1] This method was first developed by G. B. Dantzig and later (independently) by C. van de Panne. Cf. G. B. Dantzig (1961) and (1963), Ch. 24.4; C. van de Panne (1962); and C. van de Panne and A. Whinston (1964) and (1969).

negative values in the x_0 column. Since the variable to become basic at each step is not determined by the coefficients of f, there is no need to introduce a row for the preference function.

The rules for changing the basis are as follows:

(i) If a tableau is *in standard form* so that no pair of corresponding variables (x_j, v_j) or (u_i, y_i) are in the basis, select as the variable to be *introduced* the "primal variable" (x_j or y_i) whose corresponding dual variable (v_j or u_i) is most negative in the basic solution. The variable to be *replaced* is selected in accordance with the rules of the common simplex method for LP, except that the ratios are calculated only in the rows of the primal basic variables and in the row of the most negative dual variable.

(ii) In a *nonstandard* tableau there will be one "basic pair" of corresponding variables in the basis and one "nonbasic pair". The dual variable of the nonbasic pair is the variable to be *introduced*; the variable to be *replaced* is selected by applying the usual criterion to the rows of the primal basic variables and to the row of the dual variable of the basic pair.

Applying these rules to (16)–(19), problem (13) is solved in four steps, cf. Tableaux I–IV below. The first two tableaux are in standard form, whereas III is a nonstandard tableau with the basic pair (x_1, v_1) and the nonbasic pair (u_1, y_1). The solution in Tableau IV is a nonnegative standard solution and therefore an optimal one[1].

		x_0	x_1	x_2	y_1	y_2	u_1	u_2	v_1	v_2
I	v_1	-8	-2				-1	-1	1	
	v_2	-10		**-4**			-1	-2		1
	y_1	5	1	1	1					
	y_2	8	1	2		1				
II	v_1	-8	-2				-1	-1	1	
	x_2	5/2		1			1/4	1/2		$-1/4$
	y_1	5/2	**1**		1		$-1/4$	$-1/2$		1/4
	y_2	3	1			1	$-1/2$	-1		1/2
III	v_1	-3			2		**$-3/2$**	-2	1	1/2
	x_2	5/2		1			1/4	1/2		$-1/4$
	x_1	5/2	1		1		$-1/4$	$-1/2$		1/4
	y_2	1/2			-1	1	$-1/4$	$-1/2$		1/4
IV	u_1	2			$-4/3$		1	4/3	$-2/3$	$-1/3$
	x_2	2		1	1/3			1/6	1/6	$-1/6$
	x_1	3	1		2/3			$-1/6$	$-1/6$	1/6
	y_2	1			$-4/3$	1		$-1/6$	$-1/6$	1/6

[1] **Exercise 10:** Compare in detail Tableaux I–IV with the simplex tableaux used with Wolfe's method above.

The quadratic simplex method does not require f to be strictly concave; it is sufficient that the quadratic form is negative semidefinite so that f is concave (in maximization problems).

3. Like Wolfe's algorithm, the simplex method for quadratic programming must be slightly modified to be applicable to *minimization* problems.

Consider, for example, problem (22) and its Kuhn-Tucker conditions (23)–(27). With an initial basis of slack variables only, the v_j will now be positive in the basic solution whereas y is negative ($= -72$), contrary to the rule that only dual variables are allowed to be negative in a tableau. However, the problem can be solved by the procedure described above if the v_j and the u_i in (23)–(25) are treated as if they were primal variables, while the x_j and the y_i are treated as dual variables. Starting from an initial tableau with the slack variables v_j and y_i as basic variables for the linear equations (23)–(25), rules (i)–(ii) are applied to change the basis from each tableau to the next, but *with the rôles of primal and dual variables interchanged.* Only the x_j and the y_i—now considered as dual variables—are now allowed to assume negative values in the x_0 column.

This modification of the Dantzig-van de Panne algorithm is called the *dual simplex method for QP* because what we actually do is to solve the dual of the problem within the framework (i.e., the simplex tableaux) of the primal problem. The dual of a QP problem is also a quadratic problem[1].

If we prefer to go on considering the x_j and the y_i as primal variables and the v_j and u_i as dual variables, the rules (i)–(ii) can be formulated as follows:

(i′) If a tableau is *in standard form,* the variable to be *introduced* is the dual variable v_j or u_i with the most negative primal variable x_j or y_i. The variable to be *replaced* is selected as in the simplex procedure for LP, applied only to the rows of the dual basic variables (v_j and u_i) and to the row of the most negative primal variable.

(ii′) In a *nonstandard* tableau, the primal variable of the nonbasic pair is the variable to be *introduced*; the variable to be *replaced* is selected as in the common simplex method, but considering only the rows of the dual basic variables (v_j and u_i) and the row of the primal variable of the basic pair.

Only primal variables (x_j, y_i) are allowed to take negative values.

Applying this to problem (22), the optimal solution comes out in the fourth tableau[2].

---

[1] Cf. Ch. II, p. 21.

[2] **Exercise 11:** Illustrate problem (22) geometrically after the fashion of Fig. 7.

		x_0	x_1	x_2	y	v_1	v_2	u
	v_1	2	− 2			1		**10**
I	v_2	8		− 4			1	16
	y	− 72	− 10	− 16	1			
	u	1/5	− 1/5			1/10		1
II	v_2	24/5	**16/5**	− 4		− 8/5	1	
	y	− 72	− 10	− 16	1			
	u	1/2		− 1/4			1/16	1
III	x_1	3/2	1	− 5/4		− 1/2	5/16	
	y	− 57		**− 57/2**	1	− 5	25/8	
	u	1			− 1/114	5/114	2/57	1
IV	x_1	4	1		− 5/114	− 16/57	10/57	
	x_2	2		1	− 2/57	10/57	− 25/228	

Tableau I is in standard form, whereas the pair (u, y) are both basic in Tableau II and III, the nonbasic pair being (x_1, v_1) and (x_2, v_2) respectively. Tableau IV is in standard form, and the solution is positive in all basic variables and therefore represents the optimal solution to (22).

F. Beale's Method

1. The algorithms of Wolfe and Dantzig-van de Panne apply a modified simplex procedure to the linear Kuhn-Tucker conditions for a QP problem. Another possible approach—natural enough in view of the fact that the feasible region is of the same form as in LP problems—is to exploit the basic principles of the simplex method in constructing a simplicial procedure which can be applied directly to QP problems. An algorithm based on this approach has been developed by E. M. L. Beale.

Like the simplex method for LP, *Beale's method*[1] is an iterative procedure starting out from an initial basic feasible solution, i.e., a corner of the feasible region. Substituting the solution for the basic variables into the preference function f, we can examine whether the solution can be improved by introducing some nonbasic variable x_j into the basis; this will be so if $\partial f/\partial x_j$ (no longer a constant as in LP but a linear function) is positive, in which case it pays to move to the next basis. The process is repeated until the solution can no longer be improved. However, the concept of a basis will have to be modified in the process because the optimal solution is not necessarily a corner of the feasible

[1] Cf. E. M. L. Beale (1955), (1959), and (1968), Ch. 13. See also H. P. Künzi and W. Krelle (1962), Ch. 7, and S. Vajda (1961), pp. 224—230.

region (cf. point S in Fig. 7). As we shall see, this is done by introducing auxiliary variables and corresponding additional constraints during the computations.

2. We shall now solve the numerical problem (13) using Beale's method.

With an initial basis of slack variables (y_1, y_2) we have

$$\begin{aligned} y_1 &= 5 - x_1 - x_2 \\ y_2 &= 8 - x_1 - 2x_2 \\ f &= 0 + 8x_1 + 10x_2 - x_1^2 - 2x_2^2 \end{aligned} \tag{28}$$

where the constant terms represent the basic solution. Corresponding to the simplex coefficients in the linear simplex method we now have

$$\partial f/\partial x_1 = 8 - 2x_1, \quad \partial f/\partial x_2 = 10 - 4x_2,$$

both of which are positive for $x_1 = x_2 = 0$ so that f is an increasing function of x_1 and x_2 in the neighbourhood of the basic solution. Since $\partial f/\partial x_2$ is the greater of the two derivatives ($10 > 8$) we choose x_2 to become positive, keeping x_1 at zero.

Thus far we have only followed the simplex procedure for LP; the quadratic terms in f—i.e., the linear terms in the derivatives $\partial f/\partial x_j$—have made no difference. But there are now three upper limits to the increase in x_2, namely, the two values at which a basic variable becomes zero (as in linear programming) and that for which $\partial f/\partial x_2 = 0$ so that f no longer increases with x_2:

$$\begin{aligned} (y_1 =)\ 5 - x_2 &\geqslant 0, &\quad \text{i.e. } x_2 &\leqslant 5 \\ (y_2 =)\ 8 - 2x_2 &\geqslant 0, &\quad \text{i.e. } x_2 &\leqslant 4 \\ (\partial f/\partial x_2 =)\ 10 - 4x_2 &\geqslant 0, &\quad \text{i.e. } x_2 &\leqslant 5/2. \end{aligned}$$

The third is the effective limit. For $x_2 = 5/2$ we have $y_1 = 5/2$ and $y_2 = 3$ (and still $x_1 = 0$); since there are now three positive variables, this point does not represent a basic solution. Geometrically, it is not a corner of the feasible region OCPB in Fig. 7 but a point on OC.

To make good this deficiency, introduce an auxiliary variable z_1, defined by $z_1 = \partial f/\partial x_2$, so that we have

$$z_1 = 10 - 4x_2. \tag{29}$$

Considering (29) as an additional constraint—introduced with retrospective application, as it were—the initial solution can be thought of as a basic solution to the enlarged problem (28)–(29), with z_1 as a third basic variable; and the next solution, in which $x_2 = 5/2$ so that z_1 has been reduced to 0, will be another basic solution to the enlarged problem. Solving (29) for the basic variable x_2 in terms of z_1 and substituting into (28)—an operation corresponding to what we do in LP when the basis is changed, except that f is now a quadratic function—we have

$$\begin{aligned} x_2 &= \frac{5}{2} \qquad\quad - \frac{1}{4} z_1 \\ y_1 &= \frac{5}{2} - x_1 + \frac{1}{4} z_1 \\ y_2 &= 3 - x_1 + \frac{1}{2} z_1 \\ f &= \frac{25}{2} + 8x_1 - x_1^2 - \frac{1}{8} z_1^2 \end{aligned} \tag{30}$$

where the constant terms represent the new basic solution.

We are now ready to proceed to the third basis. It must be borne in mind, though, that from now on z_1 is a *free* variable, not restricted as to sign[1]. It was only in the neighbourhood of (0, 0) that the linear expression z_1 [cf. (29)] represented $\partial f/\partial x_2$ which was required to be nonnegative; and if z_1 returns to the basis at a later step, the corresponding equation for z_1 can be left out as being redundant.

In (30) we have for $x_1 = z_1 = 0$

$$\partial f/\partial x_1 = 8 - 2x_1 = 8, \qquad \partial f/\partial z_1 = 0 - \frac{1}{4} z_1 = 0$$

so that x_1 is the variable to be introduced into the basis; the upper limits are

$$\begin{aligned} (y_1 =)\, \frac{5}{2} - x_1 &\geqslant 0 \quad \text{for} \quad x_1 \leqslant \frac{5}{2} \\ (y_2 =)\, 3 - x_1 &\geqslant 0 \quad \text{for} \quad x_1 \leqslant 3 \\ (\partial f/\partial x_1 =)\, 8 - 2x_1 &\geqslant 0 \quad \text{for} \quad x_1 \leqslant 4 \end{aligned}$$

($x_2 \geqslant 0$ sets no limit to the increase in x_1). The effective limit is set by $y_1 \geqslant 0$ so that x_1 replaces y_1 in the basis. The solution for the new

[1] It follows that, should $\partial f/\partial z_1$ become negative at some later iteration, the preference function can be increased by reducing z_1 from zero to a negative value.

basic variables becomes

$$
\begin{aligned}
x_1 &= \frac{5}{2} - y_1 + \frac{1}{4} z_1 \\
x_2 &= \frac{5}{2} \qquad - \frac{1}{4} z_1 \\
y_2 &= \frac{1}{2} + y_1 + \frac{1}{4} z_1 \\
f &= \frac{105}{4} - 3y_1 - y_1^2 + \frac{3}{4} z_1 - \frac{3}{16} z_1^2 + \frac{1}{2} y_1 z_1 ;
\end{aligned}
\tag{31}
$$

no further auxiliary variable is needed at this step. Since $\partial f/\partial y_1 = -3$ and $\partial f/\partial z_1 = 3/4$ for $y_1 = z_1 = 0$, z_1 is the variable now to become basic.

By (31), only $x_2 \geqslant 0$ and $\partial f/\partial z_1 \geqslant 0$ set limits to the increase in z_1; the latter sets the effective limit. This requires a new auxiliary variable, $z_2 = \partial f/\partial z_1$, the definition of which becomes an additional constraint

$$
z_2 = \frac{3}{4} - \frac{3}{8} z_1 + \frac{1}{2} y_1 . \tag{32}
$$

Replacing z_2 by z_1 as a basic variable in the system (31)–(32) we have corresponding to the new (fourth) basis

$$
\begin{aligned}
z_1 &= 2 + \frac{4}{3} y_1 - \frac{8}{3} z_2 \\
x_1 &= 3 - \frac{2}{3} y_1 - \frac{2}{3} z_2 \\
x_2 &= 2 - \frac{1}{3} y_1 + \frac{2}{3} z_2 \\
y_2 &= 1 + \frac{4}{3} y_1 - \frac{2}{3} z_2 \\
f &= 27 - 2y_1 - \frac{2}{3} y_1^2 + 0 z_2 - \frac{4}{3} z_2^2 + 0 y_1 z_2
\end{aligned}
\tag{33}
$$

where the first equation can be left out since from now on it serves no purpose to keep z_1 in the set of variables.

For $y_1 = z_2 = 0$, (33) gives a solution in which we have

$$
\partial f/\partial y_1 = -2, \quad \partial f/\partial z_2 = 0.
$$

It follows that the value of f will be reduced if the *sign-restricted* nonbasic variable y_1 is given a positive value rather than the value zero (as in the basic solution); negative values are not permitted[1]. Moreover, f is a maximum with respect to the *free* nonbasic variable z_2. This combined criterion guarantees that the basic solution corresponding to (33)—cf. point S in Fig. 7—is an optimal solution[2].

Thus we have solved the problem in four steps. Starting from the origin in Fig. 7, we moved up the vertical axis until point $T = (0, 5/2)$ where $\partial f/\partial x_2 = 0$; at this point we found that $\partial f/\partial x_1 > 0$, and therefore moved to the right (increasing x_1). At the point (5/2, 5/2) the first side condition became effective. Proceeding down this capacity line we eventually reached the optimal point, (3, 2)[3].

The computations can be performed in a standard tabular form similar to the simplex tableaux of the linear simplex method[4].

The method will lead to a global maximum if the preference function is concave (in a minimization problem, convex). When f is not concave (convex), the solution attained at the final step is a local optimum which may or may not be a global optimum.

G. Computer Solution

Wolfe's method is essentially a modification of the simplex method for linear programming, and as such suited for any system for solving LP problem on electronic computers. Beale's method and the Dantzig-van de Panne algorithm (in several versions) can be implemented in various MP computer systems.

Numerical experiments with a number of randomly generated QP problems of various sizes have shown[5] that, broadly speaking, the simplex method for quadratic programming (Dantzig) requires fewer iterations than Beale's method, which in turn is far more efficient than the Wolfe algorithm in this respect. A modified version of Wolfe's method (using only one artificial variable for the initial solution) turned out to be nearly as efficient as Beale's method as far as the number of iterations is concerned.

---

[1] Compare the simplex criterion, which is a special case (no quadratic terms in f).

[2] Cp. the Kuhn-Tucker conditions for an unconstrained maximum of a function of nonnegative variables x_j and free variables z_k:

$$\partial f/\partial x_j \leq 0, \; x_j \geq 0, \; x_j \cdot (\partial f/\partial x_j) = 0$$

and

$$\partial f/\partial z_k = 0.$$

[3] In this case the path followed is the same as for the Wolfe and Dantzig-van de Panne algorithms, cf. the tableaux above.

[4] Cf. H. P. Künzi and W. Krelle (1962), Ch. 7.

[5] See R. J. Braitsch (1972).

H. Some Industrial Applications

1. Since quadratic programming differs from linear programming only as regards the preference function, the catalogue of industrial applications is much the same for the two methods. Whereas, for example, problems in production optimization can be handled by LP techniques when the technological input-output coefficients a_{ij} (representing the amount of input no. i required per unit of output no. j) and the prices of inputs and outputs are constant, quadratic programming becomes applicable if the selling prices depend linearly on the quantities to be sold[1].

Problem (3)–(4) with (5b)—the same as problem (13)—is an example of this important application of QP. The technology is linear, but the market for the firm's products is such that the selling prices p_1 and p_2 can be approximated by linear functions of the outputs x_1 and x_2 respectively so that the function to be optimized—total profit per period—becomes a quadratic function of x_1 and x_2. The problem of *optimal utilization of machine capacities* (or of determining the optimal product mix) can therefore be solved by QP; it was shown in sections C—F how this is done, using a variety of algorithms for quadratic programming.

Somewhat more generally, each selling price may depend linearly on both outputs so that the two commodities are interdependent in demand, say

$$\begin{aligned} p_1 &= 65 - 0.25x_1 + 0.30x_2 \\ p_2 &= 170 + 0.20x_1 - 1.00x_2. \end{aligned}$$

Let variable cost per unit of output be 20 and 50 respectively. Then total profit becomes a quadratic function with a cross product term,

$$\begin{aligned} f &= p_1x_1 + p_2x_2 - 20x_1 - 50x_2 \\ &= 45x_1 + 120x_2 - 0.25x_1^2 - 1.00x_2^2 + 0.50x_1x_2, \end{aligned} \tag{34}$$

which is to be maximized subject to three capacity constraints

$$\begin{aligned} x_1 + 2x_2 &\leqslant 200 \\ 0.5x_1 + 4x_2 &\leqslant 160 \\ x_1 &\leqslant 180, \end{aligned} \tag{35}$$

the two products being produced on three machines each of which has

---

[1] Cf. Ch. I above.

a limited capacity (in hours per period). (34)–(35) is a problem in QP[1].

Quadratic terms in the profit function may also be due to nonlinearities in the cost functions for the products. Let total variable costs be of the form

$$c_1(x_1) = 2x_1 + x_1^2, \quad c_2(x_2) = 3x_2 + x_2^2$$

(or approximated by these functions), whereas selling prices are constant, $p_1 = 10$ and $p_2 = 9$. With capacity restrictions as in problem (13) above this means that the optimization problem becomes

$$\begin{aligned} f &= p_1x_1 - c_1(x_1) + p_2x_2 - c_2(x_2) \\ &= 8x_1 + 6x_2 - x_1^2 - x_2^2 = \max \qquad (36) \\ & x_1 + x_2 \leqslant 5 \\ & x_1 + 2x_2 \leqslant 8 \end{aligned}$$

which is also a QP problem[2].

2. In these examples, the two products were technically independent except that they shared the limited capacities of the machines ("alternative production"): it was possible to produce only one of the commodities, should this be more profitable. Now consider the following example of *joint production in fixed proportions* where two products are manufactured in the technologically given proportion 1 : 2,

$$x_2 = 2x_1 \quad \text{(units produced per period).}$$

Let the variable costs of production be

$$c(x_1) = 6x_1 \qquad (\$ \text{ per period}),$$

i.e., the cost of producing one unit of the first commodity and two units of the second per period is \$ 6, and let the capacity of the process unit be

$$x_1 \leqslant 15 \quad (\text{and thus also } x_2 \leqslant 30).$$

The selling prices depend linearly on the quantities to be *sold* per period, s_1 and s_2:

$$p_1 = 30 - s_1, \quad p_2 = 80 - 2s_2.$$

Sales per period cannot exceed production; quantities produced but

---

[1] **Exercise 12:** Show that (34) is a strictly concave function (cf. pp. 37f. above), and solve the problem by the Theil-van de Panne algorithm (section C. 3 above).

[2] **Exercise 13:** Solve problem (36) by the guessing procedure of section C. 1 above.

not sold are disposed of. Eliminating x_2, this leads to a quadratic problem in s_1, s_2, and x_1:

$$\begin{aligned} f &= p_1 s_1 + p_2 s_2 - c\,(x_1) \\ &= 30 s_1 + 80 s_2 - s_1^2 - 2 s_2^2 - 6 x_1 = \max \qquad (37) \\ & s_1 \leqslant x_1 \\ & s_2 \leqslant 2 x_1 \\ & x_1 \leqslant 15 \end{aligned}$$
[1, 2].

3. The following example illustrates the application of quadratic programming to a problem of *inventory planning*.

A company is planning how much to produce of a commodity in each quarter of a year, estimated sales s_t ($t = 1, 2, 3, 4$) being as follows.

t	s_t (units)	s_t, cumulated
1	600	600
2	700	1,300
3	500	1,800
4	1,200	3,000

At the beginning of the year, inventory y_0 is $= 0$; inventory y_t at the end of each quarter ($t = 1, 2, 3, 4$) is required to be nonnegative, no delays in meeting demand being admissible. Then we have, with x_t denoting production in the tth quarter[3],

$$\begin{aligned} x_1 \qquad\qquad\qquad\quad & - y_1 = 600 \\ x_1 + x_2 \qquad\qquad\quad & - y_2 = 1{,}300 \qquad (38) \\ x_1 + x_2 + x_3 \qquad & - y_3 = 1{,}800 \\ x_1 + x_2 + x_3 + x_4 & - y_4 = 3{,}000 \end{aligned}$$

where $x_t, y_t \geqslant 0$. (The y_t can be thought of as slack variables.) The costs of production and storage in a quarter are $0.005 x_t^2$ and $1.000 y_{t-1}$ respectively. The problem now is to determine production x_t and inventory y_t ($t = 1, 2, 3, 4$) such that the sales requirements are met at

[1] **Exercise 14:** Formulate the Kuhn-Tucker conditions for problem (37) and solve the problem by guessing.

[2] **Exercise 15:** Show that if p_1 and p_2 are constant, the optimization problem will be trivial and everything produced will also be sold. Explain in general terms why we must distinguish between production and sales when the selling prices depend on the quantities sold.

[3] Cp. the inventory model (6) in Ch. III above.

minimum total cost of production and storage, i. e., the total cost function

$$c = 0.005 \cdot (x_1^2 + x_2^2 + x_3^2 + x_4^2) + 1.000 \cdot (y_1 + y_2 + y_3) \quad (39)$$

is to be minimized subject to (38) and to $x_t, y_t \geqslant 0$. This is a quadratic programming problem in the x_t when the y_t are eliminated in the preference function [but kept as slack variables in (38)][1].

4. QP techniques may be applied to solve *blending problems* in which the side conditions representing the "technology" of the blending process are linear but where the prices of inputs and/or outputs depend on the quantities used or sold.

For example[2], suppose that two products are made by blending the same three raw materials which are available in limited supplies, say 15, 10, and 55 units per period. Each output can be made from any one of the inputs or by blending the inputs in arbitrary proportions, only the proportions must be such that certain quality specifications for the products are satisfied. Let the specific gravities of the two products be required to be 0.6 and 0.5 respectively, gravity being an important quality characteristic (as is frequently the case in the chemical industries). The specific gravities of the ingredients are 1.0, 0.8, and 0.4 respectively. Then the gravity specification for the first product will be

$$\frac{1.0x_{11} + 0.8x_{21} + 0.4x_{31}}{x_{11} + x_{21} + x_{31}} = 0.6$$

where x_{ij} is the quantity of input no. i entering into the jth output ($i = 1, 2, 3$; $j = 1, 2$), the x_{ij} being measured in units of volume[3]. This equation can be rewritten as a linear equation,

$$0.4x_{11} + 0.2x_{21} - 0.2x_{31} = 0. \quad (40)$$

Similarly, for product no. 2 we get

$$0.5x_{12} + 0.3x_{22} - 0.1x_{32} = 0. \quad (41)$$

The "capacity limitations" on the supply of raw materials are linear inequalities,

$$\begin{aligned} x_{11} \quad + x_{12} \quad &\leqslant 15 \\ x_{21} \quad + x_{22} \quad &\leqslant 10 \\ x_{31} \quad + x_{32} \quad &\leqslant 55. \end{aligned} \quad (42)$$

[1] **Exercise 16:** Derive the Kuhn-Tucker conditions and solve the problem by (a) the guessing procedure, (b) the Dantzig-van de Panne algorithm for minimization problems.

[2] Cf. S. Danø (1974), pp. 37ff.

[3] Cf. the definition of specific gravity. It is assumed that no change of volume occurs when the ingredients are mixed.

Now, if the prices of inputs and outputs are constant, total profit per period will be a linear function of the x_{ij} and the optimization problem will an LP problem in these variables[1]. Suppose, however, that only the prices q_i of the inputs (raw materials) are constant whereas the outputs can be sold at prices which depend linearly on the quantities produced and sold, x_1 and x_2:

$$p_j = a_j - b_j x_j \quad (j = 1, 2).$$

Then total profit per period becomes

$$f = (a_1 - b_1 x_1)\, x_1 + (a_2 - b_2 x_2)\, x_2 - q_1 (x_{11} + x_{12}) - q_2 (x_{21} + x_{22}) - \\ - q_3 (x_{31} + x_{32}) \qquad (43)$$

where

$$x_1 = x_{11} + x_{21} + x_{31} \qquad (44)$$

$$x_2 = x_{12} + x_{22} + x_{32}.$$

The maximization of (43) subject to (40)–(42) and (44) is a quadratic problem in the variables x_{ij}.

---

[1] Cf. S. Danø (1974), p. 38. Problems of this formal type occur, for example, in the petroleum refinery industry.

V. Dynamic Programming and Multistage Optimization

1. Optimization problems consist in selecting from among the feasible alternatives one which is economically optimal. A problem of this nature is solved by formulating a mathematical model of the problem, typically a maximization model in which a preference function is to be maximized subject to a number of side conditions, and applying a method of solution tailored to the particular kind of problem. The variables of the model, interdependent through the side relations, are determined *simultaneously* in the solution.

Consider, for example, the linear programming problem

$$\begin{aligned} f = 8x_1 + 10x_2 &= \max \\ 4x_1 + \ \ 2x_2 &\leqslant 12 \\ x_1, x_2 &\geqslant 0, \end{aligned} \tag{1}$$

to be interpreted as a problem of optimal capacity utilization. x_1 and x_2 are quantities produced per period of two commodities which require 4 and 2 machine hours per unit, and the right-hand side of the side condition is maximum available machine time per period; the coefficients in the preference function are unit profits. Solving by the simplex method (or, what is simpler in such a trivial case, geometrically or by numerical inspection) we get

$$x_1 = 0, \quad x_2 = 6; \quad f = 60. \tag{2}$$

The optimal values of the two decision variables are found simultaneously in the solution procedure.

2. An alternative approach is to determine the variables *one at a time* (sequentially), *decomposing* the problem into a series of *stages* each corresponding to a subproblem in only one variable, and solving the two single-variable subproblems separately instead of solving the two-variable problem (1). This is the basic idea underlying *dynamic programming* (DP).

The decomposition of the problem (1) can be illustrated as shown in Fig. 8.

Let us assume for convenience that commodity no. 1 is produced "first" (stage 1). We might as well have started with the second commodity; the order in which they are arranged is purely formal in a case like this where the decomposition into stages does not reflect a sequence in time.

Now, for the production of the first commodity, 12 units of the capacity factor (machine hours) are available as shown in the flow diagram. If x_1 units are produced, $12 - 4x_1$ machine hours are available as input for the second stage. After producing x_2 units of commodity

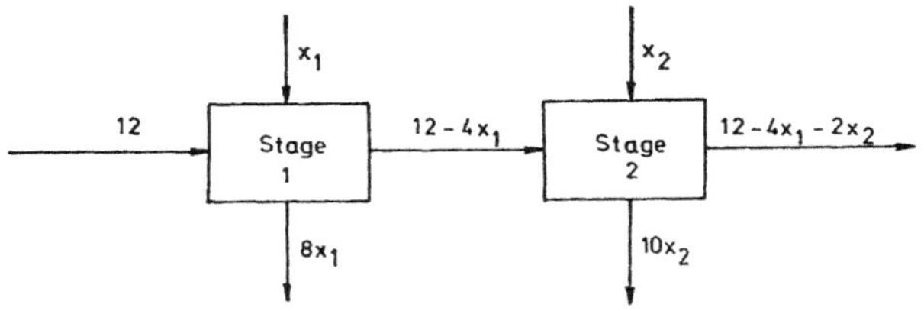

Fig. 8

no. 2, we are left with $12 - 4x_1 - 2x_2$ machine hours, corresponding to the slack variable in (1) which represents unutilized capacity. The two stages contribute $8x_1$ and $10x_2$ respectively to total profit.

We can now solve the problem *backwards*, treating x_1 as a *parameter* and optimizing *stage 2* with respect to the variable x_2. For parametric $x_1 = \bar{x}_1$ the maximal capacity left to stage 2 is $12 - 4\bar{x}_1$ machine hours so that the (parametric) subproblem of stage 2 is

$$\begin{aligned} f_1 = 10x_2 &= \max_{x_2} \\ 2x_2 &\leqslant 12 - 4\bar{x}_1 \\ x_2 &\geqslant 0, \end{aligned} \tag{3}$$

which is a linear programming problem like the total problem (1), only it is a single-variable problem. The solution is obviously

$$x_2 = 6 - 2x_1; \quad f_1^{\max} = 60 - 20\bar{x}_1 \tag{4}$$

where $\bar{x}_1$ is a parameter.

Next we optimize *stage 1* with respect to its decision variable, x_1. The capacity available is 12 machine hours. Production of x_1 units contributes $8x_1$ to total profit, but against this we have to consider that machine hours left over and used by stage 2 also affect total profit, contributing $f_1^{\max} = 60 - 20x_1$ which also depends on x_1. The optimization problem of stage 1 therefore becomes

$$\begin{aligned} f_2 = 8x_1 + f_1^{\max} = 60 - 12x_1 &= \max_{x_1} \\ 4x_1 &\leqslant 12 \\ x_1 &\geqslant 0, \end{aligned} \tag{5}$$

which is also a linear problem. Because f_2—which expresses profit contributed by the first stage plus the (parametric) maximum profit earned by the second—is a decreasing function of x_1, the solution obviously is

$$x_1 = 0; \ f_2^{\max} = 60. \tag{6}$$

Having thus found the optimal value of x_1, which is also a parameter in the solution for x_2, we substitute it into (4) to get

$$x_2 = 6 - 2x_1 = 6. \tag{7}$$

The solutions which we have found for the two variables are seen to agree with (2), and total profit $f = 60$ is seen to be equal to $f_2^{\max}$—as it should be since $f_2^{\max}$ was calculated as the total of stage contributions to profit. What we did in solving (5) was to maximize the profit of stage 1—a function of x_1—plus the maximum profit earned by stage 2 for any given value of x_1.

In this way we have solved an optimization problem in two variables by transforming it into a series, or sequence, of two single-variable problems. This is an example of *dynamic programming*. The *subproblems* corresponding to the individual stages are of the *same type as the total problem* (1)—in the present case, a linear programming problem—and they are *solved by the same method* as that applied in the simultaneous solving of the total problem (e.g. the simplex method). In other words, "dynamic programming" does not refer to a particular class of optimization problems (e.g. linear programming problems) or to a specific method of solution (like the simplex method); rather, it indicates a general procedure for *decomposing* a problem into a series of subproblems involving fewer variables, and combining their solutions to get the solution of the original problem.

3. When an optimization problem is formulated as a multistage problem to be solved by dynamic programming, it is convenient to introduce *state variables* y_n associated with the individual stages (numbered $n = 1, 2, \ldots, N$). The production process of Fig. 8 may be thought of as starting in a (given) *initial state* where $y_0 = 12$ machine hours are available; this is the input state of stage 1. Producing x_1 units of the first commodity, each of which requires 4 machine hours,

changes the state of the system: available capacity is reduced by $4x_1$ machine hours so that the *output state* of stage 1—which is also the *input state* to stage 2—becomes $y_1 = y_0 - 4x_1 = 12 - 4x_1$. Producing x_2 units of the second product, available capacity is further reduced to $y_2 = y_1 - 2x_2 = y_0 - 4x_1 - 2x_2$, which in this case represents the *final state*. ($y_2 \geqslant 0$ by definition but otherwise unknown.)

Thus, the input state of stage no. n, y_{n-1}, is transformed into an output state y_n, the change being brought about by the *decision variable*

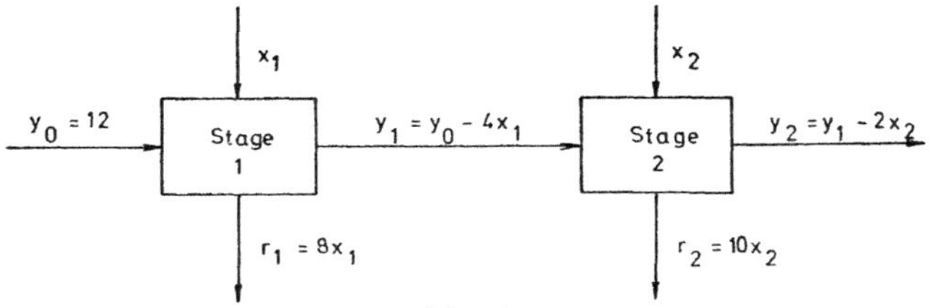

Fig. 9

of the stage, x_n. The successive changes of the state of the system can formally be described by *transformation equations* of the form

$$y_n = t_n(y_{n-1}, x_n) \quad (n = 1, 2, \ldots, N).$$

In the example they have the form

$$\begin{aligned} y_1 &= y_0 - 4x_1 \\ y_2 &= y_1 - 2x_2; \end{aligned} \tag{8}$$

together with the nonnegativity requirements x_1, x_2, y_1, $y_2 \geqslant 0$ they are equivalent to the restrictions of the original problem (1), y_0 being $= 12$ and y_2 representing the slack variable.

The *stage returns*, i.e., the contributions of the individual stages to the preference function f, will in the general case depend on the input state and the decision variable:

$$r_n = r_n(y_{n-1}, x_n) \quad (n = 1, 2, \ldots, N);$$

in the present example these *return functions* are of the simple form

$$\begin{aligned} r_1 &= 8x_1 \\ r_2 &= 10x_2. \end{aligned} \tag{9}$$

Introducing these symbols into Fig. 8, the flow diagram of the two-stage problem has the form of Fig. 9. The backward solution now proceeds as follows.

At the *first* stage of the calculations—corresponding to the last stage in the production system, $n = N = 2$—the input state y_1 is considered as a parameter, "inherited" from the previous stage of the system. The stage is optimized by maximizing its *decision function*, f_1—here equal to the stage return, $r_2(x_2)$—subject to the parametric capacity restriction $2x_2 \leqslant y_1$[1]:

$$\begin{aligned} f_1 = r_2(x_2) = 10x_2 &= \max_{x_2} \\ 2x_2 &\leqslant y_1 \\ x_2 &\geqslant 0. \end{aligned} \tag{10}$$

The solution to this parametric single-variable LP problem is

$$\begin{aligned} x_2(y_1) &= 0.5y_1 \\ F_1(y_1) &= 5y_1 \end{aligned} \tag{11}$$

where F_1 denotes the maximum value of the stage decision function, $F_1 = f_1^{\max}$.

At the *second* stage of the computations (production stage 1) we maximize the decision function $f_2 = r_1(x_1) + F_1(y_1)$ subject to the capacity limitation $4x_1 \leqslant y_0$ (i.e., $y_1 = y_0 - 4x_1 \geqslant 0$); substituting the stage transformation $y_1 = y_0 - 4x_1$, f_2 becomes a function of x_1 and y_0 so that we have the LP problem

$$\begin{aligned} f_2 &= r_1(x_1) + F_1(y_1) = 8x_1 + 5y_1 \\ &= 8x_1 + 5(y_0 - 4x_1) = 5y_0 - 12x_1 = \max_{x_1} \\ & 4x_1 \leqslant y_0 \\ & x_1 \geqslant 0. \end{aligned} \tag{12}$$

The solution is

$$\begin{aligned} x_1(y_0) &= 0 \\ F_2(y_0) &= 5y_0 \end{aligned} \tag{13}$$

when $F_2 = f_2^{\max}$.

The solution to the complete problem (1)—called *the optimal policy*—can now be determined by solving the *recursive equation system* formed by the *parametric optimum solutions* (11) and (13) and the *transformation equations* (8), starting from the initial state $y_0 = 12$:

Transformation equations $y_n = t_n(y_{n-1}, x_n)$	Parametric optimal solutions $x_n = x_n(y_{n-1})$	Maximum of decision function
$y_0 = 12$		
$y_1 = y_0 - 4x_1 = 12$	$x_1(y_0) = 0$	$F_2(y_0) = 5y_0 = 60$
$y_2 = y_1 - 2x_2 = 0$	$x_2(y_1) = 0.5y_1 = 6$	$F_1(y_1) = 5y_1 = 60$

[1] This restriction is equivalent to $y_2 = y_1 - 2x_2 \geq 0$, that is, the output state—as represented by the slack variable—must not be negative.

where the direction of the computations is the opposite of that followed above in the optimization of stages. The optimal policy emerges as $x_1 = 0$, $x_2 = 6$ and total profit is $f = F_2 = 60$. If y_0 had been a parameter, the solution—now parametric—would have been $x_1 = 0$, $x_2 = 0.5y_0$, $f = 5y_0$[1].

The decomposition by which we solved problem (1) can be described as follows. Replacing the side conditions by the equivalent formulation

$$y_1 = y_0 - 4x_1,\ y_1 \geqslant 0$$
$$y_2 = y_1 - 2x_1,\ y_2 \geqslant 0,$$

this together with the nonnegativity requirements implies

$$0 \leqslant x_1 \leqslant \frac{1}{4} y_0 \tag{14}$$

$$0 \leqslant x_2 \leqslant \frac{1}{2} y_1 \,. \tag{15}$$

Then we can write (1) in the form

$$f^{\max} = \max_{x_1, x_2} (8x_1 + 10x_2) = \max_{x_1} (8x_1 + \max_{x_2} 10x_2)$$

subject to (14)–(15); clearly this maximization problem can be decomposed into two single-variable problems, corresponding to (10) and (12):

$$F_1(y_1) = \max_{x_2}\ 10x_2 \left(0 \leqslant x_2 \leqslant \frac{1}{2} y_1\right)$$

$$F_2(y_0) = \max_{x_1}\ (8x_1 + F_1(y_1))$$
$$= \max_{x_1} \{8x_1 + F_1(y_0 - 4x_1)\} \left(0 \leqslant x_1 \leqslant \frac{1}{4} y_0\right),$$

where $f^{\max} = F_2(y_0)$. In a more general formulation the decomposition of a two-stage problem

$$f^{\max} = \max_{x_1, x_2} [r_1(y_0, x_1) + r_2(y_1, x_2)]$$

can be expressed in the *recursion equations*

$$F_1(y_1) = \max_{x_2} [r_2(y_1, x_2)] \tag{16}$$

$$F_2(y_0) = \max_{x_1} [r_1(y_0, x_1) + F_1\{t_1(y_0, x_1)\}]. \tag{17}$$

[1] For $f^{\max} = 5y_0$, where y_0 is the total capacity of the system, we have $df/dy_0 = 5$. **Exercise 17:** Interpret this result.

4. This procedure of solving a dynamic programming problem by *backward recursion* can be generalized to any number of variables. A flow diagram for an N-stage system is shown in Fig. 10.

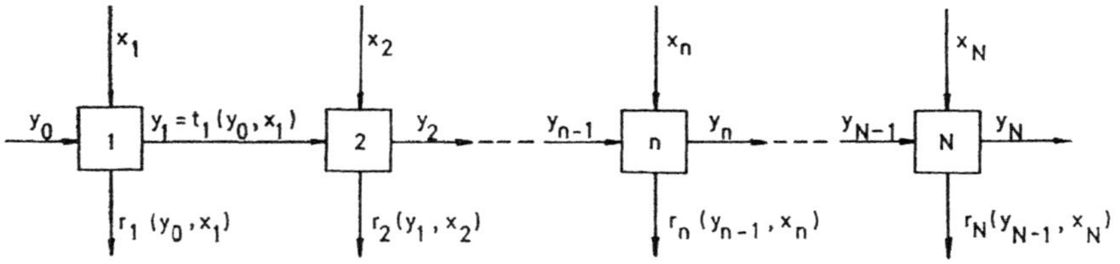

Fig. 10

The decision functions of stages $N, N-1, \ldots, 2, 1$ are respectively

$$f_1 = r_N(y_{N-1}, x_N)$$

$$f_2 = r_{N-1}(y_{N-2}, x_{N-1}) + F_1(y_{N-1}) \text{ where } y_{N-1} = t_{N-1}(y_{N-2}, x_{N-1}) \quad (18)$$

$$\cdots$$

$$f_N = r_1(y_0, x_1) + F_{N-1}(y_1) \qquad \text{where } y_1 = t_1(y_0, x_1),$$

F_j being the maximum of f_j ($j = 1, 2, \ldots, N$). Maximizing the decision function of each stage with respect to its decision variable, treating the input state as a parameter, we get the parametric stage solutions

$$x_n = x_n(y_{n-1}) \quad (n = N, N-1, \ldots, 1) \tag{19}$$

which can be "sewn together" by means of the transformation equations so that we get the parameters determined. y_0 now determines x_1 and together they determine y_1; this gives x_2, which with y_1 determines y_2; and so forth as illustrated by Fig. 11.

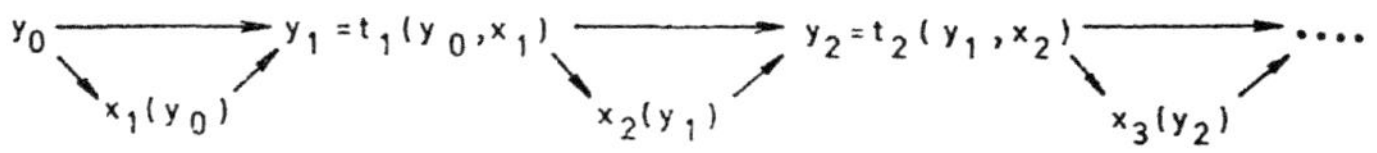

Fig. 11

It follows from (18) that the maximum of f_N represents the accumulated value of the stage returns, i.e., $F_N = f^{\max}$.

5. If the variables of a DP problem are allowed to take *discrete* values only, or if the stage returns and/or the transformation functions

are given in *tabular form* for discrete values of the variables, the problem will have to be solved by *tabular computations*.

For example, the decision variables may be required to have *integral* values ($x_n = 0, 1, 2, \ldots$) because the interpretation of the problem is such that fractional values would be meaningless. This is so in problem (1): strictly speaking it is impossible to produce a fractional number of units of a commodity, e.g. $x_1 = 2.6$. Thus, although in this case the analytical shape of the *return functions* is known, r_1 and r_2 are defined only for integral values of x_1 ($\leqslant 3$) and x_2 ($\leqslant 6$):

x_1	0	1	2	3
r_1 ($= 8x_1$)	0	8	16	24

x_2	0	1	2	3	4	5	6
r_2 ($= 10x_2$)	0	10	20	30	40	50	60

The *transformation functions* in tabular form are as follows:

	y_1 ($= y_0 - 4x_1$)			
$y_0 \backslash x_1$	0	1	2	3
12	12	8	4	0

	y_2 ($= y_1 - 2x_2$)						
$y_1 \backslash x_2$	0	1	2	3	4	5	6
0	0						
4	4	2	0				
8	8	6	4	2	0		
12	12	10	8	6	4	2	0

where y_1 is confined to the values 0, 4, 8, and 12 resulting from the first table. The blank cells in the last table correspond to combinations of values of y_1 and x_2 which are not feasible because they would imply a negative value of y_2 (cf. the sign restriction $y_2 = y_1 - 2x_2 \geqslant 0$).

The solution procedure, using backward recursion, now proceeds as follows. For the *last stage* ($n = N = 2$) we have:

Stage 2	$f_1 = r_2(x_2)$ $(= 10x_2)$									
$y_1 \diagdown x_2$	0	1	2	3	4	5	6	$F_1(y_1)$	$x_2(y_1)$	$y_2(y_1)$
0	**0**							0	0	0
4	0	10	**20**					20	2	0
8	0	10	20	30	**40**			40	4	0
12	0	10	20	30	40	50	**60**	60	*6*	*0*

where the maximal value of the decision function f_1 for each of the possible input states (values of y_1) is shown in bold-faced type[1]. These parametric optima and the optimal values of the decision variable are listed in the F_1 and x_2 columns to the right. The last column gives the resulting values of the output state y_2, computed from the transformation function (or table).

For *stage 1* we have the decision function $f_2 = r_1(x_1) + F_1(y_1)$ where the transformation gives y_1 for each value of x_1; for example, $x_1 = 2$ implies $y_1 = y_0 - 4x_1 = 4$, and the preceding table then gives $F_1(y_1) = 20$. The stage computations are done in the following table:

Stage 1	$f_2 = r_1(x_1) + F_1(y_1)$ $\{= 8x_1 + F_1(y_1)\}$						
$y_0 \diagdown x_1$	0	1	2	3	$F_2(y_0)$	$x_1(y_0)$	$y_1(y_0)$
12	**0 + 60**	8 + 40	16 + 20	24 + 0	60	*0*	*12*

These tables correspond to (10)–(11) and (12)–(13) respectively, and the optimal solution can be found similarly, starting with the last table. $y_0 = 12$ gives $x_1 = 0$ (the optimal stage solution) which leads to $y_1 = 12$ (by the transformation equation). Proceeding to the first table, $y_1 = 12$ (as just determined) gives the stage optimum $x_2 = 6$ and the output state $y_2 = 0$. These values are indicated in italics[2]. The maximal total return is $F_2(y_0) = 60$.

6. It will now be clear why it was expedient to solve the decomposed version of problem (1) *backwards*, starting with the optimization of the last stage. The procedure led to a recursive system which has the *initial state* y_0 as its starting point—as shown in Fig. 11—and it was y_0 that was given ($y_0 = 12$). This suggests that problems in which the

[1] For solution by hand these values may be put in circles.

[2] When solving such a problem by hand it is practical to underline these values in the tables, in the order in which they are determined (y_0, x_1, . . .).

final state y_N is given may be solved in the opposite direction, proceeding *forwards* from the first stage.

To show how this is done, let us redefine the state variables y_n in the example so that the final state y_2 now represents total accumulated "use" of capacity, including idle capacity; the latter is put first as the input state y_0 of the first stage of the production system[1]. Then y_1 represents the accumulated "use" of capacity, including capacity not utilized, after the first commodity has been produced. This leads to the transformations

$$\begin{aligned} y_1 &= y_0 + 4x_1 \\ y_2 &= y_1 + 2x_2 \end{aligned} \tag{20}$$

where $y_0 \geqslant 0$ and $y_2 = 12$. The stage return functions are the same as above, (9).

This dynamic programming problem is another decomposed version of problem (1). To solve it by *forward recursion* we reverse the direction

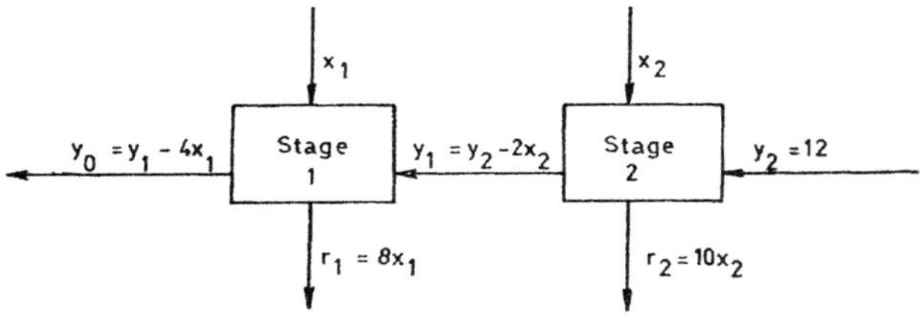

Fig. 12

of the system as shown in Fig. 12, where y_n is now to be formally treated as the input state of stage n ($n = 1, 2$) whereas the y_{n-1} become output states; we therefore write the transformation functions (20) in the inverse form

$$\begin{aligned} y_0 &= y_1 - 4x_1 \\ y_1 &= y_2 - 2x_2 \end{aligned} \tag{21}$$

(more generally,

$$y_{n-1} = t_n^* \, (y_n, x_n)$$

where t_n^* is the inverse transformation equation of stage n).

The procedure starts with the optimization of *stage 1*. The decision function $f_1 = r_1 \, (x_1)$ is to be maximized subject to $y_0 = y_1 - 4x_1 \geqslant 0$,

[1] y_0 may be thought of as the output of a fictitious (slack) stage which "absorbs" part of the total capacity.

$x_1 \geqslant 0$, where y_1—now the input state of the stage—is a parameter:

$$\begin{aligned} f_1 = r_1(x_1) = 8x_1 &= \max_{x_1} \\ 4x_1 &\leqslant y_1 \\ x_1 &\geqslant 0; \end{aligned} \tag{22}$$

the solution depends on the parameter,

$$\begin{aligned} x_1(y_1) &= 0.25y_1 \\ F_1(y_1) &= 2y_1 \end{aligned} \tag{23}$$

where $F_1 = f_1^{\max}$. At the *second stage* we have the decision function $f_2 = r_2(x_2) + F_1(y_1)$ where $y_1 = y_2 - 2x_2 \geqslant 0$, $x_2 \geqslant 0$ so that the stage optimization problem becomes

$$\begin{aligned} f_2 = 10x_2 + 2y_1 = 6x_2 + 2y_2 &= \max_{x_2} \\ 2x_2 &\leqslant y_2 \\ x_2 &\geqslant 0. \end{aligned} \tag{24}$$

The solution is

$$\begin{aligned} x_2(y_2) &= 0.5y_2 \\ F_2(y_2) &= 5y_2. \end{aligned} \tag{25}$$

Working backwards from y_2 (= 12) through the recursive system (21), (23), (25) we obtain the optimal solution:

$$\begin{aligned} y_2 &= 12 & x_2(y_2) &= 0.5y_2 = 6 \\ y_1 &= y_2 - 2x_2 = 0 & x_1(y_1) &= 0.25y_1 = 0, \\ y_0 &= y_1 - 4x_1 = 0, \end{aligned}$$

and $f^{\max} = F_2(y_2) = 5y_2 = 60$.

In the general case of N stages the decision functions are[1]

$$\begin{aligned} f_1 &= r_1(y_0, x_1) && \text{where } y_0 = t_1^*(y_1, x_1) \\ f_2 &= r_2(y_1, x_2) + F_1(y_1) && \text{where } y_1 = t_2^*(y_2, x_2) \\ &\ldots \\ f_N &= r_N(y_{N-1}, x_N) + F_{N-1}(y_{N-1}) && \text{where } y_{N-1} = t_N^*(y_N, x_N). \end{aligned}$$

The parametric stage solutions

$$x_n = x_n(y_n) \qquad (n = 1, 2, \ldots, N)$$

and the inverse transformation equations determine the optimal policy for given y_N as shown in Fig. 13.

---

[1] In the example above, r_n depends only on x_n.

It is often possible to solve by forward recursion when the initial state y_0 is given, or to apply backward recursion to DP problems with given final state y_N, using a slightly modified procedure[1]. However, when the order of the stages is arbitrary and the transformations can be inverted so that we are free to choose the direction, *backward recursion* is generally a more efficient procedure for *given* y_0, and *forward recursion* for *given* y_N (which amounts to the same thing, the only difference being the numbering of stages and variables)[2].

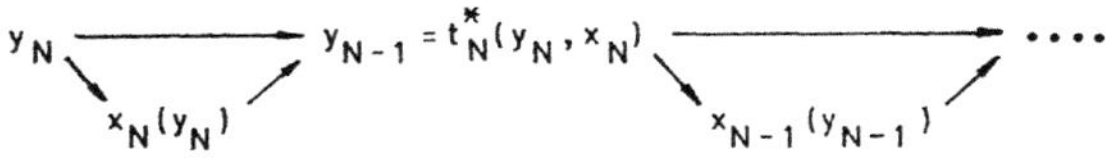

Fig. 13

7. In order for an optimization problem to be solvable by dynamic programming, the "*technical*" *structure* of the problem (as represented by the *restrictions*) must be such that it can be described by a series of successive changes of the state of the system, from the initial state y_0 to the final state y_N, each change being effected by a particular decision variable. The two-stage system of Fig. 9 above is an example of this; the transformation equations (8) together with x_1, y_1, x_2, $y_2 \geqslant 0$ and $y_0 = 12$ are an equivalent reformulation of the restrictions in problem (1), i.e., $4x_1 + 2x_2 \leqslant 12$ and $x_1, x_2 \geqslant 0$, so that the set of feasible solutions is preserved. In some cases the multistage structure represents a sequence in time—hence the name "dynamic" programming—where the stages correspond to actual processes and the direction indicates the order in which the transformations take place. This would be so in our example (1) if the two commodities were produced in separate processes and commodity no. 1 had to be made first. In many applications, however, the sequence of stages and the order in which the system passes through them are an artificial device, introduced in order to make the problem solvable by DP methods. In either case we can choose between forward and backward recursion if the direction is mathematically arbitrary.

Decomposition of a problem also requires that the *objective function* satisfies certain conditions. In general, the function to be maximized is some function of the stage returns r_n,

$$f = \varphi\,\{r_1\,(y_0, x_1), \ldots, r_N\,(y_{N-1}, x_N)\}. \tag{26}$$

---

[1] Using forward recursion for given y_0, there is no maximization at the first stage because the inverse transformation equation determines x_1 uniquely as a function of the parameter y_1 for given y_0. See Ch. X below.

[2] A survey of these recursion procedures is given in the Appendix (Ch. X).

It can be shown that two conditions on the function—separability and monotonicity[1]—together are sufficient for decomposition, i.e., for solution by means of a system of recursive equations. These conditions are automatically satisfied by a class of functions including the case of *additive returns*,

$$f = r_1 (y_0, x_1) + \ldots + r_N (y_{N-1}, x_N).$$

In this case, as we have seen above, the objective function is obviously decomposable and the recursion equations have the form (16)–(17) for a two-stage problem, readily generalized to any number of stages [cf. (18)].

8. The recursion equations can be thought of as a mathematical expression of an intuitive principle known as the "*principle of optimality*"[2]. Consider the two-stage problem shown in Fig. 9, and let $(x_1, x_2) = (\bar{x}_1, \bar{x}_2)$ be the optimal policy. The first decision, $x_1 = \bar{x}_1$, changes the state of the system from the initial state $y_0 = 12$ to $y_1 = y_0 - 4\bar{x}_1 = \bar{y}_1$. The principle of optimality now says that the remaining decision, $x_2 = \bar{x}_2$, must represent an optimal policy with respect to the state $\bar{y}_1$, i.e., it must be an optimal solution to the remaining one-stage DP problem with the initial state $\bar{y}_1$. The proof is simple: if this were not so, $(x_1, x_2) = (\bar{x}_1, \bar{x}_2)$ could not be an optimal policy.

The backward recursive procedure, as expressed in (16)–(17), by which we solved the problem is based directly on this principle. Starting by optimizing the last stage ($n = 2$), we do not know its input stage y_1, but we do know that whatever it is—i.e., whatever the first decision is—x_2 must be optimal with regard to y_1. Hence we optimize $f_2 = r_2 (y_1, x_2)$ for parametric y_1 as expressed in (16). Proceeding backwards to stage one, we optimize $f_2 = r_1 (y_0, x_1) + F_1 (y_1)$, i.e., the return of stage 1 plus the parametric optimal return of stage 2, where $y_1 = t_1 (y_0, x_1)$.

The principle of optimality in its general form states that any part of an optimal policy must be optimal; specifically, the decisions remaining after stage no. n (i.e., $x_{n+1}, \ldots, x_N$) must constitute an optimal policy for the series of stages $n + 1, \ldots, N$ with regard to the state y_n resulting from the first n decisions.

9. The multistage structures dealt with above (cf. Fig. 10) are *serial systems*, i. e., ordered sequences of stages where the output state of stage no. n is the input state to stage no. $n + 1$. Moreover, they are special in that there is *only one decision variable* x_n and *only one (output) state variable* y_n for each stage.

[1] See G. L. Nemhauser (1966), pp. 34—39.

[2] The principle of optimality was first stated by R. Bellman, the originator of dynamic programming. See R. E. Bellman (1957), p. 83.

As an obvious generalization, the x_n and the y_n may be vectors so that there are *several decision and state variables per stage*[1]. Cases of this kind are treated in Chapter VII below.

Nonserial multistage systems—important in the chemical industries—represent another generalization, characterized by branches or loops in the flow diagram[2].

A third extension of the N-stage serial multistage structure is an *infinite-stage system* where N tends to infinity. This case, relevant to some applications, is treated below in Chapter VIII.

10. The advantage of dynamic programming as a procedure for solving optimization problems is the simplification obtained by decomposition. It is often simpler and easier to solve a series of single-variable stage optimization problems, and in some cases this is the only possible procedure because "simultaneous" solution is mathematically or computationally difficult or downright impossible. Certain classes of optimization problems, however, such as linear programming problems are more efficiently solved by special algorithms without decomposition, e.g. the simplex method.

Dynamic programming has been particularly successful in its discrete version. Tabular computations are well suited for computer solution and can be used to handle problems involving irregular functions, and may be the only practicable way of solving a problem in which the variables are required to be integers. As a rough illustration of the computational advantages of DP, consider an optimization problem in N decision variables, each of which can assume m alternative discrete values (e.g. $0, 1, 2, \ldots, m - 1$). If, for lack of other methods of solution, we had to solve the problem by total enumeration, we would have to examine each of m^N alternative solutions for feasibility and optimality, whereas in a dynamic programming procedure—assuming that decomposition is possible—the number of alternatives to be enumerated would be reduced to mN, namely m for each of the N stages. Thus, roughly speaking, the computational labour increases exponentially with the number of decision variables in the case of total enumeration, but only proportionately if the problem is decomposed. For large values of m and N the computational advantages become enormous; for example, in a problem with 20 variables each of which can assume integral values from 0 to 9 we have $m^N = 10^{20}$—an astronomic number—as against $mN = 200$ possible solutions if the problem is reformulated as a 20-stage DP problem.

---

[1] In such cases the direction may not be arbitrary because inversion of the transformation equations may be difficult.

[2] See G. L. Nemhauser (1966), Ch. VI.

VI. Applications of Dynamic Programming

A. The Shortest Path through a Network

Perhaps the simplest and most straightforward application of dynamic programming is the determination of *the shortest path or route through a network*.

Consider the (stylized) road map shown in Fig. 14. A driver wants to find the shortest route from point P to point Q. There are six intermediate junctions A, B, . . ., F. The lengths of all existing road sections connecting two points in the area are indicated on the map. Any unbroken chain of road sections starting at P and ending at Q represents a possible route through this network of roads.

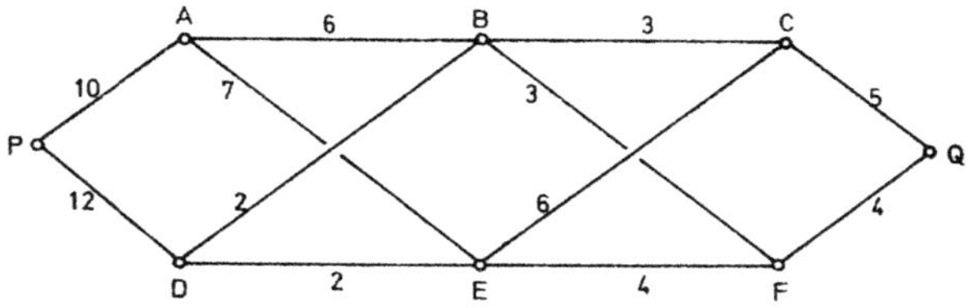

Fig. 14

Assuming that the direction of travel is always from left to right —having arrived at, say, B the driver never travels back to A or D but proceeds to either C or F—the number of possible routes is finite. The problem can therefore be solved by enumerating the alternative routes and comparing their total lengths.

Any route from P to Q is the result of *three successive decisions*. Starting at point P, the driver must decide whether he will go to A or to D. If he chooses to drive to A, say, he can proceed from A to either B or E, each of which in turn leaves him with two alternatives, C and F. Having arrived at either C or F, he has no choice but to proceed to the destination, Q. Since each decision is a choice between two alternatives and there are three consecutive decisions to be made, there are $2^3 = 8$ possible combinations, i.e., 8 alternative routes. The alternative decisions and the resulting routes can be illustrated graphically by a *decision tree* as shown in Fig. 15, where the root represents the starting point P and the branches are composed of road sections (with lengths indicated). Comparing the total lengths from root to top, it will be seen that PDBFQ is the shortest route, the total length being $12 + 2 + 3 + + 4 = 21$.

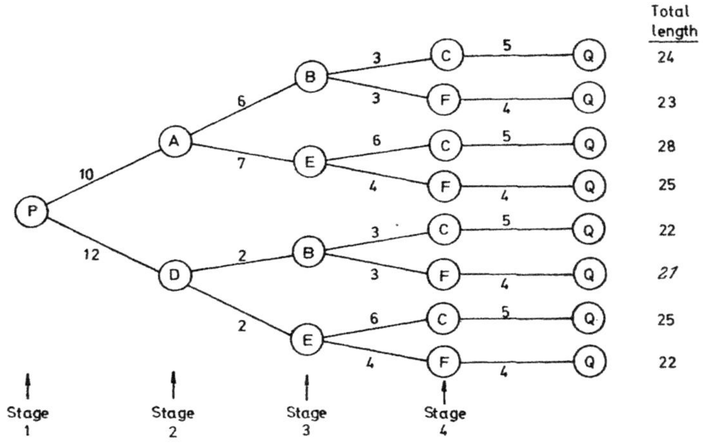

Fig. 15

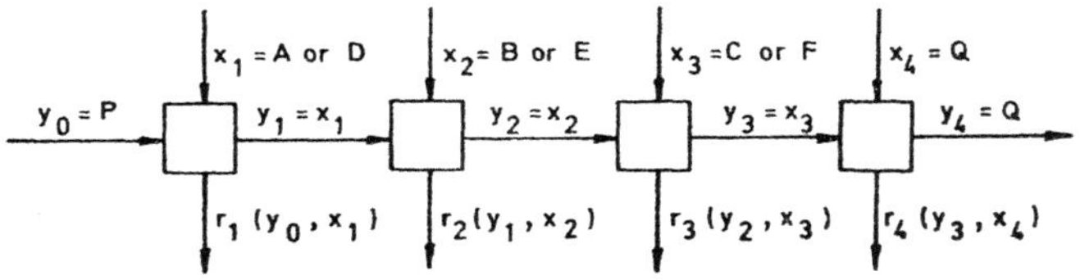

Fig. 16

This decision structure clearly represents a multistage decision system. The driver's geographical position—the points on the map—represents the state of the system, which is to be changed from the given initial state P to the given final state Q through a sequence of stage decisions in such a way as to minimize the total "return", i.e., the total distance covered. Starting from point P, i.e., the initial state $y_0 = \text{P}$, the two alternatives open to the driver can be represented by two values of a decision variable x_1: $x_1 = \text{A}$ (i.e., drive to point A) and $x_1 = \text{D}$ (drive to *D*). If he chooses $x_1 = \text{A}$, he will get to this point so that the output state of the first stage will be $y_1 = \text{A}$ and the corresponding "return" $r_1\,(\text{P, A})$ will be the distance PA = 10. Similarly, $x_1 = \text{D}$

leads to $y_1 = \text{D}$ and the return will be $r_1\,(\text{P, D}) = 12$. Proceeding in this fashion, the problem can be represented by a four-stage decision structure as shown in Fig. 16. There is no choice at stage 4 since the destination—i.e., the final state $y_4 = \text{Q}$—is given.

The transformation functions are $y_n = x_n$ $(n = 1, 2, 3, 4)$. The return functions $r_n = r_n\,(y_{n-1}, x_n)$ can be written in tabular form as follows.

$r_1(y_0, x_1)$			$r_2(y_1, x_2)$			$r_3(y_2, x_3)$			$r_4(y_3, x_4)$	
$y_0 \diagdown x_1$	A	D	$y_1 \diagdown x_2$	B	E	$y_2 \diagdown x_3$	C	F	$y_3 \diagdown x_4$	Q
P	10	12	A	6	7	B	3	3	C	5
			D	2	2	E	6	4	F	4

Using backward recursion, the problem is solved by tabular computations as follows.

Stage 4	$f_1 = r_4(y_3, x_4)$	$F_1(y_3)$	$x_4(y_3)$	$y_4(y_3)$
$y_3 \diagdown x_4$	Q			
C	5 (= CQ)	5	Q	Q
F	4 (= FQ)	4	*Q*	*Q*

Stage 3	$f_2 = r_3(y_2, x_3) + \text{F}_1(y_3)$		$F_2(y_2)$	$x_3(y_2)$	$y_3(y_2)$
$y_2 \diagdown x_3$	C	F			
B	3 + 5	**3 + 4**	7	*F*	*F*
E	6 + 5	**4 + 4**	8	F	F

Stage 2	$f_3 = r_2(y_1, x_2) + F_2(y_2)$		$\text{F}_3(y_1)$	$x_2(y_1)$	$y_2(y_1)$
$y_1 \diagdown x_2$	B	E			
A	**6 + 7**	7 + 8	13	B	B
D	**2 + 7**	2 + 8	9	*B*	*B*

Stage 1	$f_4 = r_1(y_0, x_1) + F_3(y_1)$		$\text{F}_4(y_0)$	$x_1(y_0)$	$y_1(y_0)$
$y_0 \diagdown x_1$	A	D			
P	10 + 13	**12 + 9**	21	*D*	*D*

Starting with $y_0 = \text{P}$, the solution is determined by the recursive equation system formed by the parametric stage solutions $x_n = x_n(y_{n-1})$ and the transformations $y_n = x_n$. The last table gives $x_1(y_0) = \text{D}$ and $y_1 = x_1 = \text{D}$; for $y_1 = \text{D}$, the table for stage 2 gives $x_2 = \text{B}$, $y_2 = \text{B}$; and so on. The optimal values—italicized in the tables—are

n	y_n	x_n
0	P	
1	D	D
2	B	B
3	F	F
4	Q	Q

The optimal sequence of states $y_0, y_1, \ldots, y_4$ indicates that the shortest path through the network is PDBFQ; the total length of this route is $F_4(y_0) = 21$.

This solution procedure can be translated into a graphical method, making use of a decision tree like that of Fig. 15. After making the three first decisions the driver finds himself at point C or F. No matter how he got there he will have to proceed to Q, so we draw the eight top branches of the tree; none of them can be eliminated at this stage since the preceding decisions have not yet been determined.

Going one stage back, the first two decisions have taken the driver to either B or E. If he has arrived at B, he can get to his destination Q either through C or F; the best course is to go to F since BFQ $= 3 + 4 = 7$ whereas BCQ $= 3 + 5 = 8$. Therefore, no matter which way he may have got to B, he will never proceed to C, so the branches from B to C can be eliminated and we need only draw the branches going from B to F. This is an application of Bellman's principle of optimality: if the optimal route from P to Q passes through B, the remaining part of the route (from B to Q) must also be optimal; the optimal route from P to Q cannot contain BCQ because there is a shorter route from B to the destination. Similarly, if the driver is at point E after the first two decisions, he will proceed to F because EFQ $= 4 + 4 = 8 <$ ECQ $= 6 + 5 = 11$, so ECQ can be eliminated.

Applying a similar reasoning to the state attained after the first decision, it is seen that the branches AE and DE need not be drawn; the shortest path from A to Q is ABFQ $= 6 + 7 = 13$ and the shortest path from D to Q is DBFQ $= 2 + 7 = 9$. Finally, at the starting point the choice is between PA + ABFQ $= 10 + 13 = 23$ and PD + DBFQ $= 12 + 9 = 21$; the latter alternative represents the shortest total route and there is no need to draw the branch PA.

This procedure is illustrated in Fig. 17, where the road sections which were eliminated are not drawn. The only unbroken chain of road sections left is PDBFQ, which represents the shortest total route[1].

The shortest-path DP model is also applicable to optimization problems having a similar structure but a different interpretation; the concept of a network is not confined to road systems.

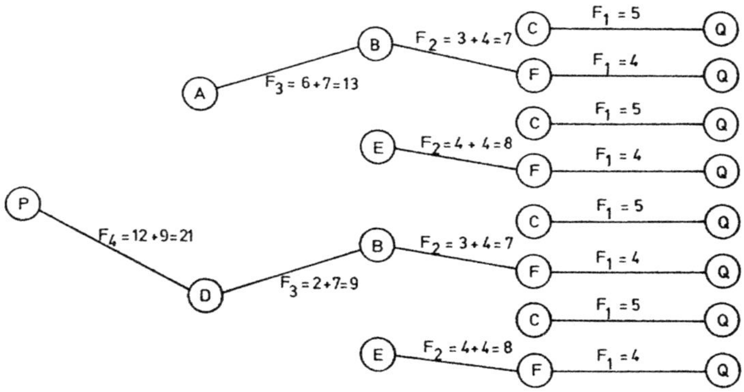

Fig. 17

B. Production Planning

1. Dynamic programming can be applied with advantage to a variety of optimization problems in the planning of production. The first example to be shown has a structure similar to that of the shortest-route problem.

A *job*—e.g. a commodity lot to be manufactured—is to be *scheduled through three successive stages of processing* at minimum total cost. At each stage there is a choice of three alternative machines. The costs of processing a unit of product on each of the nine machines are as follows:

Costs, \$/unit	Stage no.		
	1	2	3
Machine no. 1	6	10	2
2	9	12	5
3	8	8	6

[1] The procedure can be illustrated on a map (Fig. 14) instead of a tree. **Exercise 18:** Do this.

Now if any machine at one stage could be combined with any machine at the next, there would be no problem: the optimal policy would obviously be to use at each stage the machine having the lowest cost per unit, i.e., the optimal sequence of machines would be 1, 3, 1 and total cost per unit of product would be $6 + 8 + 2 = 16$. However,

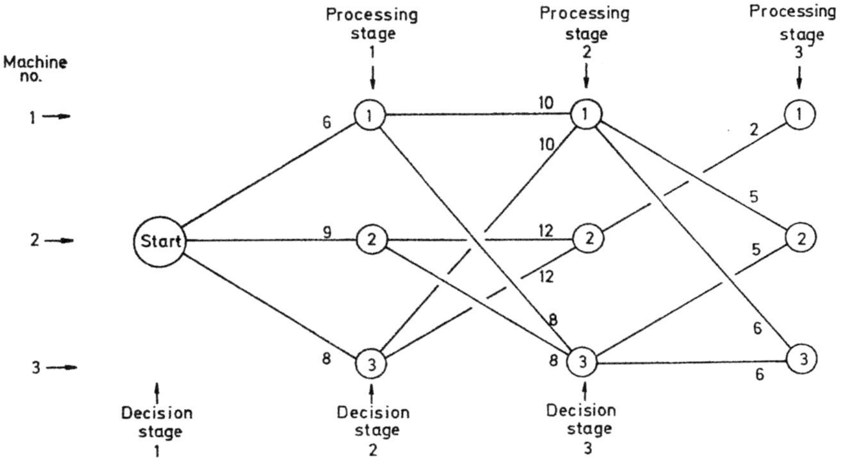

Fig. 18

not all of the $3^3 = 27$ combinations may be technically feasible, and if the sequence 1, 3, 1 is not among the feasible combinations some other method must be resorted to.

The problem is obviously sequential in nature. Any feasible policy consists in making three consecutive decisions by which each unit of product is taken through a network where the nodes represent the various machines; any route through the network represents a sequence of machines. This is illustrated in Fig. 18, where only those routes which correspond to feasible machine sequences are drawn[1].

At the starting point the system is in its initial state, which may be denoted by $y_0 = 0$ ("ready"). The first decision is to be taken here; the decision variable x_1 can take the discrete values 1, 2, or 3, indicating the number of machine to be used at the first processing stage. The decision will change the state from $y_0 = 0$ to $y_1 = 1, 2$, or 3 respectively;

[1] There are $3^3 = 27$ possible combinations but only 10 of them represent feasible sequences (routes). For example, machine no. 1 at the first processing stage cannot be followed by machine no. 2 at the next stage.

for example, $y_1 = 1$ means that the item is processed first on machine no. 1. The cost associated with this transformation—analogous to the length of a road segment in a network of roads—is indicated on the line connecting the two nodes. Proceeding in this manner, except that x_2 and x_3 are restricted to one or two values, we get to the final state y_3 (= 1, 2, or 3). The transformations functions have the form

$$y_n = x_n \quad (n = 1, 2, 3)$$

and the stage returns are functions of the decision variables only,

$$r_n = r_n(x_n) \quad (n = 1, 2, 3);$$

the return functions are tabulated in the columns of the cost table above. The problem is seen to be formally analogous to the shortest-

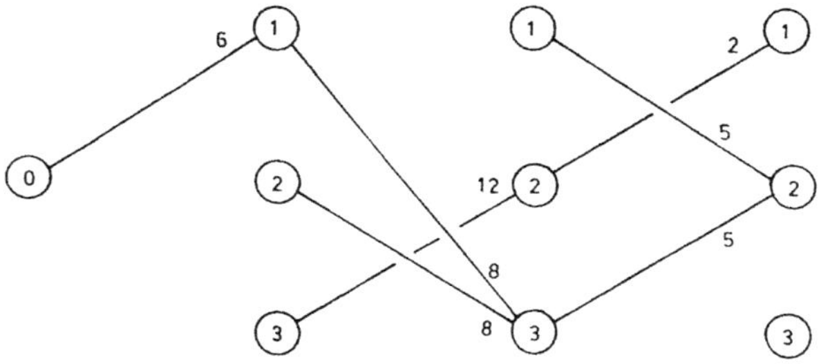

Fig. 19

path problem of Fig. 14, except that the stage returns are independent of the input state y_{n-1}, and that the final state is not given[1]. The optimal policy is represented by the "shortest" route through the network of Fig. 18, i.e., the path of least total cost, and can be computed by the same methods.

Applying the (backward) graphical method illustrated in Fig. 17 (using the network of Fig. 18 instead of a tree), the optimal sequence of machines turns out to be 1, 3, 2 as shown in Fig. 19. The accumulated cost of this sequence is $6 + 8 + 5 = 19$.

Alternatively, the problem may be solved by tabular DP computations[2].

---

[1] There would be no point in adding a point "finish" corresponding to Q in Fig. 14 since the lot is finished after being processed on whichever machine is third in the sequence. The "costs" of getting to this point from the last stage would be zero.

[2] **Exercise 19:** Show how this is done, and compare with solution by enumeration.

2. It was shown in Chapter V how a linear problem of *optimal utilization of capacity* could be formulated and solved as a dynamic programming problem. We shall now consider a simple quadratic programming problem with a similar interpretation.

Let two commodities be produced on the same machine whose capacity is 5 machine hours per period. Each commodity requires one machine hour per unit produced and the machine is to be operated at full capacity. The commodities are sold at prices depending linearly on the quantities produced and sold,

$$p_1 = 12 - x_1, \quad p_2 = 13 - 2x_2 \quad (\$/\text{unit});$$

unit variable costs of production are \$ 4.00 and \$ 3.00 respectively. Then total profit is

$$f = 8x_1 - x_1^2 + 10x_2 - 2x_2^2 \quad (\$/\text{period})$$

which is to be maximized subject to the capacity constraint

$$x_1 + x_2 = 5$$

and to $x_1, x_2 \geqslant 0$.

This problem can be turned into a two-stage problem as shown in Fig. 20. The state of the system is represented by available capacity

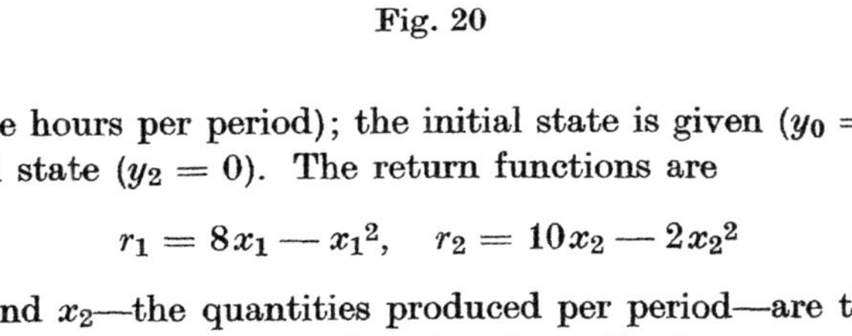

Fig. 20

(in machine hours per period); the initial state is given ($y_0 = 5$) and so is the final state ($y_2 = 0$). The return functions are

$$r_1 = 8x_1 - x_1^2, \quad r_2 = 10x_2 - 2x_2^2$$

where x_1 and x_2—the quantities produced per period—are the decision variables. The transformation functions have the form

$$\begin{aligned} &(y_0 = 5) \\ &y_1 = y_0 - x_1 \\ &y_2 = y_1 - x_2 \ (= 0) \end{aligned} \tag{1}$$

where $x_1, x_2, y_1 \geqslant 0$.

Solving by *backward* recursion, we have for stage 2

$$f_1 = 10x_2 - 2x_2^2 = \max_{x_2}$$

subject to

$$y_2 = y_1 - x_2 = 0, \text{ i.e., } x_2 = y_1;$$

there is no optimization at this stage since x_2 is uniquely determined for given parametric y_1[1], so we get

$$\begin{aligned} x_2(y_1) &= y_1 \\ F_1(y_1) &= 10y_1 - 2y_1^2. \end{aligned} \tag{2}$$

For stage 1 we have

$$f_1 = 8x_1 - x_1^2 + 10y_1 - 2y_1^2$$

or, substituting $y_1 = y_0 - x_1 = 5 - x_1$,

$$f_1 = 18x_1 - 3x_1^2 = \max_{x_1}$$

subject to

$$\left.\begin{aligned} y_1 &= 5 - x_1 \geqslant 0 \\ x_1 &\geqslant 0 \end{aligned}\right\} \quad \text{or} \quad 0 \leqslant x_1 \leqslant 5.$$

Now f_1 is an unconstrained maximum for

$$df_1/dx_1 = 18 - 6x_1 = 0, \quad \text{i.e., } x_1 = 3$$

which is in the admissible region $0 \leqslant x_1 \leqslant 5$. Therefore

$$\begin{aligned} x_1(y_0) &= 3 \\ F_2(y_0) &= 27. \end{aligned} \tag{3}$$

Going back through the recursive system (1)–(3) we get the optimal solution

$$\begin{aligned} y_0 &= 5 \\ & \qquad x_1 = 3 \\ y_1 &= 2 \\ & \qquad x_2 = 2 \\ y_2 &= 0 \end{aligned}$$

which yields the profit $f = F_2(y_0) = 27$.

If x_1 and x_2 are required to be integers, the problem has to be solved in tabular form, the return functions being

[1] In general, when the initial and the final state are both given there will be only $N - 1$ stage optimizations. **Exercise 20:** Explain why.

x_1	0	1	2	3	4	5
r_1	0	7	12	15	16	15

x_2	0	1	2	3	4	5
r_2	0	8	12	12	8	0

(x_1 and x_2 must not exceed 5). For stage 2 we now have the following tabular calculations.

Stage 2	$f_1 = 10x_2 - 2x_2^2$						$F_1(y_1)$	$x_2(y_1)$	$y_2(y_1)$
$y_1 \diagdown x_2$	0	1	2	3	4	5			
0	0						0	0	0
1		8					8	1	0
2			12				12	2	0
3				12			12	3	0
4					8		8	4	0
5						0	0	5	0

where only the diagonal cells are filled in because $y_2 = y_1 - x_2 = 0$ so that x_2 is uniquely determined for each value of y_1; again, there is no optimization at this stage. For stage 1 we have, recalling that $y_1 = 5 - x_1$,

Stage 1	$f_2 = 8x_1 - x_1^2 + F_1(y_1)$						$F_2(y_0)$	$x_1(y_0)$	$y_1(y_0)$
$y_0 \diagdown x_1$	0	1	2	3	4	5			
5	0 + 0	7 + 8	12 + 12	**15 + 12**	16 + 8	15 + 0	27	3	2

Going back through the tables, starting with $y_0 = 5$, we get the same solution as above.

Alternatively, the problem may be solved by *forward* recursion, using the inverse transformation functions

$$y_0 = y_1 + x_1$$
$$y_1 = y_2 + x_2$$

where $y_0 = 5$ and $y_2 = 0$. The decision function of the first stage is

$$f_1 = 8x_1 - x_1^2$$

where, by the first transformation equation, $x_1 = 5 - y_1$ so that we have

$$x_1(y_1) = 5 - y_1$$
$$F_1(y_1) = 15 + 2y_1 - y_1^2.$$

For stage two we have

$$f_2 = 10x_2 - 2x_2^2 + 15 + 2y_1 - y_1^2$$

or, substituting $y_1 = y_2 + x_2 = x_2$,

$$f_2 = 15 + 12x_2 - 3x_2^2 = \max_{x_2}$$

where $x_2 \geqslant 0$. f_2 is a maximum for

$$df_2/dx_2 = 12 - 6x_2 = 0, \quad \text{i.e., } x_2 = 2$$

which is positive. Therefore

$$x_2(y_2) = 2$$
$$F_2(y_2) = 27.$$

The solution is again $y_2 = 0$, $x_2 = 2$, $y_1 = 2$, $x_1 = 3$, $y_0 = 5$, $f = 27$.

The corresponding tabular computations for integral x_1 and x_2 are as follows:

Stage 1	$f_1 = 8x_1 - x_1^2$						$F_1(y_1)$	$x_1(y_1)$	$y_0(y_1)$
$y_1 \setminus x_1$	0	1	2	3	4	5			
0						15	15	5	5
1					16		16	4	5
2				15			15	3	5
3			12				12	2	5
4		7					7	1	5
5	0						0	0	5

Stage 2	$f_2 = 10x_2 - 2x_2^2 + F_1(y_1)$						$F_2(y_2)$	$x_2(y_2)$	$y_1(y_2)$
$y_2 \setminus x_2$	0	1	2	3	4	5			
0	0 + 15	8 + 16	**12 + 15**	12 + 12	8 + 7	0 + 0	27	2	2

In general, dynamic programming is not the most efficient procedure for solving quadratic programming problems when other methods are applicable. For one thing, problems with several linear constraints require several state variables, which may render solution by DP difficult[1]. However, in cases where the variables are required to be integers, the standard algorithms for quadratic programming cannot be applied and dynamic programming may be the only practicable method.

[1] Cf. Ch. VII below.

3. Still another type of problem of production planning which can be solved by dynamic programming is the following. A firm has two plants or machines at its disposal, e.g. normal equipment and stand-by equipment, both of which can produce the same commodity. Total costs in \$ *per day* are

$$c_1(u) = \begin{cases} 0.50 + 5.00u + 0.10u^2 & \text{for } u > 0 \\ 0 & \text{for } u = 0 \end{cases} \tag{4}$$

and

$$c_2(v) = \begin{cases} 0.16 + 5.10v + 0.15v^2 & \text{for } v > 0 \\ 0 & \text{for } v = 0 \end{cases} \tag{5}$$

where u and v are the quantities produced per day by the respective plants or machines. The constant terms in the cost functions represent setup costs, incurred only on days of active operation (u or $v > 0$).

Now the firm wishes to produce *6 units* of the commodity within a period of *3 days*. The problem is *how to allocate the total production requirement to the two plants such as to minimize total costs.*

Let t_1 and t_2 denote the number of days of active operation of the plants. Then the optimization problem can be formulated as follows:

$$C = t_1 \cdot c_1(u) + t_2 \cdot c_2(v) = \text{minimum} \tag{6}$$

subject to

$$\begin{gathered} t_1 u + t_2 v = 6 \\ t_1 \leqslant 3,\ t_2 \leqslant 3 \\ t_1, t_2, u, v \geqslant 0 \end{gathered} \tag{7}$$

where it is natural to require all four variables to be integral ($= 0, 1, 2, \ldots$).

The problem would be simple enough if capacity utilization were indivisible in the time dimension so that each plant had to be operated every day of the period or else not at all (i.e., t_1 and t_2 could only be 3 or 0). Then there would be only three possibilities to be considered, namely (i) $t_1 = 3$, $t_2 = 0$, $C = 3 \cdot c_1(2) = 32.70$; (ii) $t_1 = 0$, $t_2 = 3$, $C = 3 \cdot c_2(2) = 32.88$; and (iii) $t_1 = t_2 = 3$, $C = 3 \cdot c_1(1) + 3 \cdot c_2(1) = 33.03$ (\$/period), of which case (i) would represent the cheapest allocation[1]. But if no such restriction is imposed, a wider range of choice is open to the firm because t_1 and t_2 can now take all (integral) values from 0 to 3; for example, by producing $u = 2$ and $v = 1$ units per day

---

[1] If integrality of u and v is not insisted upon, $u = 1$ and $v = 1$ will not be the exact solution in case (iii). Minimizing $c_1(u) + c_2(v)$ subject to $u + v = 2$ for $u, v > 0$ yields $u = 1.4$, $v = 0.6$.

in each of two days the total cost could be reduced to $C = 2 \cdot c_1(2) + + 2 \cdot c_2(1) = 32.62$. The optimal solution now determines not only *the optimal allocation of production to the plants* ($t_1 u$ and $t_2 v$) but also, for each plant separately, *the optimal allocation of production in time*. Producing more per day in fewer days of active operation, the plant will incur higher costs of production per unit, but this may be offset by the fact that the setup cost is saved for each day the plant is not operated.

(6)–(7) with (4)–(5) is a nonlinear programming problem, which may be solved by Kuhn-Tucker optimization, deriving the Kuhn-Tucker conditions and applying a combinatorial procedure to them[1]. Because of the discontinuity of the cost functions (4) and (5) at $u = 0$ and $v = 0$ respectively this must be done separately for each of three cases: (a) $t_1, u > 0$, $t_2 = v = 0$, (b) $t_1 = u = 0$, $t_2, v > 0$, and (c) $t_1, u, t_2, v > 0$; the value of the cost function c is calculated for each of the three solutions which satisfy the conditions and the optimal solution is that of least total cost[2].

However, in applying this procedure we must treat t_1, t_2, u, and v as continuous variables. We have no guarantee that the solution will be integral in all four variables (actually it is not in the present example), and rounding off to the "nearest" integral solution is a tricky affair in a problem like this.

Dynamic programming offers an alternative procedure for solving the problem, and one which will automatically ensure an integral solution[3]. Let each day of the period represent a stage, $n = 1, 2, 3$, and let x_n ($n = 1, 2, 3$) be total production on the nth day. With state variables y_n representing accumulated production we have the given initial state $y_0 = 0$ and the given final state $y_3 = 6$, and the transformation equations will have the simple form

$$y_n = y_{n-1} + x_n$$

or (since we shall use forward recursion)

$$y_{n-1} = y_n - x_n \quad (n = 1, 2, 3). \tag{8}$$

The return functions

$$r_n = c(x_n) \quad (n = 1, 2, 3)$$

---

[1] Cf. Ch. II. B above.

[2] **Exercise 21:** Solve the problem by this method, disregarding the integrality requirements.

[3] I am indebted to Torben Warnich-Hansen, University of Copenhagen, for suggesting the following DP formulation.

represent the minimum cost of producing x_n units on the nth day (utilizing only one of the plants or both, whichever is cheaper)[1]. The function $c(x)$ is determined by minimizing total cost per day,

$$c = c_1(u) + c_2(v),$$

subject to

$$u + v = x$$

$$u, v \geqslant 0 \text{ and integral}$$

for all relevant values of x (0, 1, . . ., 6). This can be done in tabular form. For integer values of u and v the daily cost functions of the two plants are [cf. (4) and (5)]

u	0	1	2	3	4	5	6
$c_1(u)$	0	5.60	10.90	16.40	22.10	28.00	34.10

and

v	0	1	2	3	4	5	6
$c_2(v)$	0	5.41	10.96	16.81	22.96	29.41	36.16

from which we calculate $c_1(u) + c_2(v)$ for every set (u, v):

	$c_1(u) + c_2(v)$						
$u \diagdown v$	0	1	2	3	4	5	6
0	*0.00*	*5.41*	10.96	16.81	22.96	29.41	36.16
1	5.60	11.01	16.56	22.41	28.56	35.01	
2	*10.90*	*16.31*	21.86	27.71	33.86		
3	16.40	*21.81*	*27.36*	33.21			
4	22.10	27.51	*33.06*				
5	28.00	33.41					
6	34.10						

$x = u + v$ is constant along every diagonal of this table ($x = 0, 1, \ldots, 6$). The smallest figure in a diagonal—indicated by italics—is the minimum cost of producing x units in a day. Hence the daily cost function $c(x)$ is as follows

[1] **Exercise 22:** Draw the flow diagram of this three-stage structure.

x	0	1	2	3	4	5	6
$c(x)$	0.00	5.41	10.90	16.31	21.81	27.36	33.06
u	0	0	2	2	3	3	4
v	0	1	0	1	1	2	2

where the optimal allocation of x to the plants is indicated in the last two lines of the table.

$c(x)$ is to be used as the return function at every stage. It is tabulated for integral values of x only and the corresponding values of u and v are integers. Integrality of t_1 and t_2 is ensured by the definition of the stages; t_1 is simply the number of days for which u is positive in the solution (x_1, x_2, x_3), and similarly for t_2 and v. (By (8), the y_n will also be integers.)

We are now ready to solve the problem, using forward recursion. The decision function of *stage 1* is $f_1 = c(x_1)$; the transformation equation $y_0 = y_1 - x_1$ with the given initial state $y_0 = 0$ determines the decision variable uniquely for parametric y_1, so we get

$$x_1(y_1) = y_1$$

$$F_1(y_1) = c(y_1)$$

or in tabular form

Stage 1 y_1	$F_1(y_1)$	$x_1(y_1)$	$y_0(y_1)$
0	0.00	0	0
1	5.41	1	0
2	10.90	2	0
3	16.31	3	0
4	21.81	4	0
5	27.36	5	0
6	33.06	6	0

For *stage 2* we have the stage optimization problem

$$f_2 = c(x_2) + F_1(y_1) = \min_{x_2}$$

subject to

$$\left.\begin{array}{l} y_1 = y_2 - x_2 \geqslant 0 \\ x_2 \geqslant 0 \end{array}\right\} \quad \text{or} \quad 0 \leqslant x_2 \leqslant y_2,$$

and similarly for *stage 3*. Solving by tabular computations we get

Stage 2	$f_2 = c(x_2) + F_1(y_1)$							$F_2(y_2)$	$x_2(y_2)$	$y_1(y_2)$
$y_2 \diagdown x_2$	0	1	2	3	4	5	6			
0	**0.00** + **0.00**							0.00	0	0
1	0.00 + 5.41	**5.41** + **0.00**						5.41	1	0
2	0.00 + 10.90	**5.41** + **5.41**	10.90 + 0.00					10.82	1	1
3	0.00 + 16.31	5.41 + 10.90	10.90 + 5.41	**16.31** + **0.00**				16.31	3	0
4	0.00 + 21.81	5.41 + 16.31	10.90 + 10.90	**16.31** + **5.41**	21.81 + 0.00			21.72	3	1
5	0.00 + 27.36	5.41 + 21.81	10.90 + 16.31	**16.31** + **10.90**	21.81 + 5.41	27.36 + 0.00		27.21	3	2
6	0.00 + 33.06	5.41 + 27.36	10.90 + 21.81	**16.31** + **16.31**	21.81 + 10.90	27.36 + 5.41	33.06 + 0.00	32.62	*3*	*3*

Stage 3	$f_3 = c(x_3) + F_2(y_2)$							$F_3(y_3)$	$x_3(y_3)$	$y_2(y_3)$
$y_3 \diagdown x_3$	0	1	2	3	4	5	6			
6	**0.00** + **32.62**	5.41 + 27.21	10.90 + 21.72	16.31 + 16.31	21.81 + 10.82	27.36 + 5.41	33.06 + 0.00	32.62	*0*	*6*

Starting with the given final state $y_3 = 6$, we go back through the three tables to find the optimal solution (indicated by italics):

$$\begin{array}{ll} y_3 = 6 & \\ & x_3 = 0 \\ y_2 = 6 & \\ & x_2 = 3 \\ y_1 = 3 & \\ & x_1 = 3 \\ y_0 = 0 & \end{array}$$

and $C^{\min} = F_3(y_3) = 32.62$ (\$ per period). However, there are alternate optima at the last two stages, and therefore multiple solutions to the complete allocation problem. Each of the following nine solutions represents an optimal policy with $C^{\min} = 32.62$[1].

	1°	2°	3°	4°	5°	6°	7°	8°	9°
x_1	3	3	2	3	1	3	2	1	0
x_2	3	2	3	1	3	0	1	2	3
x_3	0	1	1	2	2	3	3	3	3

Three of these solutions are seen to be identical in the sense that three units are produced on each of two days; the way the problem is formulated is does not matter which of the three days the plants are standing idle. The remaining six solutions represent the six possible permutations of daily outputs 1, 2, and 3 units. In terms of the model (6)–(7) the nine solutions are equivalent since they all translate into $t_1 = 2$, $t_2 = 2$, $u = 2$, $v = 1$; they differ only with respect to the sequence in time:

Solutions 1°, 6°, 9°:		
x_n	u_n	v_n
3	2	1
3	2	1
0	0	0

Solutions 2°–5° and 7°–8°:		
x_n	u_n	v_n
1	0	1
2	2	0
3	2	1

In any case both plants will be in operation for 2 days of the three-day period, producing 2 and 1 units per day respectively.

[1] **Exercise 23:** Derive the solutions from the three stage tables. (The first solution is the one shown above.)

In problems of greater dimension, particularly when the planning period is long, the sequence of active and idle days may not be indifferent because of inventory costs and deadlines for delivery. In such cases the firm may apply a secondary criterion of optimality in chosing the best solution, for example, minimization of inventory cost subject to the observance of delivery dates.

The example illustrates some of the advantages of a dynamic programming approach. The fact that the preference function (6) is highly irregular—it is discontinuous at u or $v = 0$ and it is not convex—causes no difficulties in the DP formulation; and the problem can be solved even if the analytical shape of the functions $c_1(u)$ and $c_2(v)$ is not known. All that is needed for solving the problem is a table of the functions for discrete (integral) values of u and v, and tabular solution based on this information will automatically provide an integer solution. The DP procedure is also well suited for computer solution of large-scale problems of this nature.

4. Finally, consider the following problem of *optimal allocation of machines which are subject to attrition.* At the beginning of the planning period (4 weeks) a manufacturing firm has $y_0 = 100$ machines at its disposal. The machines can do two different jobs. From past experience the company knows that the probability of breakdown after a week's operation is 1/3 for machines doing the first job and 1/10 for machines doing job no. 2. This means that, when x_1 machines are used for job 1 during the first week and $y_0 - x_1$ for job 2, the number of machines available in the second week (y_1) will be

$$y_1 = y_0 - \frac{1}{3}x_1 - \frac{1}{10}(y_0 - x_1) = \frac{9}{10}y_0 - \frac{7}{30}x_1 .$$

The number of machines available will be similarly reduced by breakdowns in the second week (using x_2 and $y_1 - x_2$ machines for the two jobs), and so on. Each machine yields a profit of \$ 10.00 when doing job no. 1 in a week, and \$ 7.00 when doing the second job. The problem is *to allocate the machines to the two jobs in such a way as to maximize total profit over the four-week period.*

This is clearly a four-stage problem with transformation functions

$$y_n = \frac{9}{10}y_{n-1} - \frac{7}{30}x_n \qquad (n = 1, 2, 3, 4)$$

where the state variable y_n represents the number of machines available at the end of the nth week (with $y_0 = 100$) and the decision variable x_n

is the number of machines doing the first job in that week. The return functions are

$$r_n(y_{n-1}, x_n) = 10x_n + 7(y_{n-1} - x_n) = 3x_n + 7y_{n-1}.$$

The variables are restricted by $x_n \geqslant 0$, $y_{n-1} - x_n \geqslant 0$, i.e.,

$$0 \leqslant x_n \leqslant y_{n-1}.$$

Solving by backward recursion, we have for stage 4

$$f_1 = 3x_4 + 7y_3 = \max_{0 \le x_4 \le y_3}$$

i.e., the stage optimum is

$$x_4(y_3) = y_3, \qquad F_1(y_3) = 10y_3.$$

Proceeding to stage 3 we have

$$f_2 = 3x_3 + 7y_2 + 10\left(\frac{9}{10}y_2 - \frac{7}{30}x_3\right)$$

$$= \frac{2}{3}x_3 + 16y_2 = \max_{0 \le x_3 \le y_2}$$

where the solution is

$$x_3(y_2) = y_2, \qquad F_2(y_2) = \frac{50}{3}y_2.$$

For stages 2 and 1 we get by a similar procedure

$$x_2(y_1) = 0, \qquad F_3(y_1) = 22y_1$$

and

$$x_1(y_0) = 0, \qquad F_4(y_0) = 26.8y_0.$$

Setting $y_0 = 100$, the optimal stage solutions and the transformation equations determine the total solution:

$$\begin{array}{lll}
y_0 = 100 & & \\
 & x_1 = 0 & y_0 - x_1 = 100 \\
y_1 = 90 & & \\
 & x_2 = 0 & y_1 - x_2 = 90 \\
y_2 = 81 & & \\
 & x_3 = 81 & y_2 - x_3 = 0 \\
y_3 = 54 & & \\
 & x_4 = 54 & y_3 - x_4 = 0 \\
y_4 = 36. & &
\end{array}$$

Thus, all available machines should be applied to job no. 2 in the first two weeks and to job no. 1 in the remaining two weeks. Total profit for the four-week period will be $F_4(y_0) = 26.8y_0 = \$\,2{,}680$.

C. Inventory Problems

1. Dynamic programming lends itself well to solving many problems of inventory planning. One reason for this is the fact that, for any period, inventory at the end of the period (y_n) is by definition equal to initial inventory plus production or purchase (x_n) minus sales (s_n):

$$y_n = y_{n-1} + x_n - s_n, \tag{9}$$

which can be regarded as a simple transformation of the state of the inventory effected by decision variables x_n and/or s_n. For a planning horizon composed of a sequence of N periods and with given initial and/or terminal inventory, equations (9) for $n = 1, 2, \ldots, N$ represent the transformation functions of a very simple multistage structure.

Consider the following simple example[1]. A company is planning its production for a period of one year; expected sales are estimated on a quarterly basis as follows.

Quarter no.	Estimated sales, units	Cumulated sales, units
1	600	600
2	700	1,300
3	500	1,800
4	1,200	3,000

Let x_n denote production in the nth quarter, and y_n denote inventory at the end of this quarter. The cost of producing x_n units is \$ $0.005\,x_n{}^2$ and storage costs are \$ 1.00 per unit per quarter. Initial inventory y_0 is $= 0$.

The planning problem consists in *determining quarterly production* x_n *and inventory* y_n ($n = 1, 2, 3, 4$) *such as to meet the given sales requirements at minimum total costs of production and storage.* Let each quarter represent a stage. Then the transformation equations have the form (9) for $n = 1, 2, 3, 4$ where sales s_n are given by the table above, and the return function of the nth quarter is

$$r_n\,(y_{n-1}, x_n) = 0.005 x_n{}^2 + 1.00 y_{n-1} \tag{10}$$

where the last term is the approximate storage cost in the nth quarter. Clearly we can set $y_4 = 0$ since, with a horizon limited to one year, there would be no point in producing more than can be sold during the year.

[1] Cf. Ch. IV. H above.

Solution by backward recursion proceeds as follows. The decision function of stage 4 is

$$f_1 = 0.005x_4^2 + y_3$$

where

$$y_4 = y_3 + x_4 - 1{,}200 = 0$$

determines x_4 so that we get

$$\begin{aligned} x_4(y_3) &= 1{,}200 - \quad y_3 \\ F_1(y_3) &= 7{,}200 - 11y_3 + 0.005y_3^2. \end{aligned} \tag{11}$$

For stage 3 we have

$$f_2 = 0.005x_3^2 + y_2 + 7{,}200 - 11y_3 + 0.005y_3^2 = \min_{x_3}$$

subject to

$$y_3 = y_2 + x_3 - 500 \geqslant 0, \quad x_3 \geqslant 0.$$

After substituting the transformation equation, differentiate f_2 to get the necessary condition for a minimum:

$$df_2/dx_3 = 0.020x_3 - 16 + 0.010y_2 = 0 \text{ or } x_3 = 800 - 0.5y_2.$$

We can safely assume that $y_2 \leqslant 1{,}600$ so that $x_3 \geqslant 0$ is satisfied; hence

$$\begin{aligned} x_3(y_2) &= 800 - 0.5y_2 \\ F_2(y_2) &= 7{,}550 - 7y_2 + 0.0025y_2^2. \end{aligned} \tag{12}$$

For stages 2 and 1 we get similarly

$$f_3 = 0.005x_2^2 + y_1 + F_2(y_2) = \min_{x_2}$$

with the solution

$$\begin{aligned} x_2(y_1) &= 700 - \frac{1}{3}y_1 \\ F_3(y_1) &= 10{,}000 - 6y_1 + \frac{0.005}{3}y_1^2 \end{aligned} \tag{13}$$

and

$$f_4 = 0.005x_1^2 + y_0 + F_3(y_1) = \min_{x_1}$$

which gives

$$\begin{aligned} x_1(y_0) &= 600 \\ F_4(y_0) &= 11{,}800. \end{aligned} \tag{14}$$

The optimal solution as determined by (11)–(14) and the transformation equations (9) is

$$\begin{aligned} y_0 &= 0 \\ y_1 &= 0 \qquad x_1 = 600 \\ y_2 &= 0 \qquad x_2 = 700 \\ y_3 &= 300 \qquad x_3 = 800 \\ y_4 &= 0 \qquad x_4 = 900 \end{aligned}$$

and total cost is $F_4(y_0) = \$\,11{,}800$[1].

2. In the following example, quarterly sales s_n as well as the x_n are unknown quantities to be determined by optimization.

A commercial enterprise is *planning sales* (s_n) *and purchases* (x_n) *of a commodity on a quarterly basis for a period of one year*. The objective of the firm is to *maximize profits*. The prices at which the commodity is bought and sold are expected to fluctuate as follows.

	Quarter no.			
	1	2	3	4
Selling price p_n, \$/unit	12	14	10	6
Purchase price q_n, \$/unit	8	20	6	9

At the beginning of the year the firm has 5 units in stock. Inventories must at any time be nonnegative and less than the storage capacity, 10 units. The distribution of sales and purchases over time within each quarter is unknown, so to keep on the right side of storage capacity the company is basing its planning on the assumption that purchases are made in the first half of each quarter while sales take place during the second half. Storage costs are negligible. Terminal inventory at the end of the year is to be zero[2].

The structure of the problem can be represented by an eight-stage

[1] If we had required y_4 to be ≥ 0 instead of setting it $= 0$, y_4 would have appeared as another parameter in the stage solutions; the last solution, (14), would have given x_1 and F_4 as functions of y_0 *and* y_4. The optimal value of y_4 would then have to be determined by minimizing $F_4(y_0, y_4)$ with respect to y_4 subject to $y_4 \geq 0$. This would of course give $y_4 = 0$.

[2] Another possible interpretation is that x_n represents production in the nth quarter. "Purchase prices" then become unit costs of production.

system as illustrated in Fig. 21, where z_n is an interposed state variable representing inventory in the middle of the nth quarter (i.e., after purchasing) and y_n is inventory at the end of the quarter (after selling). x_n and s_n are the decision variables.

The transformation equations have the form

$$z_n = y_{n-1} + x_n \tag{15}$$

$$y_n = z_n \quad - s_n \quad (n = 1, 2, 3, 4) \tag{16}$$

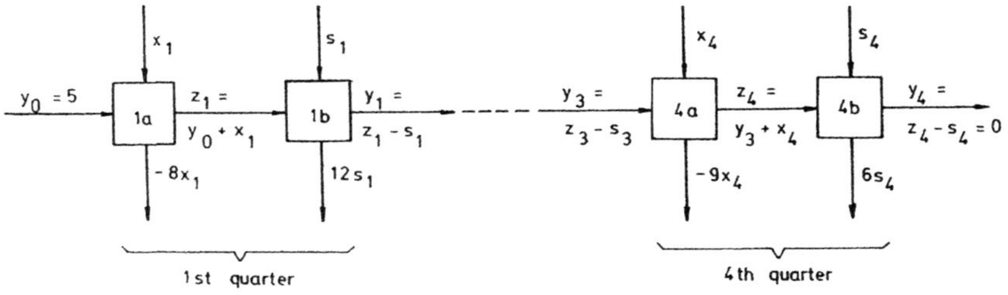

Fig. 21

and the return functions—representing contributions to total profit—are for stages 1a, 2a, . . .

$$r_n^a = - q_n x_n$$

and for stages 1b, 2b, . . .

$$r_n^b = p_n s_n$$

where p_n and q_n are the prices listed above.

The variables are restricted by the following inequalities:

$$x_n \geqslant 0, \quad s_n \geqslant 0, \quad 0 \leqslant z_n \leqslant 10, \quad 0 \leqslant y_n \leqslant 10$$

which—by (15)–(16)—are seen to imply

$$0 \leqslant x_n \leqslant 10 - y_{n-1} \tag{17}$$

$$0 \leqslant s_n \leqslant z_n \qquad (n = 1, 2, 3, 4). \tag{18}$$

(17)–(18) define the range of variation of the decision variables at each stage.

Using backward recursion, we have for stage 4b:

$$f_1 = 6s_4 \quad \text{where } y_4 = z_4 - s_4 = 0, \text{ i.e., } s_4 = z_4$$

so that

$$s_4(z_4) = z_4$$

$$F_1(z_4) = 6z_4.$$

For stage 4a we have

$$f_2 = -9x_4 + 6z_4$$

or, substituting the transformation (15) for $n = 4$,

$$f_2 = -3x_4 + 6y_3 = \max_{0 \leq x_4 \leq 10 - y_3}$$

i.e.,

$$x_4(y_3) = 0$$

$$F_2(y_3) = 6y_3.$$

Proceeding to stage 3b, the decision function is

$$f_3 = 10s_3 + 6y_3 = 4s_3 + 6z_3 = \max_{0 \leq s_3 \leq z_3}$$

so that

$$s_3(z_3) = z_3$$

$$F_3(z_3) = 10z_3.$$

The remaining stage optimizations are done in a similar way and we get

$$\begin{aligned} x_3 &= 10 - y_2, & F_4 &= 40 + 6y_2 \\ s_2 &= z_2, & F_5 &= 40 + 14z_2 \\ x_2 &= 0, & F_6 &= 40 + 14y_1 \\ s_1 &= 0, & F_7 &= 40 + 14z_1 \\ x_1 &= 10 - y_0, & F_8 &= 100 + 8y_0. \end{aligned}$$

Working backwards from $y_0 = 5$, the solution is seen to be

n	1	2	3	4
x_n	5	0	10	0
z_n	10	10	10	0
s_n	0	10	10	0
y_n	10	0	0	0

and total profit is $F_8(y_0) = 140$ (\$/year).

3. In the next example to be demonstrated expected sales in each quarter, s_n units ($n = 1, 2, 3, 4$), are estimated as follows:

n	1	2	3	4	Total
s_n	250	200	100	200	750

The rate of demand is assumed to be constant over each quarter, whereas the commodity is purchased (or produced) in lots of x_n units *at the beginning* of the quarters; total purchase or production is planned to be 750 units, initial and terminal inventories being $= 0$. The lot sizes x_n to be considered are the s_n or sums thereof; for example, x_1 can be 250, 450, 550, or 750 units. The problem is *to determine the four lots* x_n ($n = 1, 2, 3, 4$) *in such a way as to meet demands at minimum total cost of storage and ordering;* the cost of storing a unit for a quarter is \$ 1.00

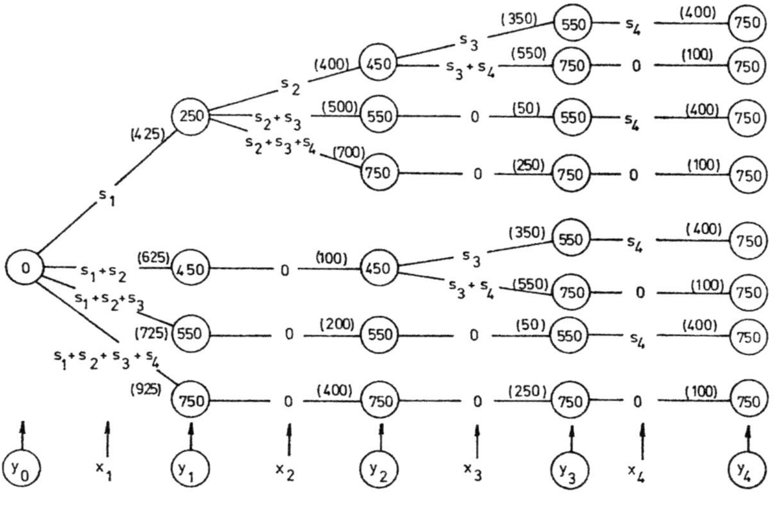

Fig. 22

and the ordering cost (or the fixed cost associated with producing a lot) is \$ 300 per lot regardless of the lot size[1].

Let the state variables y_n represent accumulated purchases or production so that $y_0 = 0$, $y_4 = s_1 + s_2 + s_3 + s_4 = 750$, and let the x_n be the decision variables of the four stages (quarters). The feasible alternatives—the sets of x_n which will meet demands—can be illustrated by a decision tree as shown in Fig. 22. Clearly demands can only be met if $y_1 \geqslant s_1 = 250$, $y_2 \geqslant s_1 + s_2 = 450$, and $y_3 \geqslant s_1 + s_2 + s_3 = 550$ (i.e., if inventory is always nonnegative at the end of a quarter)[2].

---

[1] The total purchase price (or variable cost of production) for the 750 units can be disregarded since it is constant and cannot affect the solution.

[2] There are more feasible alternatives than those shown in Fig. 22. For example, $x_1 = s_1$, $x_2 = s_2 + s_3$, $x_3 = s_4$, $x_4 = 0$ will meet all demands; but such a solution would clearly be uneconomical since buying s_4 units

It is obvious that total inventory costs are at a minimum for $x_n = s_n$ ($n = 1, 2, 3, 4$); then the average number of units kept in stock in the nth quarter will be $\frac{s_n + 0}{2}$ so that the total storage costs will be $1.00 \times \sum s_n/2 = 375$. However, this solution will also imply maximum costs of ordering, $300 \times 4 = 1{,}200$. The optimal solution must be some sort of a compromise.

All we have to do now is to associate returns (costs) $r_n (y_{n-1}, x_n)$ with each branch of the decision tree; having done this we can solve the problem as a shortest-route problem, either by tabular computations or by the graphical method.

Consider, for instance, the policy

$$x_1 = s_1 + s_2 = 450, \quad x_2 = 0, \quad x_3 = s_3 + s_4 = 300, \quad x_4 = 0$$

(no. 3 from below in Fig. 22). Costs of *ordering* are incurred only for $x_n > 0$; they are \$ 300.00 in the first and the third quarter and otherwise zero. *Storage* costs are computed for each quarter as \$ 1.00 times the average number of units held in stock, z_n. For the policy considered, there are $x_1 = 450$ units in stock at the beginning of the first quarter (after purchasing this lot); at the end of the quarter there are $x_1 - s_1 = 200$ units left, so average inventory is $z_1 = (450 + 200)/2 = 325$ units and storage cost is \$ 325.00. Proceeding in this fashion we have for the policy in question:

n	1	2	3	4
x_n	450	0	300	0
z_n	$\frac{450 + 200}{2}$	$\frac{200 + 0}{2}$	$\frac{300 + 200}{2}$	$\frac{200 + 0}{2}$
r_n	325 + 300	100	250 + 300	100

and similarly for all other branches. The r_n are indicated in brackets in Fig. 22[1]. Using the graphical procedure for backward recursion, eliminating inoptimal subpolicies, it appears that there are multiple optimal solutions:

before they are required will only increase total storage costs without saving any cost of ordering. A lot should not be purchased or produced until at least some of it is required for sale.

[1] Note that there are only three values of y_2 so that everything to the right of y_2 appears twice, a fact which reduces the computational labour.

	x_1	x_2	x_3	x_4
1°	250	300	0	200
2°	450	0	300	0
3°	550	0	0	200

all of which have a total cost of \$ 1,375.00[1].

4. A company is planning its purchases and inventories of a commodity for a period of three months (90 days). Initial inventory is zero and the rate of demand is constant, $s = 100$ units per day. To meet the total demand of $s \cdot 90 = 9{,}000$ units, three lots of x_1, x_2, and

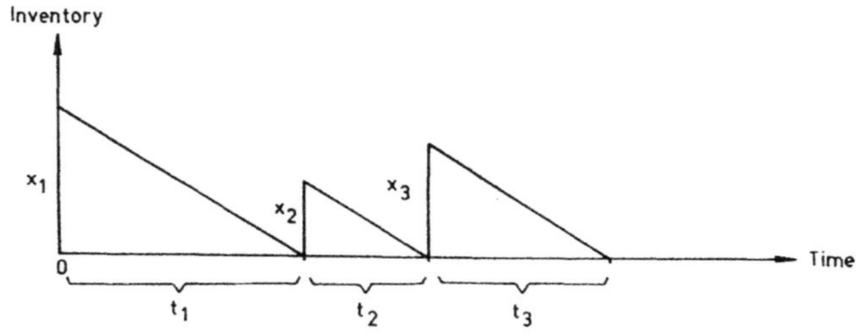

Fig. 23

x_3 units are purchased ($x_1 + x_2 + x_3 = 9{,}000$); the first order is placed at the beginning of the period and the stock is replenished twice when it has come down to zero. Then the pattern of inventories will be as shown in Fig. 23.

The intervals between purchases are t_1, t_2, and t_3, where $x_n = 100 t_n$ ($n = 1, 2, 3$). The purchase price is \$ 0.50 per unit plus \$ 125.00 per order, and the costs of storage are \$ 0.10 per unit per day. The problem is *to determine the three lot sizes such that total cost is a minimum.*

In a DP formulation of the problem, let the state variables y_n represent time and let the intervals between purchases (t_n) be the decision variables of the three stages. Then the (inverse) transformation equations are

$$y_{n-1} = y_n - t_n \quad (n = 1, 2, 3) \tag{19}$$

where $y_0 = 0$ and $y_3 = 90$; the variation of t_n is restricted by the sign requirements $t_n \geqslant 0$, $y_{n-1} \geqslant 0$, that is

$$0 \leqslant t_n \leqslant y_n.$$

[1] **Exercise 24:** Demonstrate the solutions in Fig. 22, and check by tabular solution.

The return functions (stage costs) are—since $x_n = 100\, t_n$ and average inventory for stage n is $x_n/2 = 50t_n$—

$$r_n = 0.50 \times 100t_n + 125 + 0.10 \times 50t_n \times t_n$$
$$= 125 + 50t_n + 5t_n^2.$$

Total cost is $c = \sum_n r_n$, which is to be minimized.

Applying forward recursion we have for stage 1:

$$f_1 = 125 + 50t_1 + 5t_1^2$$

where $t_1 = y_1 - y_0 = y_1$ so that there is no optimization at this stage, hence

$$t_1(y_1) = y_1$$
$$F_1(y_1) = 125 + 50y_1 + 5y_1^2. \qquad (20)$$

For stage 2 we have

$$f_2 = 125 + 50t_2 + 5t_2^2 + 125 + 50\,(y_2 - t_2) + 5\,(y_2 - t_2)^2 = \min_{0 \le t_2 \le y_2}$$

$$df_2/dt_2 = 20t_2 - 10y_2 = 0 \quad \text{for} \quad t_2 = \frac{1}{2} y_2$$

$$t_2\,(y_2) = \frac{1}{2} y_2 \qquad (21)$$

$$F_2\,(y_2) = 2 \cdot 125 + 50y_2 + 5 \cdot \frac{1}{2} \cdot y_2^2$$

and for stage 3

$$f_3 = 125 + 50t_3 + 5t_3^2 + 2 \cdot 125 + 50\,(y_3 - t_3) + 5 \cdot \frac{1}{2} \cdot (y_3 - t_3)^2 = \min_{0 \le t_3 \le y_3}$$

$$df_3/dt_3 = 15t_3 - 5y_3 = 0 \quad \text{for} \quad t_3 = \frac{1}{3} y_3$$

$$t_3\,(y_3) = \frac{1}{3} y_3 \qquad (22)$$

$$F_3\,(y_3) = 3 \cdot 125 + 50y_3 + 5 \cdot \frac{1}{3} \cdot y_3^2\,.$$

For $y_3 = 90$, (19)–(22) determine the optimal policy

$$t_1 = t_2 = t_3 = 30; \quad c^{\min} = F_3(90) = 18{,}375$$
$$x_1 = x_2 = x_3 = 100t_n = 3{,}000.$$

Thus the company should buy in equal lots of 9,000/3 = 3,000 units at equal intervals of 90/3 = 30 days.

This is the optimal policy for $N = 3$; but we cannot be sure that the best policy is to replenish the stock 3 times during the 90-day period rather than, for example, 2 or 5 times. To determine the optimal number of purchases we can treat N as a parameter and minimize the parametric solution $F_N(y_N)$ with respect to N[1].

We have already computed $F_N(y_N)$ for $N = 1$, 2, and 3 because we used forward recursion in solving the three-stage problem. For $N = 1$ the procedure would terminate with (20), which for $y_N = y_1 = 90$ gives the solution $c = F_1(90) = 45{,}125$. For $N = 2$, (21) gives $c = F_2(90) = 25{,}000$; and for $N = 3$ we found above $c = F_3(90) = 18{,}375$. So far, total cost decreases with the number of stages.

To find a general expression for $F_N(y_N)$, we observe that (20)–(22) suggest the form

$$F_N(y_N) = N \times 125 + 50 \times y_N + 5 \times \frac{1}{N} \times y_N^2, \text{ where } y_N = 90; \tag{23}$$

this is also the form we would expect, for the cost of ordering N lots is $N \times 125$, the total purchase price is 0.50 times the total purchase $100 \times y_N$, and provided that all lots are of equal size, storage costs will be 0.10 times storage time y_N times average inventory $\frac{1}{2} x_n = \frac{1}{2} \times 100 y_N/N$. It is easily proved by induction that (23) is in fact correct; assuming that F_N has the form (23), F_{N+1} as obtained by maximizing $r_{N+1} + F_N$ turns out to be of the same form.

The optimal value of N is determined by minimizing (23) with respect to N, setting the derivative $= 0$:

$$d\,F_N(y_N)/dN = 125 - (5/N^2) \cdot y_N^2 = 0$$

which yields

$$N = \sqrt{\frac{5 y_N^2}{125}} = 0.2 y_N = 18, \tag{24}$$

that is, the company should buy 500 units every fifth day. Substituting (24) into (23) we get the total cost

$$c = F_N(y_N) = 100 y_N = 9{,}000,$$

which represents a minimum because $d^2 F_N/dN^2$ is seen to be positive. (24) is the "square root formula" known from inventory theory.

Note that y_N/N $(= 5)$ is constant, that is, the intervals between purchases (t_n) are independent of the length of the planning period, and so are the lot sizes $(x_n = 100 t_n)$.

---

[1] Cf. G. L. Nemhauser (1966), p. 86 (Exercise 11).

D. Investment Planning

1. Dynamic programming can be applied to determine *optimal equipment replacement policies*, as the following example will illustrate.

A company is considering undertaking an investment, i.e., buying (at time $t = 0$) a piece of equipment—for example, a machine—which is expected to generate future cash flows. The net present value (C_1) of the investment, defined as the sum of discounted net cash proceeds minus the initial cost of the equipment plus the discounted salvage value, will depend on its economic life (x_1). At time $t = x_1$ (years) the equipment is replaced, i.e., a new investment is undertaken whose net present value at $t = x_1$ is $C_2(x_2)$ where x_2 is the life of the new equipment; and so on. The total net present value of the replacement chain, discounted back to $t = 0$, is

$$f = C_1(x_1) + (1+i)^{-x_1} C_2(x_2) + (1+i)^{-(x_1+x_2)} C_3(x_3) + \ldots \qquad (25)$$

where i is the rate of interest. The chain may have a finite or an infinite number of terms, depending on the horizon for which the company chooses to plan. It is assumed that the company's objective is to maximize the net present value of the chain. Then the problem is *to determine the lives of the successive investments* ($x_1, x_2, \ldots$) *such as to maximize* $f = f(x_1, x_2, \ldots)$; the solution implicitly determines the times at which replacements are to take place ($x_1, x_1 + x_2, x_1 + x_2 + x_3, \ldots$).

Consider an initial investment which is expected to generate annual net cash proceeds $a_t = 4 - 0.5t$ ($t = 1, 2, \ldots$); the equipment costs 12 and the salvage value is $11 - t$ (all in \$ 1,000,000). Then, assuming an interest rate of 8 per cent, the net present value of the investment is

$$C(x_1) = \sum_{\tau=1}^{x_1} (4 - 0.5\tau) \cdot 1.08^{-\tau} - 12 + (11 - x_1) \cdot 1.08^{-x_1} \qquad (26)$$

where x_1 is integer. The function is tabulated below for $x_1 = 1, 2, \ldots, 5$.

x_1	1	2	3	4	5	(years)
$C(x_1)$	0.500	1.529	2.148	2.413	2.372	(\$ 1,000,000)

The company is planning to replace the equipment twice by identical equipment after x_1 and $x_1 + x_2$ years, so $C_1(x) = C_2(x) = C_3(x) = C(x)$. The total net present value of this replacement chain is

$$f = C(x_1) + 1.08^{-x_1} C(x_2) + 1.08^{-(x_1+x_2)} C(x_3) \qquad (27)$$

which is to be maximized with respect to x_1, x_2, and x_3 (all integers).

In this three-stage decision system, let the state variable y_n represent time ($y_0 = 0$). Then the transformation equations have the simple form

$$y_n = y_{n-1} + x_n \quad (n = 1, 2, 3)$$
$$(y_0 = 0)$$

where the lives x_n are decision variables. The return functions—the net present values at the start of each investment—are

$$r_n = C(x_n) \quad (n = 1, 2, 3).$$

For backward solution the decision functions, discounted to the times at which the respective decisions are made, are

$$f_1 = r_3 = C(x_3)$$
$$f_2 = r_2 + 1.08^{-x_2} F_1 = C(x_2) + 1.08^{-x_2} F_1$$
$$f_3 = r_1 + 1.08^{-x_1} F_2 = C(x_1) + 1.08^{-x_1} F_2;$$

for example, the value of the last two investments, discounted to $t = y_1$, is $C(x_2)$ plus the optimal value F_1 of the third investment discounted back x_2 years, cf. Fig. 24.

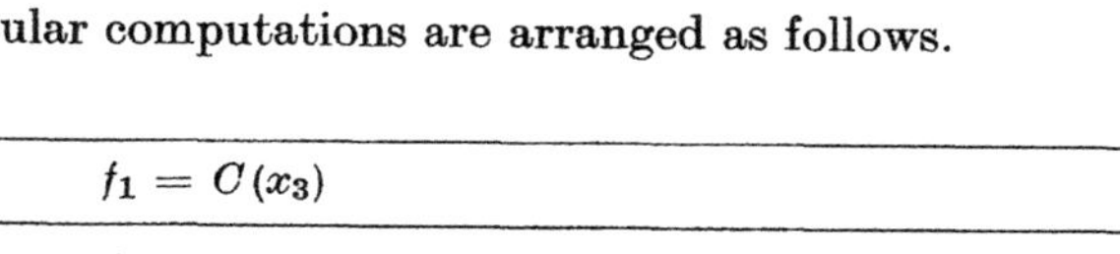

Fig. 24

The tabular computations are arranged as follows.

Stage 3	$f_1 = C(x_3)$						F_1	x_3
$y_2 \diagdown x_3$	1	2	3	4	5	...		
all values	0.500	1.529	2.148	**2.413**	2.372	...	2.413	4

Stage 2	$f_2 = C(x_2) + 1.08^{-x_2}F_1$						F_2	x_2
$y_1 \diagdown x_2$	1	2	3	4	5	...		
all values	0.500 + 2.234	1.529 + 2.069	2.148 + 1.916	**2.413** + **1.774**	2.372 + 1.642	...	4.187	4

Stage 1	$f_3 = C(x_1) + 1.08^{-x_1}F_2$						F_3	x_1
$y_0 \diagdown x_1$	1	2	3	4	5	...		
0	0.500 + 3.877	1.529 + 3.590	2.148 + 3.324	**2.413** + **3.078**	2.372 + 2.850	...	5.491	4

The optimal policy is seen to be

$$x_1 = 4, \ x_2 = 4, \ x_3 = 4$$

and the total net present value of the replacement chain is $f = 5.491$ million dollars. The equipment should be replaced 4 and 8 years after the start[1].

Thus in this case the lives of the three successive identical investments are the same. This result, however, is due to the fact the x_n are allowed to take integral values only. In a finite replacement chain of this type (N finite) the optimal lives will be an increasing sequence

$$x_1 < x_2 < \ldots < x_N$$

when non-integral values of the x_n are allowed. This would come out if the calculations were done on a half-yearly basis, say. Or better still—though the data are unlikely to warrant such a refined procedure—the x_n might be treated as continuous variables. In the latter case we have[2]

$$C(x_1) = \int_0^{x_1} (4 - 0.5t)\, e^{-0.08t}\, dt - 12 + (11 - x_1) \cdot e^{-0.08x_1} \tag{28}$$

or, after performing the integration,

$$C(x_1) = e^{-0.08x_1} \cdot (39.125 + 5.25x_1) - 40.125.$$

---

[1] Observe that this DP problem is an example of decomposition with nonadditive stage returns; the total return f is the sum of *discounted* stage returns r_n. If we defined the stage returns as net present values discounted to $t = 0$,

$$r_n = 1.08^{-y_{n-1}} \cdot C(n) \quad (n = 1, 2, 3; \ y_0 = 0),$$

the stage returns would add up to the total return f. The result would be the same but the calculations would be more laborious. **Exercise 25:** Solve the problem in this way.

[2] Strictly speaking, when the interest rate is $i = 0.08$ (8 per cent) compounded annually, the equivalent rate in the case of interest compounded continuously is not 0.08 but $\rho = \ln 1.08 = 0.0770$, equivalence (in terms of growth factors) being defined by $1 + i = e^{\rho}$.

Then the net present value of the chain ($N = 3$) is

$$f = C(x_1) + e^{-0.08x_1} C(x_2) + e^{-0.08(x_1+x_2)} C(x_3)$$

and the three-stage DP problem can be solved analytically. For the last stage we have the decision function

$$f_1 = C(x_3)$$

which is a maximum for

$$C'(x_3) = e^{-0.08x_3} \cdot (2.12 - 0.42x_3) = 0,$$

i.e.,

$$x_3 = 5.0, \quad F_1 = C(x_3) = 3.697.$$

For stage two we have

$$f_2 = C(x_2) + e^{-0.08x_2} \cdot F_1 = \max_{x_2}$$

so that x_2 is determined by

$$C'(x_2) = e^{-0.08x_2} \cdot (2.12 - 0.42x_2) = 0.08 \cdot 3.697 \cdot e^{-0.08x_2}$$

which gives

$$x_2 = 4.3, \; C(x_2) = 3.617, \; F_2 = 6.238.$$

Similarly, for stage one

$$f_3 = C(x_1) + e^{-0.08x_1} \cdot F_2 = \max_{x_1}$$

$$C'(x_1) = e^{-0.08x_1} \cdot (2.12 - 0.42x_1) = 0.08 \cdot 6.238 \cdot e^{-0.08x_1},$$

i.e.,

$$x_1 = 3.9, \; C(x_1) = 3.502, \; F_3 = 8.068.$$

The optimal life of the last investment in a finite chain as determined by $C'(x_N) = 0$ is the value of x that maximizes $C(x)$; as we go backwards, the lives get shorter because the right-hand side of the optimum condition

$$C'(x_n) = 0.08 \cdot F_{N-n} \cdot e^{-0.08x_n}$$

increases with F_{N-n}.

Even with integral x_n a similar result will emerge if we add further links to the chain. With four investments of the type (26), i.e., $N = 4$, the lives can be computed by increasing the subscripts of the x_n and y_n by one in the three tables above and adding a fourth table:

	$f_4 = C(x_1) + 1.08^{-x_1}F_3$							
$y_0\diagdown x_1$	1	2	3	4	5	...	F_4	x_1
0	0.500 + 5.084	1.529 + 4.708	**2.148** + **4.359**	2.413 + 4.036	2.372 + 3.737	...	6.507	3

so that the first replacement takes place after 3 years[1].

Similar procedures can of course be applied to problems in which the planning period starts when the initial equipment has been in operation for some time; then x_1 is to be interpreted as the remaining life of the equipment. They can also be applied to more general cases of the type (25) where the replacements are not identical repetitions of the initial investment because the company anticipates changes in the technology, but in such cases we have to make the rather unrealistic assumptions that the optimal sequence of replacements (types of equipment) is known beforehand and that the corresponding net present values C_n are independent of calendar time and depend only on the lives, $C_n = C_n(x_n)$. The latter assumption, which implies that the initial cost of an investment is constant whereas the salvage value and the annual net cash proceeds depend only on the age of the equipment, is also basic to the above model of identical replacements—cf. (26) and (27)—but it is of course more questionable in the case of technological improvement.

2. In a DP model for optimizing the replacement chain (27) the *planning horizon* is defined by the number of stages, N. In the numerical example above, N (= 3) was *the number of consecutive investments* of

[1] For $N \to \infty$ all x_n converge to a common limit $\bar{x}$, i.e., all replacements take place at intervals of $\bar{x}$ years so that the net present value of the (infinite) chain becomes

$$f = \frac{C(\bar{x})}{1 - 1.08^{-\bar{x}}}$$

where $\bar{x}$ is determined by maximizing f; in the present case (26) we get $\bar{x} = 2$ years, $f = 10.718$. In the continuous case (28) we have for $N \to \infty$

$$f = \frac{C(\bar{x})}{1 - e^{-0.08\bar{x}}}$$

which is a maximum for $\bar{x} = 2.25$ years, corresponding to $f = 14.700$.

Dynamic programming with an infinite horizon is dealt with further in Ch. VIII below.

the type (26), cf. (27). This means that the length of the planning period ($= x_1 + x_2 + x_3$) cannot be fixed beforehand but will be determined by the optimization.

In most cases, it seems a more realistic approach to the replacement chain problem to define the (finite) horizon in terms of *a planning period of given length, N* years. This requires a reformulation of the problem (27) such that stage no. n now represents the nth year of the planning period ($n = 1, 2, \ldots, N$). At the beginning of year n the age of the current equipment is y_{n-1} years and the company has to decide whether to replace it by new equipment of the same type or to keep it and use it in year n; thus the decision variable x_n can take two values, say $x_n = 1$ (*replace* at the beginning of the year) and $x_n = 2$ (*keep*). It follows that the transformation equations have the form

$$y_n = \begin{cases} 1 & \text{for } x_n = 1 \\ y_{n-1} + 1 & \text{for } x_n = 2 \end{cases} \tag{29}$$

where the output state y_n represents the age of the equipment used in year n at the end of this year (i.e., at $t = n$). Conforming to the previous formulation (27) it is assumed that the initial equipment has been purchased at the beginning of the first year, so $y_0 = 0$.

To derive the stage returns we need the following data contained in (26):

The *current net cash proceeds* in year n depend on the age of the equipment at the end of the year,

$$a(y_n) = 4 - 0.5 y_n;$$

in accordance with (26) they are assumed to be concentrated at the end of the year, i.e., at $t = n$. The *salvage value* at the beginning of year n (i.e., at $t = n - 1$) depends on the age at $t = n - 1$,

$$S(y_{n-1}) = 11 - y_{n-1}.$$

The *price* of a unit of equipment at the beginning of year n ($t = n - 1$) is constant,

$$A = 12.$$

The payments due in year n are shown in Figs. 25a and b for $x_n = 1$ and 2 respectively.

If $x_n = 1$ (*replace*), cf. Fig. 25a, the old equipment is sold at the beginning of the year at a salvage value of $11 - y_{n-1}$ and a new piece of equipment is purchased and installed at the price 12; the current net cash proceeds are $4 - 0.5 y_n$ or, since $y_n = 1$ for $x_n = 1$, $4 - 0.5 \cdot$

$\cdot 1 = 3.5$. Discounting this amount back to $t = n - 1$, the stage return is seen to be

$$r_n = 11 - y_{n-1} - 12 + 1.08^{-1} \cdot 3.5 = 2.241 - y_{n-1}.$$

The return function for the last year of the period has an additional term because the equipment is sold at the end of the horizon (i.e., at $t = N$), the salvage value being $11 - y_N = 10$ for $y_N = 1$; discounted to $t = N - 1$ we have $1.08^{-1} \cdot 10 = 9.259$, i.e.,

$$r_N = 2.241 - y_{N-1} + 9.259.$$

For $x_2 = 2$ (*keep*), cf. Fig. 25b, no payments take place at the beginning of the year. At the end of the year we have the current net

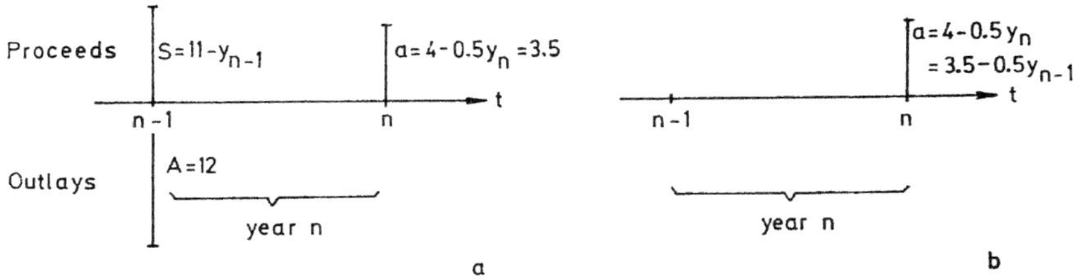

Fig. 25a–b

cash proceeds $4 - 0.5y_n = 4 - 0.5(y_{n-1} + 1) = 3.5 - 0.5y_{n-1}$ or, discounted to $t = n - 1$,

$$r_n = 1.08^{-1}(3.5 - 0.5y_{n-1}).$$

At the end of year N the equipment is sold at a salvage price of $11 - y_N = 11 - (y_{N-1} + 1) = 10 - y_{N-1}$ so that we get

$$r_N = 3.241 - 0.463y_{N-1} + 1.08^{-1}(10 - y_{N-1}).$$

This leads to the following return functions $r_n(y_{n-1}, x_n)$;

$$r_n(y_{n-1}, 1) = \begin{cases} 2.241 - y_{n-1} & (n = 1, 2, \ldots, N-1) \\ 11.500 - y_{n-1} & (n = N) \end{cases} \tag{30a}$$

$$r_n(y_{n-1}, 2) = \begin{cases} 3.241 - 0.463y_{n-1} & (n = 1, 2, \ldots, N-1) \\ 12.500 - 1.389y_{n-1} & (n = N). \end{cases} \tag{30b}$$

Using the return functions (30a–b) and the transformations (29) we shall now solve the problem backwards for a horizon of $N = 12$ years. The decision functions are

$$f_1 = r_{12}(y_{11}, x_{12})$$
$$f_2 = r_{11}(y_{10}, x_{11}) + 1.08^{-1} \cdot F_1(y_{11})$$
$$\ldots\ldots$$
$$f_{12} = r_1(y_0, x_1) + 1.08^{-1} \cdot F_{11}(y_1),$$

recalling that r_{11} is discounted to $t = 10$ and F_1 to $t = 11$, and similarly for the decision functions $f_3, f_4, \ldots$ $(1.08^{-1} = 0.925926)$. The values of the input state y_{n-1} to be listed in the stubs of the tables are $y_{n-1} = 1, 2, \ldots, n-1$ (but $y_0 = 0$ in the last table), as will be seen from the tree shown in Fig. 26.

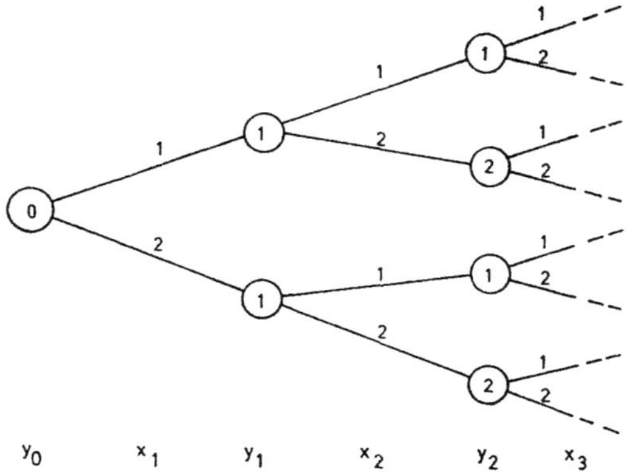

Fig. 26

The tabular calculations proceed as follows:

	$f_1 = r_{12}$				
$y_{11} \diagdown x_{12}$	1	2	$F_1(y_{11})$	$x_{12}(y_{11})$	$y_{12}(y_{11})$
1	10.500	11.111	11.111	2	2
2	9.500	9.722	9.722	2	3
3	8.500	8.333	8.500	1	1
4	7.500	6.944	7.500	1	1
5	6.500	5.555	6.500	1	1
6	5.500	4.166	5.500	1	1
7	4.500	2.778	4.500	1	1
8	3.500	1.389	3.500	1	1
9	2.500	0.000	2.500	1	1
10	1.500	− 1.389	1.500	1	1
11	0.500	− 2.778	0.500	1	1

$y_{10} \diagdown x_{11}$	$f_2 = r_{11} + 0.925926 \cdot F_1(y_{11})$: 1	2	$F_2(y_{10})$	$x_{11}(y_{10})$	$y_{11}(y_{10})$
1	1.241 + 10.288	2.778 + 9.002	11.780	2	2
2	0.241 + 10.288	2.315 + 7.870	10.529	1	1
3	— 0.759 + 10.288	1.852 + 6.944	9.529	1	1
4	— 1.759 + 10.288	1.389 + 6.019	8.529	1	1
5	— 2.759 + 10.288	0.926 + 5.093	7.529	1	1
6	— 3.759 + 10.288	0.463 + 4.167	6.529	1	1
7	— 4.759 + 10.288	0.000 + 3.241	5.529	1	1
8	— 5.759 + 10.288	— 0.463 + 2.315	4.529	1	1
9	— 6.759 + 10.288	— 0.926 + 1.389	3.529	1	1
10	— 7.759 + 10.288	— 1.389 + 0.463	2.529	1	1

$y_9 \diagdown x_{10}$	$f_3 = r_{10} + 0.925926 \cdot F_2(y_{10})$: 1	2	$F_3(y_9)$	$x_{10}(y_9)$	$y_{10}(y_9)$
1	1.241 + 10.907	2.778 + 9.749	12.527	2	2
2	0.241 + 10.907	2.315 + 8.823	11.148	1	1
3	— 0.759 + 10.907	1.852 + 7.897	10.148	1	1
4	— 1.759 + 10.907	1.389 + 6.971	9.148	1	1
5	— 2.759 + 10.907	0.926 + 6.045	8.148	1	1
6	— 3.759 + 10.907	0.463 + 5.119	7.148	1	1
7	— 4.759 + 10.907	0.000 + 4.194	6.148	1	1
8	— 5.759 + 10.907	— 0.463 + 3.268	5.148	1	1
9	— 6.759 + 10.907	— 0.926 + 2.342	4.148	1	1

$y_8 \diagdown x_9$	$f_4 = r_9 + 0.925926 \cdot F_3(y_9)$: 1	2	$F_4(y_8)$	$x_9(y_8)$	$y_9(y_8)$
1	1.241 + 11.599	2.778 + 10.322	13.100	2	2
2	0.241 + 11.599	2.315 + 9.396	11.840	1	1
3	— 0.759 + 11.599	1.852 + 8.470	10.840	1	1
4	— 1.759 + 11.599	1.389 + 7.544	9.840	1	1
5	— 2.759 + 11.599	0.926 + 6.619	8.840	1	1
6	— 3.759 + 11.599	0.463 + 5.693	7.840	1	1
7	— 4.759 + 11.599	0.000 + 4.767	6.840	1	1
8	— 5.759 + 11.599	— 0.463 + 3.841	5.840	1	1

$y_7 \diagdown x_8$	$f_5 = r_8 + 0.925926 \cdot F_4(y_8)$: 1	2	$F_5(y_7)$	$x_8(y_7)$	$y_8(y_7)$
1	1.241 + 12.130	2.778 + 10.963	13.741	2	2
2	0.241 + 12.130	2.315 + 10.037	12.371	1	1
3	— 0.759 + 12.130	1.852 + 9.111	11.371	1	1
4	— 1.759 + 12.130	1.389 + 8.185	10.371	1	1
5	— 2.759 + 12.130	0.926 + 7.259	9.371	1	1
6	— 3.759 + 12.130	0.463 + 6.333	8.371	1	1
7	— 4.759 + 12.130	0.000 + 5.407	7.371	1	1

$y_6 \diagdown x_7$	$f_6 = r_7 + 0.925926 \cdot F_5(y_7)$ 1	2	$F_6(y_6)$	$x_7(y_6)$	$y_7(y_6)$
1	1.241 + 12.723	2.778 + 11.455	14.233	2	2
2	0.241 + 12.723	2.315 + 10.529	12.964	1	1
3	— 0.759 + 12.723	1.852 + 9.603	11.964	1	1
4	— 1.759 + 12.723	1.389 + 8.677	10.964	1	1
5	— 2.759 + 12.723	0.926 + 7.751	9.964	1	1
6	— 3.759 + 12.723	0.463 + 6.825	8.964	1	1

$y_5 \diagdown x_6$	$f_7 = r_6 + 0.925926 \cdot F_6(y_6)$ 1	2	$F_7(y_5)$	$x_6(y_5)$	$y_6(y_5)$
1	1.241 + 13.178	2.778 + 12.004	14.782	2	2
2	0.241 + 13.178	2.315 + 11.078	13.419	1	1
3	— 0.759 + 13.178	1.852 + 10.152	12.419	1	1
4	— 1.759 + 13.178	1.389 + 9.226	11.419	1	1
5	— 2.759 + 13.178	0.926 + 8.300	10.419	1	1

$y_4 \diagdown x_5$	$f_8 = r_5 + 0.925926 \cdot F_7(y_5)$ 1	2	$F_8(y_4)$	$x_5(y_4)$	$y_5(y_4)$
1	1.241 + 13.687	2.778 + 12.425	15.203	2	2
2	0.241 + 13.687	2.315 + 11.499	13.928	1	1
3	— 0.759 + 13.687	1.852 + 10.573	12.928	1	1
4	— 1.759 + 13.687	1.389 + 9.647	11.928	1	1

$y_3 \diagdown x_4$	$f_9 = r_4 + 0.925926 \cdot F_8(y_4)$ 1	2	$F_9(y_3)$	$x_4(y_3)$	$y_4(y_3)$
1	1.241 + 14.077	2.778 + 12.896	15.674	2	2
2	0.241 + 14.077	2.315 + 11.970	14.318	1	1
3	— 0.759 + 14.077	1.852 + 11.044	13.318	1	1

$y_2 \diagdown x_3$	$f_{10} = r_3 + 0.925926 \cdot F_9(y_3)$ 1	2	$F_{10}(y_2)$	$x_3(y_2)$	$y_3(y_2)$
1	1.241 + 14.513	2.778 + 13.257	16.035	2	2
2	0.241 + 14.513	2.315 + 12.331	14.754	1	1

$y_1 \diagdown x_2$	$f_{11} = r_2 + 0.925926 \cdot F_{10}(y_2)$ 1	2	$F_{11}(y_1)$	$x_2(y_1)$	$y_2(y_1)$
1	1.241 + 14.847	2.778 + 13.661	16.439	2	2

	$f_{12} = r_1 + 0.925926 \cdot F_{11}(y_1)$				
$y_0 \diagdown x_1$	1	2	$F_{12}(y_0)$	$x_1(y_0)$	$y_1(y_0)$
0	2.241 + 15.221	3.241 + 15.221	18.462	2	1

The optimal policy is seen to be

$$x_3 = x_5 = x_7 = x_9 = x_{11} = 1, \text{ all other } x_n = 2; \ F_{12} = 18.462.$$

In other words, the equipment is to replaced at the beginning of year 3, 5, 7, 9, and 11, i.e., at $t = 2, 4, 6, 8, 10$. The optimal policy corresponds to a chain of six identical investments each of which has an economic life of 2 years; the total net present value of the chain is 18.462 million dollars or, if we deduct the initial cost of 12.000 (assumed to have been paid just before $t = 0$), 6.462 million dollars[1]. This corresponds to the net present value of a replacement chain of six successive investments each of which has an economic life of two years (where $C(2) = 1.529$),

$$f = C(2) + 1.08^{-2}C(2) + \ldots + 1.08^{-10}C(2) = 6.462.$$

Thus is makes quite a difference whether the stages and the horizon are defined in terms of the number of investments or in terms of years. In the former case, $N = 3$ led to a chain of three investments of the type (26), each with an optimal life of 4 years so that the length of the chain in time was 12 years; in the latter case, a horizon of 12 years led to six consecutive investments of the same type, each with a life of 2 years. When the horizon is extended to infinity ($N \to \infty$), however, the difference between the two approaches vanishes and all the lives in the infinite replacement chain converge to the same limit, 2 years[2].

Again, the model applies equally well to cases where the initial equipment has been in operation for some time.

Moreover, this kind of DP replacement model can be extended to cover cases in which the payments entering into the stage returns also depend on *calendar time* and not only on the *age* of the equipment. This generalization, important as it is in itself, is particularly suited to take technological improvement into account because technological change is a process that takes place in calendar time as represented here by the stage number, n. As the technology changes, the price

[1] Alternatively, we might have deducted the initial cost (= 12) from r_1, both for $x_1 = 1$ and for $x_1 = 2$, in the last table.

[2] Cf. Ch. VIII below.

of purchasing and installing a new machine (assumed roughly to serve the same purpose as the previous piece of equipment) at the beginning of year n will depend on n, so instead of A = constant we write $A = A_n$ ($n = 1, 2, \ldots, N$). Similarly, the salvage value and the current net cash proceeds will depend on the year in which the current equipment was purchased as well as on its age, i.e. they will be functions of calendar time and age[1]:

$$S = S_n(y_{n-1}), \qquad a = a_n(y_n) \qquad (n = 1, 2, \ldots, N).$$

In this case Fig. 25 must be replaced by Figs. 27a and b (corresponding to $x_n = 1$ and 2 respectively):

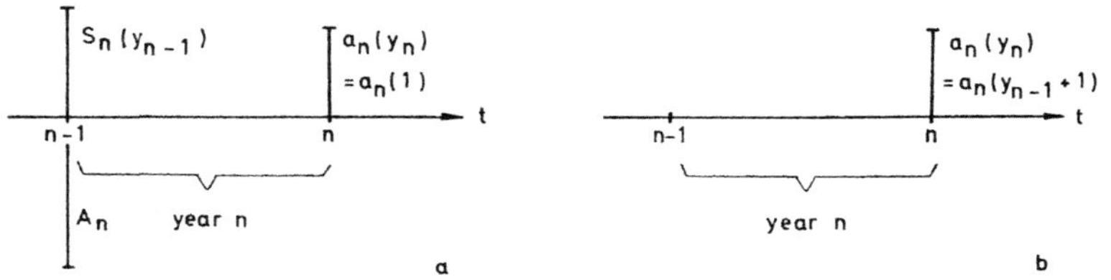

Fig. 27a–b

The stage return functions $r_n(y_{n-1}, x_n)$ now have the form

$$\left.\begin{aligned} r_n(y_{n-1}, 1) &= S_n(y_{n-1}) - A_n + 1.08^{-1} a_n(1) \\ r_n(y_{n-1}, 2) &= 1.08^{-1} a_n(y_{n-1} + 1) \end{aligned}\right\} (n = 1, 2, \ldots, N - 1)$$

and depend on calendar time, n. They require estimates of the following data[2]:

	$a_n(y_n)$ (at $t = n$)			
$y_n \diagdown n$	1	2	3	...
1	$a_1(1)$	$a_2(1)$	$a_3(1)$	...
2	$a_1(2)$	$a_2(2)$	$a_3(2)$	...
3	$a_1(3)$	$a_2(3)$	$a_3(3)$	...
⋮	⋮			

[1] If a piece of equipment purchased at $t = \tau$ is used in year n, we have $\tau + y_n = n$ and the net cash proceeds can be written as a function of any two of these three variables, i.e., $a(\tau, y_n)$ or $a(\tau, n - \tau)$ or $a(n - y_n, y_n) = a_n(y_n)$; a similar reasoning applies to the salvage value.

[2] For a numerical example of this type see H. P. Künzi, O. Müller, and E. Nievergelt (1968), pp. 43ff.

	$S_n(y_{n-1})$ (at $t = n - 1$)			
$y_{n-1} \diagdown n$	1	2	3	...
0	$S_1(0)$	$S_2(0)$	$S_3(0)$	...
1	$S_1(1)$	$S_2(1)$		
2	$S_1(2)$			
⋮	⋮			

	A_n (at $t = n - 1$)			
n	1	2	3	...
	A_1	A_2	A_3	...

The model can be further generalized to cover cases in which there are more than two possible alternative decisions at each stage (year). For example, the possibility of overhauling the existing equipment (at a certain cost) may be represented by $x_n = 3$ (overhaul and keep). Or there may be alternative types of new equipment to choose from, each to be represented by a particular value of the decision variable x_n[1]. Still another possibility is to replace by used equipment so that there will be a particular value of x_n for each age or vintage considered[2].

E. Allocation of Salesmen

A company is planning how to allocate 4 salesman to 3 geographically separate sales districts. The extra profit $r_n(x_n)$ obtained per month by assigning x_n salesmen to district no. n is indicated in the following table:

	$r_n(x_n)$, 1,000 dollars per month				
$n \diagdown x_n$	0	1	2	3	4
1	0	16	25	30	32
2	0	12	17	21	22
3	0	10	14	16	17

This type of allocation problem can be solved by dynamic programming, letting each district represent a stage ($n = 1, 2, 3$) where x_n—the

[1] See e.g. G. Hadley (1964), pp. 439ff.

[2] For a numerical example (automobile replacement under stationary conditions, i.e., no technological improvements) see M. J. Beckmann (1968), pp. 26ff.

number of salesmen allocated to district no. n—is the decision variable. The state variable y_n denotes the accumulated number of salesmen allocated to districts $1, 2, \ldots, n$, so the transformation equations are

$$y_n = y_{n-1} + x_n \quad (n = 1, 2, 3)$$

where

$$y_0 = 0, \; y_3 = 4.$$

The decision variables x_n and the state variables y_1 and y_2 can have the values $0, 1, \ldots, 4$. The return function for these values of x_n are the rows of the table above.

Using the inverse transformations,

$$y_{n-1} = y_n - x_n \; (\geqslant 0),$$

we shall solve the problem by forward recursion.

At stage 1 there is no optimization, for $y_0 = y_1 - x_1 = 0$ so that $x_1(y_1) = y_1$ and $F_1(y_1) = r_1(y_1)$:

$x_1 = y_1$	0	1	2	3	4
$F_1(y_1)$	0	16	25	30	32

For stages 2 and 3 we have

	$f_2 = r_2(x_2) + F_1(y_2 - x_2)$				$F_2(y_2)$	$x_2(y_2)$	$y_1(y_2)$
$y_2 \diagdown x_2$ 0	1	2	3	4			
0	**0 + 0**				0	0	0
1	**0 + 16**	12 + 0			16	0	1
2	0 + 25	**12 + 16**	17 + 0		28	1	1
3	0 + 30	**12 + 25**	17 + 16	21 + 0	37	1	2
4	0 + 32	**12 + 30**	**17 + 25**	21 + 16	22 + 0	42	1 (2)	3 (2)

$y_2 \diagdown x_2$	0	1	2	3	4	$F_2(y_2)$	$x_2(y_2)$	$y_1(y_2)$

$y_3 \diagdown x_3$	0	1	2	3	4	$F_3(y_3)$	$x_3(y_3)$	$y_2(y_3)$
	$f_3 = r_3(x_3) + F_2(y_3 - x_3)$							
4	0 + 42	**10 + 37**	14 + 28	16 + 16	17 + 0	47	1	3

The optimal policy is to assign two salesmen to the first district and one salesman to each of the other two districts, yielding a total extra profit of \$ 47,000.00 per month.

The second-best policy yields \$ 42,000.00 per month, the next largest value of f_3 in the last table being 42, which occurs in two places

($x_3 = 0$ and 2). Going back through the tables we find that there are three policies leading to this result:

Policy	x_1	x_2	x_3
(1°)	3	1	0
(2°)	2	2	0
(3°)	1	1	2

F. Cargo Loading and the Knapsack Problem

1. The so-called *"knapsack" problem*, a classical problem in dynamic programming, can be stated as follows. A hiker has made a list of items (no. 1, 2, . . ., N) which he would like to carry in his knapsack.

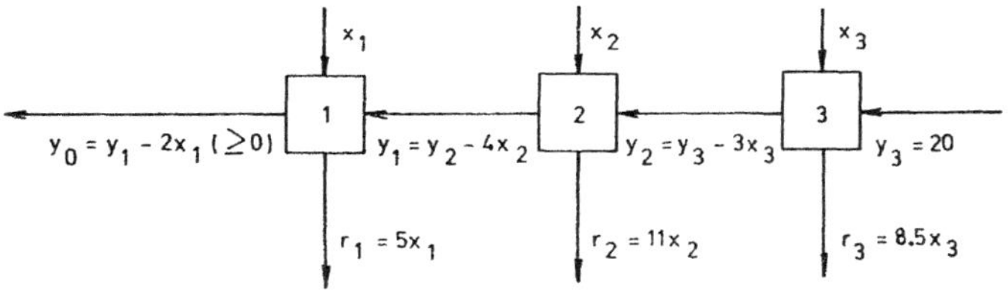

Fig. 28

Given the weight per unit of each item and the "value" per unit—a measure of the utility he can derive from carrying it—his problem is to find the number of units of each item to be put in the knapsack such as to maximize the total "value" of its content, subject to the constraint that the total weight must not exceed a specified upper limit.

Suppose the maximum total weight is 20 lbs., and let weight and value per unit be as follows:

Item no.	Weight, lbs./unit	Value per unit
1	2	5
2	4	11
3	3	8.5

Denoting the (integer) number of units of the nth item by x_n, this knapsack problem can be solved by linear programming with integer variables x_n[1]. Another approach is to formulate it as one of dynamic programming with a stage for each item ($n = 1, 2, 3$) and with decision variables x_n, cf. Fig. 28.

[1] **Exercise 26:** Show this.

The state variable y_n ($\geqslant 0$) is to be interpreted as accumulated weight including the slack y_0 ($\geqslant 0$). The inverted transformation equations are indicated in Fig. 28.

For stage 1 we have the decision function

$$f_1 = 5x_1 = \max_{x_1} \text{ subject to } y_1 - 2x_1 \geqslant 0.$$

Clearly f_1 is a maximum for $x_1 = \frac{1}{2} y_1$ if y_1 is even (so that $\frac{1}{2} y_1$ is integer); if y_1 is odd, x_1 will be equal to the nearest smaller integer $\left(= \frac{1}{2} y_1 - \frac{1}{2}\right)$. Hence we have[1]

y_1	0	1	2	3	4	5	6	7	8	9	10	11	12	13	14	15	16	17	18	19	20
$x_1(y_1)$	0	0	1	1	2	2	3	3	4	4	5	5	6	6	7	7	8	8	9	9	10
$F_1(y_1)$	0	0	5	5	10	10	15	15	20	20	25	25	30	30	35	35	40	40	45	45	50

For stage 2 we have

$$f_2 = 11x_2 + F_1(y_1) = 11x_2 + F_1(y_2 - 4x_2) = \max_{x_2}$$

where

$$y_1 = y_2 - 4x_2 \geqslant 0.$$

There is no need to tabulate f_2 for all integer values of y_2 up to 20, for since $y_2 = 20 - 3x_3 \geqslant 0$ and x_3 is to be integer (or zero), y_2 can take only the values 20, 17, 14, . . ., 2. Hence the values of x_2 to be considered are 0, 1, 2, 3, 4, 5. The stage table then looks as follows.

	$f_2 = 11x_2 + F_1(y_2 - 4x_2)$							
$y_2 \diagdown x_2$	0	1	2	3	4	5	$F_2(y_2)$	$x_2(y_2)$
2	**0** + **5**						5	0
5	0 + 10	**11** + **0**					11	1
8	0 + 20	11 + 10	**22** + **0**				22	2
11	0 + 25	11 + 15	**22** + **5**				27	2
14	0 + 35	11 + 25	22 + 15	**33** + **5**			38	3
17	0 + 40	11 + 30	22 + 20	33 + 10	**44** + **0**		44	4
20	0 + 50	11 + 40	22 + 30	33 + 20	44 + 10	**55** + **0**	55	5

[1] Actually a few of these values of y_1 cannot occur (explain why!), but on the other hand there is no harm in including them in the table.

Finally, stage 3 is optimized:

	$f_3 = 8.5x_3 + F_2(y_3 - 3x_3)$							$F_3(y_3)$	$x_3(y_3)$
$y_3 \diagdown x_3$	0	1	2	3	4	5	6		
20	0 + 55	8.5 + 44	17 + 38	25.5 + 27	**34 + 22**	42.5 + 11	**51 + 5**	56	4 (6)

There are two optimal policies[1], both with $F_3 = 56$:

	x_1	x_2	x_3
(1°)	0	2	4
(2°)	1	0	6

2. A similar procedure can obviously be applied to problems of *cargo loading*. If a ship having a maximum capacity in terms of volume is to be loaded with items which differ as to volume and value per unit, the problem of maximizing the total value of the cargo is analogous to the knapsack problem and can be solved by the same method (if necessary, on a computer)[2,3].

[1] **Exercise 27:** What difference would it make to the calculations and to the result if the hiker insisted on carrying at least one unit of each item in the knapsack?

[2] When there are two capacity limitations, maximum total weight and maximum total volume, the DP formulation requires two state variables per stage, accumulated weight and volume. (Cf. Ch. VII below.)

[3] A related but more complicated problem is that of stocking a ship with spare parts. It is assumed that storage space is limited and that the demand for each type of spare part is a stochastic variable characterized by a known probability distribution; the stockout costs—i.e., the costs incurred if a spare part is required but not available—are known for each type. Then the problem is to minimize the total expected stockout cost. For a numerical example see G. Hadley (1964), pp. 362ff., and H. P. Künzi, O. Müller, and E. Nievergelt (1968), pp. 31ff.

VII. Several Decision and State Variables

1. The basic idea underlying dynamic programming is that of decomposing an optimization problem into a series of stage problems each of which involves fewer variables than the total problem, and combining the parametric stage solutions to get the solution to the original problem.

So far we have only considered examples in which the stage problems were single-variable problems, but the application of DP is by no means confined to this special case. Stage decomposition will in many cases lead to stage optimization problems involving *several decision variables per stage* so that x_n is not a single decision variable but a vector of such variables.

As an example, consider the problem of optimal allocation of machines subject to attrition (Ch. VI. B. 4, pp. 91 f.). There are really two decision variables at each stage, the number of machines allocated to job no. 1 (x_n) and to job no. 2 (z_n). With two decision variables the transformations have the form

$$y_n = y_{n-1} - \frac{1}{3} x_n - \frac{1}{10} z_n \tag{1}$$

where the feasible region for stage n is defined by

$$\begin{aligned} x_n + z_n &= y_{n-1} \\ x_n, z_n &\geqslant 0. \end{aligned} \tag{2}$$

What we did above was to eliminate z_n,

$$z_n = y_{n-1} - x_n,$$

so that (2) could be replaced by the equivalent stage restrictions

$$0 \leqslant x_n \leqslant y_{n-1}$$

and (1) became

$$y_n = \frac{9}{10} y_{n-1} - \frac{7}{30} x_n.$$

The stage returns

$$r_n = 10 x_n + 7 z_n \tag{3}$$

were similarly reduced to

$$r_n = 3x_n + 7y_{n-1}.$$

With two decision variables per stage, the problem can be solved by backward recursion as follows.

For stage 4 we have the decision problem

$$f_1 = 10x_4 + 7z_4 = \max_{x_4, z_4}$$

subject to

$$x_4 + z_4 = y_3$$

$$x_4, z_4 \geqslant 0$$

which is a (parametric) linear programming problem in two variables. The solution obviously is

$$x_4(y_3) = y_3, \qquad z_4(y_3) = 0, \qquad F_1(y_3) = 10y_3; \qquad y_4(y_3) = \frac{2}{3}y_3.$$

The problem at stage 3 is

$$f_2 = 10x_3 + 7z_3 + F_1\left(y_2 - \frac{1}{3}x_3 - \frac{1}{10}z_3\right) = \frac{20}{3}x_3 + 6z_3 + 10y_2 = \max$$

subject to

$$x_3 + z_3 = y_2$$

$$x_3, z_3 \geqslant 0$$

which has the solution

$$x_3(y_2) = y_2, \qquad z_3(y_2) = 0, \qquad F_2(y_2) = \frac{50}{3}y_2; \qquad y_3(y_2) = \frac{2}{3}y_2.$$

For stages 2 and 1 we have

$$f_3 = 10x_2 + 7z_2 + F_2(y_2) = \frac{40}{9}x_2 + \frac{16}{3}z_2 + \frac{50}{3}y_1 = \max$$

subject to (2) for $n = 2$, i.e.

$$x_2(y_1) = 0, \qquad z_2(y_1) = y_1, \qquad F_3(y_1) = 22y_1; \qquad y_2(y_1) = \frac{9}{10}y_1$$

and

$$f_4 = 10x_1 + 7z_1 + F_3(y_1) = \frac{8}{3}x_1 + \frac{24}{5}z_1 + 22y_0 = \max$$

subject to (2) for $n = 1$, with the solution

$$x_1(y_0) = 0, \qquad z_1(y_0) = y_0, \qquad F_4(y_0) = \frac{134}{5}y_0; \qquad y_1(y_0) = \frac{9}{10}y_0.$$

For $y_0 = 100$, the stage solutions and the transformations give the total solution

$$\begin{aligned}
y_0 &= 100 \\
& \qquad x_1 = 0, \quad z_1 = 100 \\
y_1 &= 90 \\
& \qquad x_2 = 0, \quad z_2 = 90 \\
y_2 &= 81 \\
& \qquad x_3 = 81, \quad z_3 = 0 \\
y_3 &= 54 \\
& \qquad x_4 = 54, \quad z_4 = 0 \\
y_4 &= 36
\end{aligned}$$

and total return is $F_4(y_0) = 2{,}680$, corresponding to what we found on p. 92 above.

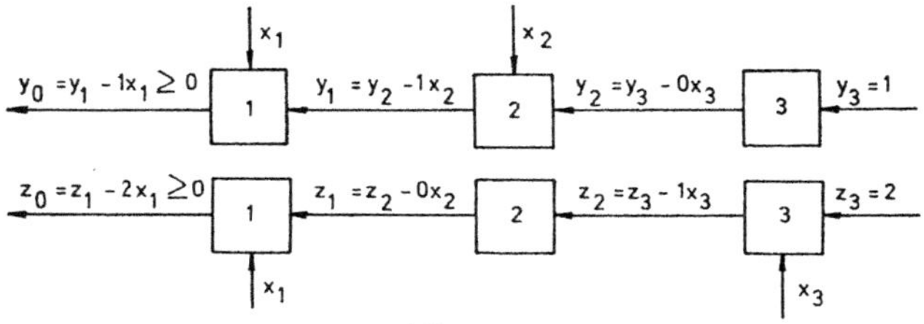

Fig. 29

Thus the fact that there were two decision variables per stage caused no trouble in this case. However, in large-scale problems with variables required to be integral, numerical solution—even computer solution—will become difficult or downright impracticable as the dimension of the decision vector x_n increases.

2. The *state variables* y_n may also be vectors in a DP problem because, in principle, each side condition will require a separate state variable.

Consider the linear problem[1]

$$\begin{aligned}
f = 4x_1 + 1x_2 + 1x_3 &= \max \\
1x_1 + 1x_2 \qquad &\leqslant 1 \\
2x_1 \qquad + 1x_3 &\leqslant 2,
\end{aligned}$$

to be interpreted as a problem of optimal capacity utilization with two capacity constraints. The variables x_n $(n = 1, 2, 3)$ are required

[1] The example is similar to one given in H. P. Künzi, O. Müller, and E. Nievergelt (1968), p. 98.

to be nonnegative integers. With a view to forward recursion the problem can be decomposed into a three-stage problem as illustrated in Fig. 29. For each of the two scarce resources successively consumed in the three production processes we introduce a particular state variable, y_n and z_n ($n = 0, 1, 2, 3$). The final state is given by $y_3 = 1$, $z_3 = 2$; for the initial state we have $y_0 \geqslant 0$, $z_0 \geqslant 0$ (i.e., the slack variables of the LP problem are to be nonnegative).

Clearly the variables can take the following values only:

x_1	x_2	x_3	y_n	z_n
0, 1	0, 1	0, 1, 2	0, 1	0, 1, 2

Solving by tabular computations (forward recursion) we have for the first stage

Stage 1		$f_1 = 4x_1$		$F_1(y_1, z_1)$	$x_1(y_1, z_1)$	$y_0(y_1, z_1)$	$z_0(y_1, z_1)$
y_1	$z_1 \diagdown x_1$	0	1				
0	0	**0**		0	0	0	0
0	1	**0**		0	0	0	1
0	2	**0**		0	0	0	2
1	0	**0**		0	0	1	0
1	1	**0**		0	0	1	1
1	*2*	0	**4**	4	*1*	*0*	*0*

(where the empty cells represent infeasible combinations), and for stages 2 and 3

Stage 2		$f_2 = 1x_2 + F_1$		$F_2(y_2, z_2)$	$x_2(y_2, z_2)$	$y_1(y_2, z_2)$	$z_1(y_2, z_2)$
y_2	$z_2 \diagdown x_2$	0	1				
0	0	**0 + 0**		0	0	0	0
0	1	**0 + 0**		0	0	0	1
0	2	**0 + 0**		0	0	0	2
1	0	0 + 0	**1 + 0**	1	1	0	0
1	1	0 + 0	**1 + 0**	1	1	0	1
1	*2*	**0 + 4**	1 + 0	4	*0*	*1*	*2*

Stage 3		$f_3 = 1x_3 + F_2$			$F_3(y_3, z_3)$	$x_3(y_3, z_3)$	$y_2(y_3, z_3)$	$z_2(y_3, z_3)$
y_3	$z_3 \diagdown x_3$	0	1	2				
1	*2*	**0 + 4**	1 + 1	2 + 1	4	*0*	*1*	*2*

The optimal policy is

$$\begin{array}{ccc} y_3 = 1 & & z_3 = 2 \\ & x_3 = 0 & \\ y_2 = 1 & & z_2 = 2 \\ & x_2 = 0 & \\ y_1 = 1 & & z_1 = 2 \\ & x_1 = 1 & \\ y_0 = 0 & & z_0 = 0 \end{array}$$

and the optimal return (total profit) is $F_3(y_3, z_3) = 4$.

The procedure used is a simple generalization of that used in the case of only one state variable per stage; the only difference is that the parametric stage solutions are now functions of both state variables, $x_n = x_n(y_n, z_n)$ and $F_n = F_n(y_n, z_n)$. The computations were simple enough and the fact that there were two state variables per stage presented no difficulties. But this was only because y_n and z_n were restricted to the values 0, 1 and 0, 1, 2 respectively so that we could do with $2 \cdot 3 = 6$ lines in the first two tables, each line corresponding to a feasible combination (y_n, z_n). If the right-hand sides of the restrictions in the LP problem had been 10 and 20, for example, each table would have required $11 \cdot 21 = 231$ rows, and the number of columns would have increased with the number of feasible values of the x_n. With a larger number of restrictions (state variables) we would be in an even worse position. In practice we can only hope to solve integer problems by dynamic programming when the number of decision variables per stage is very small (at most 4), even if a computer is applied.

This appears to be the most serious shortcoming of dynamic programming. To overcome this difficulty, methods have been developed by which the dimensionality of a given DP problem (the number of state variables) can be reduced, e.g. by use of Lagrange multipliers[1].

[1] See G. L. Nemhauser (1966), Ch. IV, or R. E. Bellman and S. E. Dreyfus (1962), Ch. II.

VIII. Infinite-Stage Problems

1. When the stage return functions and the transformations have the same form at all stages, that is,

$$r_n = r_n(y_{n-1}, x_n) = r(y_{n-1}, x_n)$$

and

$$y_n = t_n(y_{n-1}, x_n) = t(y_{n-1}, x_n)$$

for all n $(= 1, 2, \ldots, N)$, we will find that the contributions to total return obtained by adding further stages to the system will, under certain conditions, get smaller and smaller; the total return will tend to a finite limit as the number of stages (N) approaches infinity so that we have an *infinite horizon.* The same is true of the optimal x_n, which tends to become independent of the particular stage number, n.

This can be illustrated by the problem of Ch. VI. B. 4 above (pp. 91 f., optimal allocation of machines subject to breakdowns), where the stage returns and the transformation equations are

$$r_n = 3x_n + 7y_{n-1}, \qquad y_n = \frac{9}{10}y_{n-1} - \frac{7}{30}x_n \qquad (n = 1, 2, \ldots, N).$$

Using backward recursion (the initial state being given, $y_0 = 100$), the recursion equations all have the form

$$F_n(y_{N-n}) = \max(3x_{N-n+1} + 7y_{N-n} + F_{n-1}(y_{N-n+1})$$

$$(n = 1, 2, \ldots, N; \quad F_0 = 0) \tag{1}$$

where

$$0 \leqslant x_{N-n+1} \leqslant y_{N-n}.$$

We have already solved the problem for $N = 4$. Solving also for $N = 1$, 2, and 3 we obtain the following results[1]:

---

[1] **Exercise 28:** Perform the computations.

N	x_1	x_2	x_3	x_4
1	y_0			
2	y_0	$\frac{2}{3} y_0$		
3	0	$\frac{9}{10} y_0$	$\frac{2}{3} \cdot \frac{9}{10} y_0$	
4	0	0	$\left(\frac{9}{10}\right)^2 y_0$	$\frac{2}{3} \cdot \left(\frac{9}{10}\right)^2 y_0$

N	y_1	y_2	y_3	y_4	$F_N(y_0)$
1	$\frac{2}{3} y_0$				$10 y_0$
2	$\frac{2}{3} y_0$	$\left(\frac{2}{3}\right)^2 y_0$			$\frac{50}{3} y_0$
3	$\frac{9}{10} y_0$	$\frac{2}{3} \cdot \frac{9}{10} y_0$	$\left(\frac{2}{3}\right)^2 \cdot \frac{9}{10} y_0$		$22 y_0$
4	$\frac{9}{10} y_0$	$\left(\frac{9}{10}\right)^2 y_0$	$\frac{2}{3} \cdot \left(\frac{9}{10}\right)^2 y_0$	$\left(\frac{2}{3}\right)^2 \cdot \left(\frac{9}{10}\right)^2 y_0$	$\frac{134}{5} y_0$

The structure appears to be such that, for $N > 2$,

$$x_n = \begin{cases} 0 & \text{for } n = 1, 2, \ldots, N-2 \\ y_{n-1} & \text{for } n = N-1, N, \end{cases}$$

that is, all available machines are allocated to the second job (where profit is 7 per machine per stage) except at the last two stages (where profit is 10). Therefore

$$y_n = \left(\frac{9}{10}\right)^n y_0, \qquad r_n = 7 y_{n-1} = 7 \cdot \left(\frac{9}{10}\right)^{n-1} y_0$$

$$(n = 1, 2, \ldots, N-2)$$

$$y_{N-2} = \left(\frac{9}{10}\right)^{N-2} y_0, \qquad r_{N-1} = 10 y_{N-2} = 10 \cdot \left(\frac{9}{10}\right)^{N-2} y_0$$

$$y_{N-1} = \frac{2}{3} \cdot \left(\frac{9}{10}\right)^{N-2} y_0, \qquad r_N = 10 y_{N-1} = 10 \cdot \frac{2}{3} \cdot \left(\frac{9}{10}\right)^{N-2} y_0$$

and total return $F_N(y_0) = \sum_n r_n$ is

$$F_N(y_0) = 7\,y_0 \cdot \left(1 + \frac{9}{10} + \ldots + \left(\frac{9}{10}\right)^{N-3}\right) + 10\,y_0 \cdot \left(\frac{9}{10}\right)^{N-2} \left(1 + \frac{2}{3}\right) =$$

$$= 70 \cdot \left(1 - \left(\frac{9}{10}\right)^{N-2}\right) y_0 + \frac{50}{3} \cdot \left(\frac{9}{10}\right)^{N-2} y_0 =$$

$$= 70\,y_0 - \frac{160}{3} \cdot \left(\frac{9}{10}\right)^{N-2} y_0.$$

For N approaching infinity this expression converges to a limit $F(y_0)$,

$$F(y_0) = \lim_{N \to \infty} F_N(y_0) = 70\,y_0,$$

and the optimal policy $x_n(y_0)$ $(n = 1, 2, \ldots)$ approaches the limit

$$x(y_0) = 0.$$

The interpretation is that, as the number of stages goes to infinity, the last two stages at which $x_n \neq 0$ in the finite-horizon problem are put off indefinitely so that we have at all stages $x_n = 0$, $y_n = (9/10)^n\, y_0$, $r_n = 7\,y_{n-1}$, and therefore $\sum_n r_n = 7 \cdot 10\,y_0$[1].

2. In this case we were able to derive analytically the shape of $F(y_0)$ and the optimal policy $x(y_0)$ for the infinite-horizon problem. This is not always possible, however, and some *iterative numerical procedure* must be applied instead.

Consider the recursion equation (1), and substitute the transformation equation to get

$$F_n(y_{N-n}) = \max \left(3\,x_{N-n+1} + 7\,y_{N-n} + F_{n-1}\left(\frac{9}{10}\,y_{N-n} - \frac{7}{30}\,x_{N-n+1}\right)\right) \qquad (2)$$

where $0 \leqslant x_{N-n+1} \leqslant y_{N-n}$. For $N \to \infty$, $F_N(y_0)$ will approach $F(y_0)$, and $F_{N-1}(y_1)$ will approach $F(y_1)$, hence for $n = N \to \infty$ equation (2) becomes the *functional equation*

$$F(y_0) = \max_{0 \leq x_1 \leq y_0} \left(3\,x_1 + 7\,y_0 + F\left(\frac{9}{10}\,y_0 - \frac{7}{30}\,x_1\right)\right) \qquad (3)$$

---

[1] **Exercise 29:** Explain why, in the infinite-horizon problem, all machines are allocated to the job for which profit per machine per stage is *smaller* ($7 < 10$), and why the solution is different for the last two stages in the finite-horizon problem.

where the function F is unknown, to be determined together with $x_1(y_0)$. Since the recursion equations have the same form (2) for all n, (2) will be satisfied by the same function F for all n, and the optimal decision at each stage will be independent of the stage number, depending on the input state only ($x = x(y)$). Then the functional equation can be written

$$F(y) = \max_{0 \leq x \leq y} \left(3y + 7y + F\left(\frac{9}{10}y - \frac{7}{30}x\right)\right) \tag{4}$$

where y is the input state. The form of the function F is to be determined by numerical iteration, which also gives the optimal policy x.

One procedure is to start by setting $F_0(y) = 0$ as an initial guess and proceed by successive approximations as follows:

$$F_0(y) = 0$$

$$F_1(y) = \max_{0 \leq x \leq y} \left(3x + 7y + 0 \cdot \left(\frac{9}{10}y - \frac{7}{30}x\right)\right) \Rightarrow x(y) = y,\ F_1(y) = 10y$$

$$F_2(y) = \max_{0 \leq x \leq y} \left(3x + 7y + 10 \cdot \left(\frac{9}{10}y - \frac{7}{30}x\right)\right) \Rightarrow x(y) = y,\ F_2(y) = \frac{50}{3}y$$

$$F_3(y) = \max_{0 \leq x \leq y} \left(3x + 7y + \frac{50}{3} \cdot \left(\frac{9}{10}y - \frac{7}{30}x\right)\right) \Rightarrow x(y) = 0,\ F_3(y) = 22y$$

and so on. For $N \to \infty$, $F_N(y)$ will tend to the limit $F(y) = 70y$ and the optimal policy becomes $x(y) = 0$. However, this method of solving the infinite-stage problem by successive approximations—also known as *value iteration*, or approximation in return space—is not very efficient. The computations are seen to correspond to what we did above in solving the N-stage problem for $N = 1, 2, 3, \ldots$, and convergence is very slow in this case.

Another iterative procedure for solving the functional equation starts with a guess $x = x^0$ for the optimal policy and then successively improves the policy. Let $x^0(y) = y$ be the initial guess; substituting into the functional equation (4) we have

$$F^0(y) = 10y + F^0\left(\frac{2}{3}y\right) \tag{5}$$

which is to be solved for the unknown function $F^0(y)$. Now, we know (or can prove by induction) that F has the form $F = ay$ where a is a constant; hence we can set

$$F^0\left(\frac{2}{3}y\right) = \frac{2}{3} \cdot F^0(y)$$

in (5) and solve the equation to get

$$F^0(y) = 30y,$$

which is our first approximation of $F(y)$.

The next approximation, $F^1(y)$, is determined by applying F^0 to the right-hand side of the functional equation (4) and maximizing:

$$F^1(y) = \max_{0 \le x \le y} \left(3x + 7y + F^0\left(\frac{9}{10}y - \frac{7}{30}x\right)\right) =$$

$$= \max_{0 \le x \le y} \left(3x + 7y + 30 \cdot \left(\frac{9}{10}y - \frac{7}{30}x\right)\right)$$

which leads to

$$x^1(y) = 0, \quad F^1(y) = 34y.$$

The procedure is now repeated with $F^1(y) = 34y$ replacing $F^0(y) = 30y$ on the right-hand side of the functional equation:

$$F^2(y) = \max_{0 \le x \le y} \left(3x + 7y + 34 \cdot \left(\frac{9}{10}y - \frac{7}{30}x\right)\right)$$

which has the solution

$$x^2(y) = 0, \quad F^2(y) = 37.6y.$$

Proceeding in this fashion we get

$$x^3(y) = 0, \quad F^3(y) = 40.84y$$

and so forth. The procedure terminates when $F^{k+1}(y) = F^k(y)$ so that the functional equation is satisfied by $F^k(y)$, but in the present case we can stop at $k = 3$; clearly the coefficient of x in the decision function gets more and more negative, hence further iterations will give the same policy, $x(y) = 0$.

If we had started with the initial guess $x^0(y) = 0$—which would have been a natural choice in view of the finite-stage results above—we would have got

$$F^0(y) = 7y + F^0\left(\frac{9}{10}y\right), \qquad \text{i.e., } F^0(y) = 70y$$

and

$$F^1(y) = \max_{0 \le x \le y} \left(3x + 7y + 70\left(\frac{9}{10}y - \frac{7}{30}x\right)\right)$$

which has the solution

$$x^1(y) = 0, \quad F^1(y) = 70y = F^0(y).$$

The function $F(y) = 70y$ satisfies the functional equation; one iteration was sufficient and the optimal solution to the infinite-stage problem is

$$F(y_0) = 70y_0,$$

the optimal policy being $x_n(y_{n-1}) = 0$ for all n.

This procedure, known as *policy iteration* (approximation in policy space), is in general a more efficient method of solving the functional equation than value iteration.

3. In cases like the example above, it may be useful to formulate and solve the infinite-stage problem because the stages represent periods of given length and the number of such periods, N—i.e., the horizon—is arbitrary; there is no natural termination of the system in time.

But even if the horizon is finite, the infinite-stage problem may be relevant to the decision maker because it throws light upon the structure of the optimal finite-horizon policy. For very large N the computation of the optimal policy $x_n(y_{n-1})$ for all n will be a laborious task; it is much easier to compute the solution to the infinite-stage problem by policy iteration and apply it as an approximation. Doing this in the example above for $N = 4$, i.e., setting $x_n(y_{n-1}) = 0$ for $n = 1, 2, 3, 4$, we would get

$$y_n = \left(\frac{9}{10}\right)^n y_0 \qquad \text{for all } n$$

and the total return would be

$$\sum_{n=1}^{4} 7\,y_{n-1} = 7\,y_0 \cdot (1 + 0.9 + 0.9^2 + 0.9^3) = 24.073\,y_0$$

as against $(134/5)\,y_0 = 26.8y_0$ in the correct four-stage solution. A better approximation could be obtained by applying the infinite-stage solution for $n = 1, 2, 3$ and the finite-stage solution for the last stage, $n = 4$:

$$F_1(y_3) = \max_{0 \le x_4 \le y_3} (3x_4 + 7y_3), \qquad \text{i.e., } x_4(y_3) = y_3, \; F_1(y_3) = 10y_3.$$

For $x_1 = x_2 = x_3 = 0, \quad x_4 = y_3$ we get

$$y_n = \left(\frac{9}{10}\right)^n y_0 \quad (n = 1, 2, 3), \qquad y_4 = \left(\frac{9}{10}\right)^3 \cdot \frac{2}{3}\,y_0$$

and total return is seen to be

$$\sum_{n=1}^{3} 7\,y_{n-1} + 10\,y_3 = 26.26\,y_0.$$

If we used the infinite-state solution for $n = 1$ and 2 only, the solution would be identical with the correct 4-stage solution.

In order for the infinite-stage problem to be meaningful and solvable, the total return must obviously be bounded from above. The example above clearly satisfies this condition.

4. Another example is a replacement chain formed by identical repetition of the same investment[1] having the net present value

$$C(x) = \sum_{\tau=1}^{x} (4 - 0.5\,\tau) \cdot 1.08^{-\tau} - 12 + (11 - x) \cdot 1.08^{-x}$$

so that the total net present value of the chain is

$$f = C(x_1) + 1.08^{-x_1} C(x_2) + 1.08^{-(x_1+x_2)} C(x_3) + \ldots$$

where the lives $x_1, x_2, x_3, \ldots$ are required to be integers.

In the first DP approach to this problem (pp. 103–107) each investment of the chain represented a stage; the lives x_n were the decision variables and the transformation equations were $y_n = y_{n-1} + x_n$ (with the initial state $y_0 = 0$), the state variable y_n representing the sum of the first n lives (i.e., total time elapsed since the start of the chain). For a finite horizon of $N = 3$ stages we found the optimal policy to be $x_1 = x_2 = x_3 = 4$ years. Now what is the optimal policy in the infinite-horizon case, $N \to \infty$[2]?

Value iteration will not be an efficient procedure in this case. Calculating the optimal policy for $N = 1, 2, \ldots$ we find[3]:

N	x_1	x_2	x_3	x_4	x_5	x_6	...	F_N
1	4							2.413
2	4	4						4.187
3	4	4	4					5.491
4	3	4	4	4				6.507
5	3	3	4	4	4			7.313
6	3	3	3	4	4	4		7.953
⋮								⋮

Proceeding in this fashion, adding further links to the chain, we will find that for $N \geqslant 13$, the last three investments have economic lives

[1] Cf. Ch. VI. D above.

[2] The discount factor 1.08^{-x_n} ensures that the total return, f, is bounded from above.

[3] The procedure for adding further links to the chain and deriving the optimal policy is indicated on pp. 106 f.

of 4 years and the lives of the previous nine are 3 years each, while $x_n = 2$ years for $n = 1, 2, \ldots, N - 12$. (The total time horizon derived from this policy will be $T(N) = (N - 12) \cdot 2 + 9 \cdot 3 + 3 \cdot 4 = 2N + 15$ years for large N.) Thus, for $N \to \infty$ we have $x_n \to 2$, $F_N \to C(2) \cdot (1 + 1.08^{-2} + 1.08^{-4} + \ldots) = C(2)/(1 - 1.08^{-2}) = 10.718$ (and $T \to \infty$), but the convergence is slow.

Instead, we may try policy iteration. The functional equation clearly has the form

$$F(y) = \max_x \big(C(x) + 1.08^{-x} F(y + x)\big).$$

Let our first guess be, say, $x^0 = 4$. Then the first approximation of $F(y)$ will be determined by

$$F^0(y) = C(4) + 1.08^{-4} F^0(y + 4). \tag{6}$$

The unknown function F^0 can be determined by exploiting the fact that, if all investments have the same life x—as assumed in the first guess, $x = 4$—the net present value of the chain must be

$$C(x) \cdot (1 + 1.08^{-x} + 1.08^{-2x} + \ldots) = \frac{C(x)}{1 - 1.08^{-x}}$$

which is independent of y. This expression, with $x = 4$, is seen to be a solution to (6) for the unknown function F^0, so the first approximation of $F(y)$ is

$$F^0(y) = C(x) + 1.08^{-x} \cdot \frac{C(x)}{1 - 1.08^{-x}} = \frac{C(x)}{1 - 1.08^{-x}} = 9.107 \quad \text{for } x = 4.$$

Next, determine x^1 and F^1 by

$$\begin{aligned} F^1(y) &= \max_x \big(C(x) + 1.08^{-x} \cdot F^0(y + x)\big) \\ &= \max_x \left(C(x) + 1.08^{-x} \cdot \frac{C(x)}{1 - 1.08^{-x}}\right) \\ &= \max_x \frac{C(x)}{1 - 1.08^{-x}}; \end{aligned}$$

for integer values of x we have

x	1	2	3	4	...
$\dfrac{C(x)}{1 - 1.08^{-x}}$	6.750	*10.718*	10.418	9.107	...

i.e., the function is a maximum for $x = 2$ and we get

$$x^1 = 2, \qquad F^1(y) = \frac{C(x)}{1 - 1.08^{-x}} = 10.718 \quad \text{for } x = 2.$$

Further iterations will obviously give identical results. Since

$$x^2 = x^1 = 2, \quad F^2(y) = F^1(y) = 10.718$$

we have solved the problem. The optimal policy is $x_n = 2$ for all n when the horizon is extended to infinity and the solution to the functional equation is

$$F(y) = \frac{C(x)}{1 - 1.08^{-x}} = 10.718,$$

which is the limit of F_N in the table above for $N \to \infty$ [1].

For large N, even if the horizon is finite, we can therefore safely apply the solution to the infinite-horizon problem. The stationary policy $x_n = 2$ has the advantage of being simple as well as easier to compute. It is true that the optimal lives of the last investments of the finite chain will be somewhat longer, as we have seen, but this is not particularly relevant to the first decisions taken at $t = 0$, $t = x_1$, etc.—especially as the plan is more likely to be revised before expiration, the longer the horizon is. Moreover, although the planning horizon applied to practical problems is usually finite—an infinite horizon is rather in the nature of an abstraction—the planner is unlikely to be able to specify his horizon in terms of a particular value of N, as would be required for the determination of the optimal finite-horizon policy for the later stages.

Turning now to the second formulation of the replacement chain problem (pp. 107–113), where the years of the planning period represent stages and a decision has to be made at the beginning of each year whether to replace the equipment ($x_n = 1$) or keep it another year ($x_n = 2$), the optimal policy for an infinite horizon will clearly be the same; in terms of the decision variables of this approach, replacement every two years means that

$$x_1 = 2, \quad x_2 = 2, \quad x_3 = 1, \quad x_4 = 2, \quad x_5 = 1, \quad x_6 = 2, \ldots$$

i.e.,

$$x_n = \begin{cases} 2 \text{ for } n = 1 \\ 1 \text{ for } n \text{ odd } (n \neq 1) \\ 2 \text{ for } n \text{ even} \end{cases} \tag{7}$$

so that the optimal policy is a recurrent cycle having a period of 2 years.

[1] In this case, we might have done without the numerical iterations, for the guess $F = C(x)/(1 - 1.08^{-x})$—i.e., all lives are equal—is seen to satisfy the functional equation, leading to $x = 2$.

Value iteration can be performed as follows. For $N = 1$ we have $f_1 = r_1 + 1.08^{-1} \cdot 10$ (the equipment is sold at the end of the year at a price of 10), i.e.,

$y_0 \diagdown x_1$	1	2	F_1	x_1	y_1
0	2.241 + 9.259	3.241 + 9.259	12.500	2	1

For $N = 2$ we let the first table on p. 110 represent stage 2 after changing the subscripts:

$y_1 \diagdown x_2$	1	2	F_1	x_2	y_2
1			11.111	2	2
2			9.722	2	3
⋮			⋮	⋮	⋮

$y_0 \diagdown x_1$	1	2	F_2	x_1	y_1
0	2.241 + 10.288	3.241 + 10.288	13.529	2	1

(where $1.08^{-1} \cdot 11.111 = 10.288$); for $N = 3$ we use the first two tables on pp. 110f.; and so forth. This leads to the following optimal policies for $N = 1, 2, \ldots, 12$:

N	x_1	x_2	x_3	x_4	x_5	x_6	x_7	x_8	x_9	x_{10}	x_{11}	x_{12}	...	F_N
1	2													12.500
2	2	2												13.529
3	2	2	2											14.148
4	2	2	1	2										14.840
5	2	2	1	2	2									15.371
6	2	2	1	2	1	2								15.964
⋮														⋮
12	2	2	1	2	1	2	1	2	1	2	1	2	...	18.462

(where each of the F_N must be reduced by 12, the price of the initial equipment, to be comparable with the F_N of the first approach). In this case the optimal policy converges rapidly—in fact, immediately—to the infinite-stage policy, (7).

IX. Dynamic Programming under Risk

A. Risk and Multistage Optimization

1. The dynamic programming problems treated in the previous chapters were all cases of multistage decision making under *certainty* (deterministic problems): for each stage, the stage return r_n and the output state y_n were uniquely determined by the input state y_{n-1} and the decision x_n,

$$r_n = r_n(y_{n-1}, x_n)$$

$$y_n = t_n(y_{n-1}, x_n).$$

The situation is different if a stochastic variable s_n occurs in these functions. Then the return and the output state resulting from given y_{n-1} and x_n will also be stochastic variables. When the probability distributions of the s_n—assumed to be independent[1]—are known, however, we know the probabilities associated with the alternative possible values of r_n and y_n. Then we have a case of multistage optimization under *risk*[2].

2. By way of illustration, consider an inventory problem of the following type. At the beginning of period n, when the company has y_{n-1} units of the commodity in stock, x_n units are purchased (at a price of q_n per unit), which brings inventory up to $z_n = y_{n-1} + x_n$ units. During the period, s_n units are sold (at a price of p_n) so that inventory at the end of the period is reduced to $y_n = z_n - s_n$. Then the stage return is

$$r_n(x_n, s_n) = p_n s_n - q_n x_n$$

and the stage transformation is

$$\left.\begin{aligned} z_n &= y_{n-1} + x_n \\ y_n &= z_n - s_n \end{aligned}\right\} \Rightarrow y_n = t_n(y_{n-1}, x_n, s_n) = y_{n-1} + x_n - s_n,$$

cf. Fig. 30.

[1] This is clearly a prerequisite for decomposition.

[2] *Uncertainty*, as distinct from risk, is the case where the probabilities are unknown to the planner.

Now consider a simple two-period problem of this type where sales s_1 and s_2 are given in the form of probability distributions[1]:

s_1	Probability	s_2	Probability
10	0.6	10	0.5
20	0.4	20	0.5

Selling prices p_n and purchase prices q_n are $p_1 = 3$, $p_2 = 5$, $q_1 = 1$, $q_2 = 3$. The planning horizon is one year. The company buys x_1 units of the commodity at the beginning of the first six-month period and

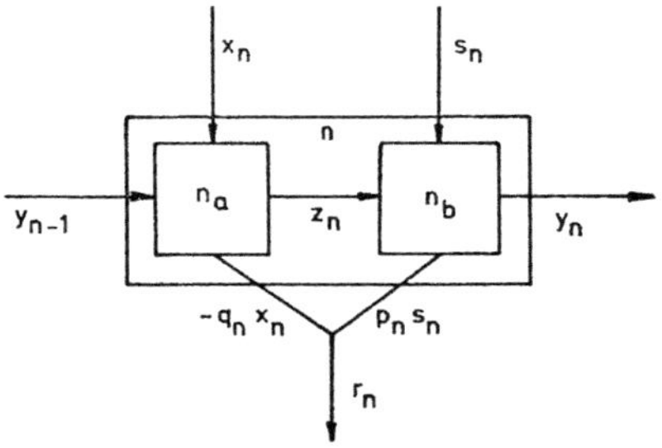

Fig. 30

x_2 units at the beginning of the second half-year. Purchases are made in lots of either 10 or 20 units. Unsold units at the end of the year (i.e., y_2) are realized at a clearance price of $p_3 = 2$ per unit.

This case can be illustrated by a decision tree as shown in Fig. 31. The company makes its decisions at y_0 and y_1, whereas the branches from z_1 and z_2 represent "decisions made by nature". The figures on the nodes and branches represent the values of the variables $(y_0, x_1, z_1, y_1, \ldots)$; the figures in brackets indicate the successive contributions to profit $(-q_1 x_1,\ p_1 s_1,\ -q_2 x_2,\ p_2 s_2,\ p_3 y_2)$. The stage returns are $r_1 = -1 x_1 + 3 s_1$ and $r_2 = -3 x_2 + 5 s_2 + 2 y_2$ (where $y_2 = y_1 + x_2 - s_2$).

There are ten possible paths from the root to the top. The total profit resulting from each path is easily calculated, but the company

[1] Cp. the problem demonstrated on pp. 93–95, where the s_n are known with certainty and the x_n (quarterly production) are determined such as to meet the sales requirements at minimum total costs of production and storage, and the next problem (pp. 95–97) in which the s_n are additional decision variables to be determined by the optimization. (It was only in the latter case that we had to introduce the intermediate state variables z_n.)

cannot simply choose the path of maximum profit because the two decisions it makes are not sufficient to define a particular path; the transition from y_0 to y_2 is subject to *risk*. We must therefore modify the criterion of optimality, assuming that the company's objective is to maximize *expected* profit.

The problem can now be solved by backward recursion. The input state of stage 2, y_1, can be either 0 or 10. Consider first $y_1 = 0$. If the

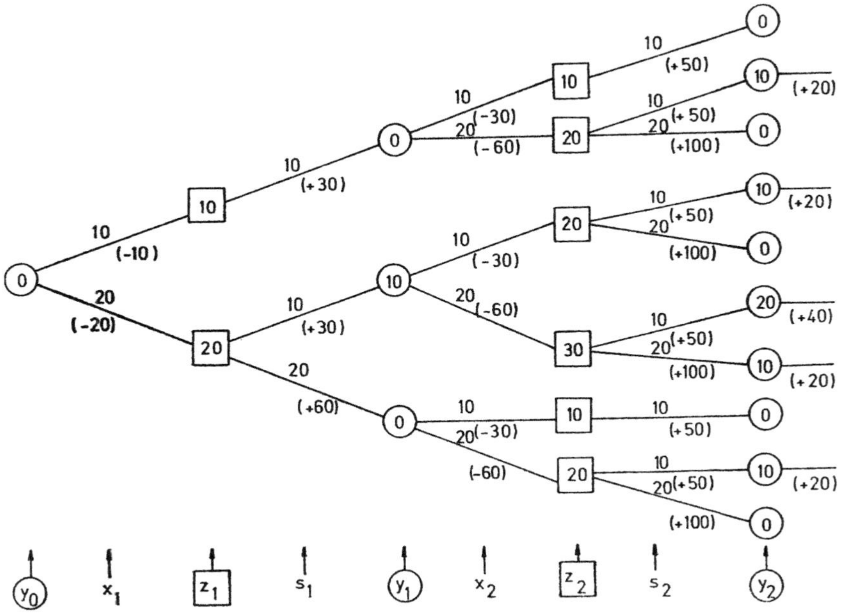

Fig. 31

company chooses the decision $x_2 = 10$, the return will be $f_1 = r_2(10, 10) = -30 + 50 = \mathit{20}$ (cf. Fig. 31). For $x_2 = 20$, the value of $r_2(x_2, s_2)$ will be either $r_2(20, 10) = -60 + 50 + 20 = 10$ or $r_2(20, 20) = -60 + 100 = 40$, depending on whether nature chooses $s_2 = 10$ or 20, the probabilities of which are both 0.5; hence the expected return in this case is $f_1 = 0.5 \cdot 10 + 0.5 \cdot 40 = \mathit{25}$. Therefore the best decision for $y_1 = 0$ is $x_2 = 20$ and we have $F_1(y_1) = 25$ for $y_1 = 0$. For the input state $y_1 = 10$ we have similarly $f_1 = 0.5 \cdot 40 + 0.5 \cdot 70 = \mathit{55}$ for $x_2 = 10$ and $f_1 = 0.5 \cdot 30 + 0.5 \cdot 60 = \mathit{45}$ for $x_2 = 20$, i.e., for $y_1 = 10$ we should choose $x_2 = 10$ and expect to get $F_1(y_1) = 55$.

Going back to stage 1, where $y_0 = 0$, the decision function is $f_2 = r_1 + F_1$. For $x_1 = 10$, the expected value of the decision function is $f_2 = -10 + 30 + F_1(0) = \mathit{45}$, whereas $x_1 = 20$ can lead to either

$y_1 = 10$ or $y_1 = 0$ with probabilities 0.6 and 0.4 respectively so that the expected value is $f_2 = -20 + 0.6(30 + F_1(10)) + 0.4(60 + F_1(0)) = 65$. The best choice is $x_1 = 20$, $F_2(0) = 65$.

This means that the company should buy $x_1 = 20$ units at the beginning of the first six-month period because this decision will lead to the maximum *expected* profit, $F_2 = 65$. The optimal decision at stage 2 will depend on how much it sells during the first six months, so the optimal purchase x_2 cannot be determined at the beginning of the year; nature's decision as to the value of s_1 is known only at the beginning of the second half-year period when the second lot is to be purchased. If nature has chosen $s_1 = 10$ so that $y_1 = 10$, the company buys $x_2 = 10$ units, whereas $s_1 = 20$ (i.e., $y_1 = 0$) leads to the decision $x_2 = 20$.

If the company follows these rules, the *actual* result will be one of the following four paths corresponding to the four possible combinations of nature's decisions[1]:

y_0	x_1	z_1	s_1	y_1	x_2	z_2	s_2	y_2	F_2 (profit)	Probability
0	20	20	10	10	10	20	10	10	50	$0.6 \times 0.5 = 0.3$
0	20	20	10	10	10	20	20	0	80	$0.6 \times 0.5 = 0.3$
0	20	20	20	0	20	20	10	10	50	$0.4 \times 0.5 = 0.2$
0	20	20	20	0	20	20	20	0	80	$0.4 \times 0.5 = 0.2$
										1.0

The *expected* value of the policy—the sum of the four values of F_2 weighted by their probabilities—is seen to be 65, but the *actual* profit earned will be either 50 or 80, the chances being even. The optimal policy boils down to this: the lots should be such that inventory at the beginning of each six-month period *after* purchase is sufficient to cover maximum sales, i.e., $z_1 = z_2 = 20$ or $x_1 = 20$, $x_2 = 20 - y_1$.

This way of solving the two-stage problem has the advantage of being flexible with respect to changes in the data. The first decision is based on estimated probability distributions of s_1 and s_2. If the estimates are revised at the end of the first six-month period—for example, if the probabilities are now estimated to be 0.3 and 0.7 for the two values of s_2—all we have to do is to revise the computation of $F_1(y_1, x_2)$ accordingly (for the value of y_1 actually realized), i.e., to determine x_2 such as to maximize expected profit for the remaining part of the planning period.

[1] **Exercise 30:** Illustrate by a decision tree, drawing only the relevant branches (cf. above).

B. Dynamic Programming and Markov Processes

1. We shall next consider a class of problems in which there is a finite number of possible states (the same for all stages) and the stage transformations are given by *transition probabilities* p_{ij} where i is the input state and j the output state. For example, if the input state is $i = 1$, the output state will be 1 or 2 with probabilities p_{11} and p_{12} respectively. The transition probabilities depend on the value of the decision variable (k), but for given k the probabilities p_{ij}^k are independent of the stage number. A given return r_{ij}^k is associated with each p_{ij}^k, representing the return from a stage transformation from state i to state j, given the decision $x_n = k$.

As an example, let a firm be planning its advertising policy for a period of four weeks. For simplicity assume that there are two possible states, $y_n = 1$ and 2, representing a high and a low sales level, and two policy alternatives (values of k), $x_n = 1$ (advertising) and $x_n = 2$ (no advertising). The transition probabilities are

p_{ij}^k	$k = 1$		$k = 2$	
	$j = 1$	$j = 2$	$j = 1$	$j = 2$
$i = 1$	0.8	0.2	0.6	0.4
$i = 2$	0.6	0.4	0.2	0.8

Thus, for example, if the firm was doing well in the previous week ($i = 1$), there is a sixty per cent probability that the sales level will also be high in the current week if the firm does not advertise; if it decides to advertise in the current week, the probability of success will be raised to eighty per cent.

The returns are based on the following data. Sales profits are 80 or 60 per week depending on whether the sales level is high or low, but if the firm chooses $k = 1$ an advertising cost of 7 must be deducted from these figures. Moreover, an extra cost of 8 is incurred if the level of production and sales is changed from one week to the next. This leads to the following returns:

r_{ij}^k	$k = 1$		$k = 2$	
	$j = 1$	$j = 2$	$j = 1$	$j = 2$
$i = 1$	73 (= 80 — 7)	45 (= 60 — 7 — 8)	80	52 (= 60 — 8)
$i = 2$	65 (= 80 — 7 — 8)	53 (= 60 — 7)	72 (= 80 — 8)	60

In a dynamic programming formulation, the problem clearly has to be solved by backward recursion. We shall number the stages in reverse order[1] so that stage $N = 4$ is put first (to the left) in the flow diagram, representing the first week. Stage n is shown in Fig. 32. The

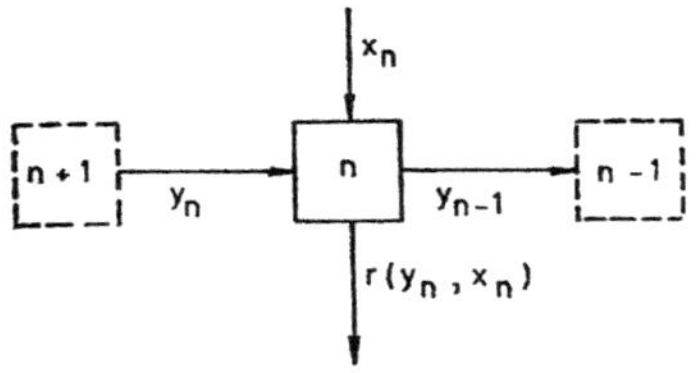

Fig. 32

transformation from $y_n = i$ to $y_{n-1} = j$ is given by the transition probabilities p_{ij}^k; r_n is the *expected* state return which has the same form for all n,

$$r_n = r(y_n, x_n) = r_i^k = p_{i1}^k r_{i1}^k + p_{i2}^k r_{i2}^k \qquad (i = y_n, k = x_n).$$

For stage 1 we have the decision function

$$f_1 = r_1 = r_i^k \qquad (i = y_1,\ k = x_1)$$

so that we get the table

$y_1 \diagdown x_1$	1	2	$F_1(y_1)$	$x_1(y_1)$
1	$0.8 \cdot 73 + 0.2 \cdot 45 = 67.4$	$0.6 \cdot 80 + 0.4 \cdot 52 = 68.8$	68.8	2
2	$0.6 \cdot 65 + 0.4 \cdot 53 = 60.2$	$0.2 \cdot 72 + 0.8 \cdot 60 = 62.4$	62.4	2

The decision function for stage 2 is the expected immediate return r_2 plus the expected value of F_1,

$$f_2 = r_i^k + p_{i1}^k F_1(1) + p_{i2}^k F_1(2) \quad (i = y_2,\ k = x_2),$$

and similarly for stages 3 and 4. The calculations are as follows.

$y_2 \diagdown x_2$	1	2	$F_2(y_2)$	$x_2(y_2)$
1	$67.4 + 0.8 \cdot 68.8 +$ $+ 0.2 \cdot 62.4$	$68.8 + 0.6 \cdot 68.8 +$ $+ 0.4 \cdot 62.4$	135.04	2
2	$60.2 + 0.6 \cdot 68.8 +$ $+ 0.4 \cdot 62.4$	$62.4 + 0.2 \cdot 68.8 +$ $+ 0.8 \cdot 62.4$	126.44	1

[1] This will turn out to be convenient later when the horizon is extended to infinity. Cf. pp. 153 f. below.

$y_3 \diagdown x_3$	1	2	$F_3(y_3)$	$x_3(y_3)$
1	$67.4 + 0.8 \cdot 135.04 + + 0.2 \cdot 126.44$	$68.8 + 0.6 \cdot 135.04 + + 0.4 \cdot 126.44$	200.72	1
2	$60.2 + 0.6 \cdot 135.04 + + 0.4 \cdot 126.44$	$62.4 + 0.2 \cdot 135.04 + + 0.8 \cdot 126.44$	191.80	1

$y_4 \diagdown x_4$	1	2	$F_4(y_4)$	$x_4(y_4)$
1	$67.4 + 0.8 \cdot 200.72 + + 0.2 \cdot 191.80$	$68.8 + 0.6 \cdot 200.72 + + 0.4 \cdot 191.80$	266.336	1
2	$60.2 + 0.6 \cdot 200.72 + + 0.4 \cdot 191.80$	$62.4 + 0.2 \cdot 200.72 + + 0.8 \cdot 191.80$	257.352	1

Thus, whatever the initial state y_4 (the sales level in the week before the planning period starts), it pays to advertise at the beginning of the first week ($x_4 = 1$). Because of the stochastic nature of the problem this decision is not sufficient to determine the output state y_3, which is the input state of the second week; y_3 is determined by nature's choice, which is known to the firm only at the beginning of the second week. However, the next optimal decision happens to be $x_3 = 1$ whether y_3 turns out to be $= 1$ or 2. The decision at the beginning of the third week is conditional on the value of y_2 chosen by nature (and known only when the decision is to be made), and similarly for the fourth week[1].

2. Now let the number of stages, N ($= 4$ in the example), approach infinity so that the problem becomes an infinite-horizon DP problem.

Since the return functions and the transformations are the same for every state, the optimal policy will tend to become independent of the stage number as further stages are added to the system. In the 4-week problem solved above we saw that the optimal policy was $x_n(y_n) = 1$ for $n = 3$ and 4, that is, it pays to advertize in all but the last two weeks, so we have reason to believe that the optimal policy with an infinite horizon is $x_n = 1$ regardless of the value of y_n.

That this is in fact so can be confirmed by *value iteration*. Extending the horizon to $N = 5, 6, \ldots$ weeks, adding further tables to the calcula-

[1] The generalization to any finite number of possible states—e.g., high, medium, and low level or, as an extreme case, the number of units sold—is obvious. Similarly there may be more than two alternative values of the decision variable x_n ($= k$), representing alternative amounts spent on advertising. However, the estimation of transition probabilities will soon become a formidable problem when the dimension of the DP problem is increased.

tions above, we will find that $x_5 = x_6 = \ldots = 1$ for either value of the initial state y_N; the first four tables are not affected.

However, in the present case we can do without further numerical computations, for it is easily shown by induction that if the optimal decision at stage n is $x_n(y_n) = 1$ for some n, i.e., if we have

$$67.4 + 0.8F_{n-1}(1) + 0.2F_{n-1}(2) > 68.8 + 0.6F_{n-1}(1) + 0.4F_{n-1}(2) \quad (1)$$

$$60.2 + 0.6F_{n-1}(1) + 0.4F_{n-1}(2) > 62.4 + 0.2F_{n-1}(1) + 0.8F_{n-1}(2) \quad (2)$$

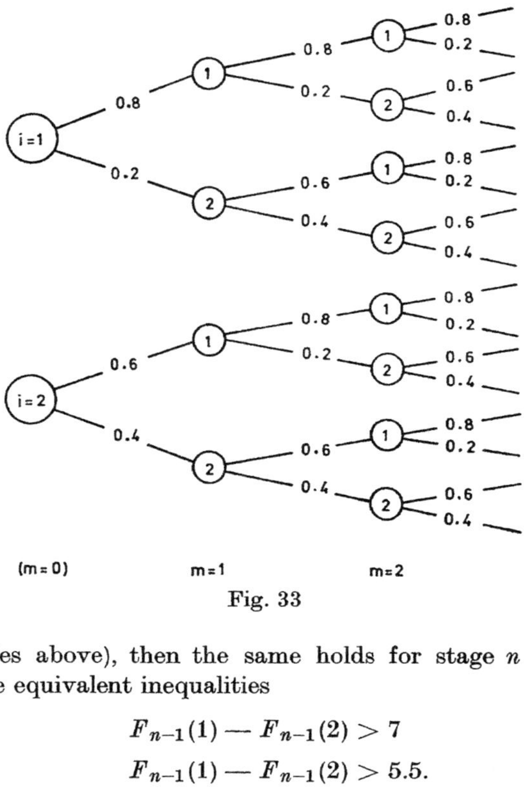

Fig. 33

(cf. the tables above), then the same holds for stage $n + 1$. (2)–(3) reduce to the equivalent inequalities

$$F_{n-1}(1) - F_{n-1}(2) > 7 \quad (3)$$

$$F_{n-1}(1) - F_{n-1}(2) > 5.5. \quad (4)$$

The left-hand sides of (1) and (2) are by definition equal to $F_n(1)$ and $F_n(2)$; their difference,

$$F_n(1) - F_n(2) = 7.2 + 0.2\left(F_{n-1}(1) - F_{n-1}(2)\right),$$

is greater than $7.2 + 0.2 \cdot 7 = 8.6$ [cf. (3)], hence (3)–(4) and the equivalent inequalities (1)–(2) are also satisfied with subscripts n so that the decision function for stage $n + 1$ is a maximum for $x_{n+1}(y_{n+1}) = 1$ for either value of y_{n+1}. Since we know from the tables above that

$x_n(y_n) = 1$ for $n = 4$ it follows that the same decision is optimal for $n = 5, 6, \ldots$, Q.E.D.

Thus, for $N \to \infty$ the optimal policy converges rapidly to the stationary policy

$$x(y) = 1 \quad \text{for} \quad y = 1, 2$$

as the last two stages are put off indefinitely.

3. Given this policy ($k = 1$), the *state probabilities* $\pi_m(j)$—i.e., the probabilities of the system being in state $j = 1$ and 2 respectively after m decisions—will depend on the transition probabilities p^1_{ij} and on the initial state, i (= 1 or 2). This can be illustrated by a tree as shown in Fig. 33.

A system of this kind is known as a *Markov chain*[1].

If the state at the beginning of the planning period is $i = 1$, the probabilities of the system being in state $j = 1$ or 2 after the first decision (i.e., at the beginning of the second week) are

$$\pi_1(1) = 0.8, \quad \pi_1(2) = 0.2.$$

After another decision we have

$$\pi_2(1) = p^1_{11}\,\pi_1(1) + p^1_{21}\,\pi_1(2) = 0.8 \cdot 0.8 + 0.6 \cdot 0.2 = 0.76$$
$$\pi_2(2) = p^1_{12}\,\pi_1(1) + p^1_{22}\,\pi_1(2) = 0.2 \cdot 0.8 + 0.4 \cdot 0.2 = 0.24.$$

Proceeding in this fashion, using the recursive expressions

$$\begin{aligned} \pi_m(1) &= p^1_{11}\,\pi_{m-1}(1) + p^1_{21}\,\pi_{m-1}(2) \\ \pi_m(2) &= p^1_{12}\,\pi_{m-1}(1) + p^1_{22}\,\pi_{m-1}(2), \end{aligned} \tag{5}$$

we have[2]

m	0	1	2	3	...	∞
$\pi_m(1)$	1	0.8	0.76	0.752	...	0.75
$\pi_m(2)$	0	0.2	0.24	0.248	...	0.25

[1] A *Markov process* is a stochastic process defined by transition probabilities p_{ij} which are independent of how the system came to be in state i. When the transitions occur at fixed intervals the process becomes a *Markov chain.*

If there is a choice among alternative matrices of transition probabilities p^k_{ij} ($k = 1, 2, \ldots$) and corresponding return matrices r^k_{ij} are introduced (as in the example above), we have a *Markov decision process.* This type of optimization model and the application of dynamic programming to it are due to Howard, cf. R. A. Howard (1960).

[2] The initial state $i = 1$ can be expressed by $\pi_0(1) = 1$, $\pi_0(2) = 0$ since the probability of the starting state being $= 1$ is unity ($i = 1$ is known with certainty), whereas $i = 2$ can be represented by $\pi_0(1) = 0$, $\pi_0(2) = 1$.

Similarly, for the initial state $i = 2$ we get

m	0	1	2	3	...	∞
$\pi_m(1)$	0	0.6	0.72	0.744	...	0.75
$\pi_m(2)$	1	0.4	0.28	0.256	...	0.25

For $m \to \infty$ *the state probabilities* $\pi_m(1)$ and $\pi_m(2)$ *converge to limits* $\pi(1)$ and $\pi(2)$ *which are independent of the initial state*[1],

$$\begin{aligned} \pi_m(1) &\to \pi(1) = 0.75 \\ \pi_m(2) &\to \pi(2) = 0.25 \end{aligned} \qquad \text{for } m \to \infty.$$

$\pi(1)$ and $\pi(2)$ are determined as the stationary solution of the system of simultaneous linear difference equations, (5). Deleting the subscripts we have

$$\pi(1) = 0.8\pi(1) + 0.6\pi(2)$$
$$\pi(2) = 0.2\pi(1) + 0.4\pi(2)$$

each of which gives

$$\pi(1) = 3\pi(2)$$

(there is only one independent equation); since the two probabilities must add up to unity we get

$$\pi(1) = 0.75, \quad \pi(2) = 0.25\,^{2}.$$

[1] A Markov chain having this property is called *ergodic*.

[2] In matrix notation, the recursive solution of (5)—as shown above for $m = 1, 2, 3$—can be written

$$\begin{aligned} \pi_1 &= \pi_0 P \\ \pi_2 &= \pi_1 P = \pi_0 P^2 \\ &\dots \\ \pi_m &= \pi_{m-1} P = \pi_0 P^m \end{aligned}$$

where $\pi_m = [\pi_m(1)\ \pi_m(2)]$ $(m = 0, 1, 2, \dots)$ and $P = \begin{bmatrix} 0.8 & 0.2 \\ 0.6 & 0.4 \end{bmatrix}$.

Now, since

$$P^m \to \begin{bmatrix} 0.75 & 0.25 \\ 0.75 & 0.25 \end{bmatrix} \qquad \text{for } m \to \infty$$

we have

$$\pi_m \to [1\ \ 0] \begin{bmatrix} 0.75 & 0.25 \\ 0.75 & 0.25 \end{bmatrix} = [0.75\ \ 0.25] \quad \text{for } i = 1$$

$$\pi_m \to [0\ \ 1] \begin{bmatrix} 0.75 & 0.25 \\ 0.75 & 0.25 \end{bmatrix} = [0.75\ \ 0.25] \quad \text{for } i = 2$$

where i is the initial state.

Thus, after a large number of decisions (m) the probabilities of the decision system being in states 1 or 2 will be 0.75 and 0.25 regardless of the initial state.

When the system has attained this state of equilibrium *the expected return per stage will also be constant and independent of the initial state.* If the input state is $i = 1$, the probability of which is $\pi(1)$, the expected return will be

$$r_1{}^1 = p_{11}^1 r_{11}^1 + p_{12}^1 r_{12}^1 = 0.8 \cdot 73 + 0.2 \cdot 45 = 67.4$$

whereas the input state 2 will give an expected return of

$$r_2{}^1 = p_{21}^1 r_{21}^1 + p_{22}^1 r_{22}^1 = 0.6 \cdot 65 + 0.4 \cdot 53 = 60.2.$$

Since the probabilities of $i = 1$ and 2 are $\pi\,(1)$ and $\pi\,(2)$, the total expected stage return will be

$$g = \pi\,(1)\, r_1{}^1 + \pi\,(2)\, r_2{}^1 = 0.75 \cdot 67.4 + 0.25 \cdot 60.2 = 65.60$$

whatever the initial state of the system[1].

4. The fact that the return per stage approaches a constant value g for a large number of stages suggests that the total expected return from n stages will approach a linear function of n,

$$F_n = g \cdot n + \text{constant} \qquad (\to \infty \text{ for } n \to \infty),$$

for large n; however, the value iteration tables above (pp. 140f.) indicate that $F_n\,(y_n)$ is greater for the initial state $y_n = 1$ than for $y_n = 2$, so the constant will depend on the initial state, $i\ (= y_n)$:

$$F_n\,(i) = g \cdot n + v_i \qquad (i = 1, 2). \tag{6}$$

These asymptotes of the total return function can be used to determine the optimal infinite-horizon policy by *policy iteration.*

The optimal decision at stage n—i.e., with n stages remaining—is determined by

$$F_n(1) = \max_{k=1,2} \left(r_1{}^k + p_{11}^k\, F_{n-1}(1) + p_{12}^k\, F_{n-1}(2)\right) \tag{7}$$

$$F_n(2) = \max_{k=1,2} \left(r_2{}^k + p_{21}^k\, F_{n-1}(1) + p_{22}^k\, F_{n-1}(2)\right). \tag{8}$$

Substitute (6), i.e.,

$$F_n\,(i) = g \cdot n + v_i, \quad F_{n-1}\,(i) = g \cdot (n - 1) + v_i \quad (i = 1, 2),$$

---

[1] **Exercise 31:** Describe the Markov chain resulting from the policy

$$x\,(y) = \begin{cases} 1 & \text{for } y = 1 \\ 2 & \text{for } y = 2, \end{cases}$$

and calculate $\pi\,(1)$, $\pi\,(2)$, and g for this policy.

into (7)–(8) and rearrange terms, recalling that $p^k_{i1} + p^k_{i2} = 1$ $(i = 1, 2)$ so that the term $g \cdot n$ cancels out; then we get

$$g = \max_{k=1,2} \left(r_1{}^k - v_1 + p^k_{11} v_1 + p^k_{12} v_2 \right) \tag{9}$$

$$g = \max_{k=1,2} \left(r_2{}^k - v_2 + p^k_{21} v_1 + p^k_{22} v_2 \right). \tag{10}$$

This means that, instead of maximizing the total return F_n (which tends to infinity for $n \to \infty$), we determine the optimal policy by maximizing the expected return per stage, g.

Policy iteration now starts with a guess for the optimal policy, say $k^0 = 1$ for $i = 1$ and 2 (corresponding to what we found above using value iteration). If this policy is the optimal one, we have by (9)–(10)

$$g = r_1{}^1 - v_1 + p^1_{11} v_1 + p^1_{12} v_2 = 67.4 - v_1 + 0.8\, v_1 + 0.2\, v_2 \tag{11}$$

$$g = r_2{}^1 - v_2 + p^1_{21} v_1 + p^1_{22} v_2 = 60.2 - v_2 + 0.6\, v_1 + 0.4\, v_2. \tag{12}$$

Because the probabilities in each equation add up to unity, (11)–(12) can be written as two equations determining g and $(v_1 - v_2)$; alternatively we can set e.g. $v_2 = 0$ and solve the equations to get

$$v_1{}^0 = 9, \quad v_2{}^0 = 0, \quad g^0 = 65.6.$$

This implies that our first approximations of $F_n(i)$ is

$$F_n{}^0(1) = 65.6n + 9, \quad F_n{}^0(2) = 65.6n + 0^1.$$

Next, to see whether the policy can be improved, we can apply these functions (with $n - 1$ replacing n) to the right-hand sides of (7)–(8) and maximize with respect to k. This is equivalent to maximizing the right-hand sides of (9)–(10) after substituting the values we have just found for v_1, v_2, and g:

$$g = \max\left((67.4 - 9 + 0.8 \cdot 9 + 0.2 \cdot 0), (68.8 - 9 + 0.6 \cdot 9 + 0.4 \cdot 0)\right) =$$
$$= \max(65.6, 65.2) = 65.6, \quad \text{i.e.,} \quad k^1(1) = 1$$

$$g = \max\left((60.2 - 0 + 0.6 \cdot 9 + 0.4 \cdot 0), (62.4 - 0 + 0.2 \cdot 9 + 0.8 \cdot 0)\right) =$$
$$= \max(65.6, 64.2) = 65.6, \quad \text{i.e.,} \quad k^1(2) = 1.$$

Thus the policy remains the same ($k^1 = k^0 = 1$ for $i = 1$ and 2), and so do v_1, v_2 and g as determined once more from (11)–(12), hence it is an optimal policy for the infinite-horizon Markov decision problem[2].

[1] Actually v_1 and v_2 are determined up to an additive constant. All we know (and all we are really interested in) is $v_1 - v_2 = 9$, i.e., the relative advantage of starting in state 1 rather than state 2.

[2] Cf. the value of g found above (p. 145) by weighting $r_1{}^1$ and $r_2{}^1$ by the stationary state probabilities $\pi(1)$ and $\pi(2)$ and adding.

If we had started by guessing $k^0(1) = 1$, $k^0(2) = 2$, equations (11)–(12) would have been replaced by

$$g = 67.4 - v_1 + 0.8 v_1 + 0.2 v_2$$
$$g = 62.4 - v_2 + 0.2 v_1 + 0.8 v_2$$

which for $v_2 = 0$ have the solution

$$v_1^0 = 12.5, \quad v_2^0 = 0, \quad g^0 = 64.9.$$

The policy can now be improved, for we have

$$g = \max\big((67.4 - 12.5 + 0.8 \cdot 12.5), (68.8 - 12.5 + 0.6 \cdot 12.5)\big) =$$
$$= \max(64.9, 63.8) = 64.9, \quad \text{i.e.,} \quad k^1(1) = 1$$
$$g = \max\big((60.2 + 0.6 \cdot 12.5), (62.4 + 0.2 \cdot 12.5)\big) =$$
$$= \max(67.7, 64.9) = 67.7, \quad \text{i.e.,} \quad k^1(2) = 1$$

so that $k^1 \neq k^0$ for $i = 2$. With the new policy we now have to solve (11)–(12); the solution is

$$v_1^1 = 9, \quad v_2^1 = 0, \quad g^1 = 65.6$$

and the next iteration (maximizing v_1 and v_2) leads to the same policy,

$$k^2(1) = 1 = k^1(1), \quad k^2(2) = 1 = k^1(2)$$

so that this policy is an optimal one[1].

5. In the problem above each value of the decision variable represented the same action regardless of the input state. For example, $k = 1$ meant "advertise" whether the firm was doing well last week or not ($i = 1$ or 2), or more specifically "spend the amount 7 on advertising"; $k = 2$ represented the absence of advertising, i.e., an advertising cost of 0, whatever the state.

Clearly the structure of the problem and the method by which it can be solved will remain the same if the decision $k = 1$ is given a different interpretation according as to whether last week's sales level was high or low. For example, the firm may choose to spend more on advertising if $i = 2$ than if $i = 1$ so that the alternative decisions are defined as follows, where c denotes advertising cost:

	$k = 1$ (advertising)	$k = 2$ (no advertising)
$i = 1$	$c = 7$	$c = 0$
$i = 2$	$c = 10$	$c = 0$

[1] **Exercise 32:** Perform the policy iteration routine with the initial guess

$$k^0(1) = 2, \quad k^0(2) = 1.$$

This would merely reduce the returns r_{21}^1 and r_{22}^1 by the amount 3; everything else in the example would remain the same (except that the corresponding transition probabilities are likely to change when more is spent on advertising).

Nor would it change the nature of the problem if $k = 1$ represented quite different actions for $i = 1$ and 2[1]:

	$k = 1$	$k = 2$
$i = 1$	advertising	no advertising
$i = 2$	research	no advertising

6. Another industrial example of a Markov decision process is the following[2]. An automobile manufacturer can find himself in one of two states: the current model was successful last year ($i = 1$) or not successful ($i = 2$). The alternative courses of action open to him are as follows:

	$k = 1$	$k = 2$
$i = 1$	keep the same model	try a new model
$i = 2$	copy the competitor's model	try a new model

If he can estimate transition probabilities p_{ij}^k and returns r_{ij}^k the decision problem can be solved by the methods demonstrated above.

An equally simple example is the following machine care problem[3]. A machine may be operating ($i = 1$) or failed ($i = 2$). There are two alternative decisions:

$i \diagdown k$	1	2
1	no maintenance	preventive maintenance
2	normal repair	express repair

The data needed for solving the decision problem for a given—finite or

[1] For a numerical example of this kind see H. P. Künzi, O. Müller, and E. Nievergelt (1968), pp. 82ff.

[2] Cf. G. Hadley (1964), pp. 460ff.

[3] Cf. M. J. Beckmann (1968), pp. 55ff.

infinite—horizon are the transition probabilities p_{ij}^k and net profits (less repair and maintenance costs) per period, r_{ij}^k.

Further applications of dynamic programming to Markov decision processes are replacement problems in which the states $i = 0, 1, 2, \ldots$ represent the age of the equipment and the decision $k = 1$ means "keep" whereas $k = 2, 3, 4 \ldots$ represent "buy new equipment aged $k - 2$", and certain problems of inventory planning[1].

[1] Cf. H. P. Künzi, O. Müller, and E. Nievergelt (1968), pp. 88—91 and 91—92.

X. Appendix:
The Recursion Procedure in Dynamic Programming

A. Stage Optimization

An optimization problem can be solved recursively by dynamic programming if it can be decomposed into a sequence of stage optimization problems. The procedure depends on the direction of the process (forward or backward recursion), and varies according as the final or the initial state or both are given.

Fig. 34 is a flow diagram of a multistage system (with stages 1, 2, . . ., N) arranged with a view to *backward* recursion. At stage n,

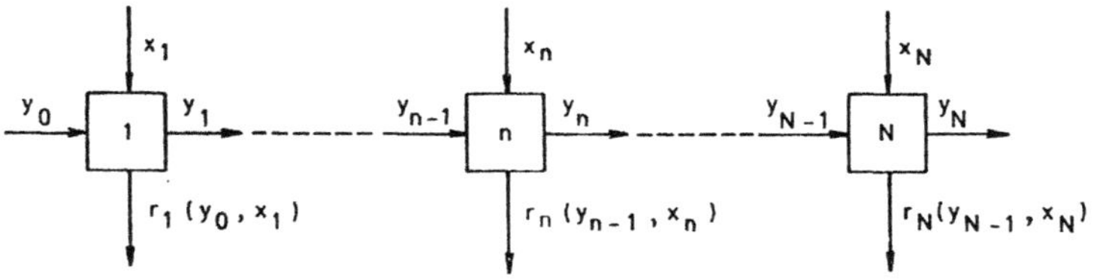

Fig. 34

the decision variable x_n transforms the input state y_{n-1} into the output state y_n, the transformation function being

$$y_n = t_n\,(y_{n-1}, x_n). \tag{1}$$

The state return is

$$r_n\,(y_{n-1}, x_n). \tag{2}$$

We first optimize stage N for parametric input y_{N-1}, and then proceed backwards through stages $N - 1$, $N - 2$, . . .

If the problem is to be solved by *forward* recursion, starting with stage 1, y_{n-1} becomes the output of stage n and y_n is the input state to be considered as a parameter when the stage is optimized. This illustrated in Fig. 35. Instead of (1) we must now use the inverse transformation equations

$$y_{n-1} = t_n^*\,(y_n, x_n) \tag{3}$$

and if the return functions too are to depend on the input state—now y_n—and x_n, we substitute (3) into (2) to get

$$r_n = r_n\left(t_n^*(y_n, x_n), x_n\right) = r_n^*(y_n, x_n); \qquad (4)$$

alternatively, we may use the return functions in the original form (2) with the inverse transformations (3) as side conditions.

For given *initial* state y_0, *backward* recursion is usually the easiest way of solving the problem, while *forward* recursion is computationally more efficient when the *final* state y_N is given.

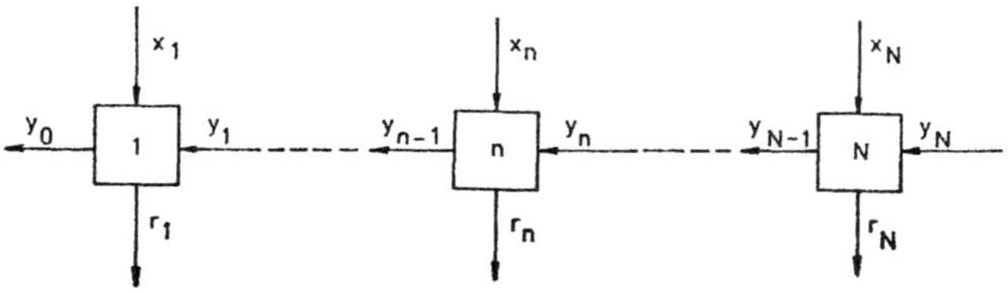

Fig. 35

B. Backward Recursion for Given Initial State

For given y_0, the backward recursion procedure starts with the optimization of stage N. The decision function is

$$f_1 = r_N(y_{N-1}, x_N) = \max_{x_N}$$

subject to whatever restrictions are imposed on the variation of x_N (e.g. a nonnegativity requirement $x_N \geqslant 0$, a capacity limitation $x_N \leqslant \leqslant b_N$, etc.). The transformation equation at this stage,

$$y_N = t_N(y_{N-1}, x_N),$$

does not as such impose any restriction but merely serves to calculate the resulting final output y_N; but if y_N is required to be nonnegative, the stage optimization has got to respect the restriction $y_N = = t_N(y_{N-1}, x_N) \geqslant 0$. Maximizing f_1 we get the optimal solution as a function of y_{N-1},

$$x_N = x_N(y_{N-1}), \quad F_1 = F_1(y_{N-1})$$

where F_1 is the maximum of f_1[1].

---

[1] The optimal x_N may be determined, for example, by $df_1/dx_N = 0$, or it may be a point on the boundary of the feasible region (e.g. $x_N = 0$ or $x_N = a$ if the region is defined by $0 \leq x_N \leq a$).

Proceeding to stage $N-1$, we maximize the decision function

$$f_2 = r_{N-1}\,(y_{N-2}, x_{N-1}) + F_1\,(y_{N-1}) = \max_{x_{N-1}}$$

(again subject to sign requirements and other stage restrictions), where y_{N-1} can be eliminated by means of the transformation equation (1) for $n = N-1$. The optimum solution at this stage will then depend on the parameter y_{N-2},

$$x_{N-1} = x_{N-1}\,(y_{N-2}), \quad F_2 = F_2\,(y_{N-2}).$$

Proceeding similarly, we eventually have for stage 1

$$f_N = r_1\,(y_0, x_1) + F_{N-1}\,(y_1) = \max_{x_1}$$

where $y_1 = t_1\,(y_0, x_1)$ so that the solution has the form

$$x_1 = x_1\,(y_0), \quad F_N = F_N\,(y_0).$$

Going back through the recursive system formed by the parametric optimum solutions and the transformation equations, starting with the given value of y_0, the total solution emerges:

$$\begin{array}{lcl} y_0 = y_0 \ \text{(given)} & \searrow & \\ & & x_1 = x_1\,(y_0) \\ & \swarrow & \\ y_1 = t_1\,(y_0, x_1) & \searrow & \\ & & x_2 = x_2\,(y_1) \\ & \swarrow & \end{array}$$

This procedure is well suited for *sensitivity analysis* of the way in which the total return F_N varies with the input state, y_0.

C. Forward Recursion for Given Initial State

The procedure now starts with stage 1, where the decision function is

$$f_1 = r_1\,(y_0, x_1)$$

subject to the inverse transformation

$$y_0 = t_1^*\,(x_1, y_1).$$

Because y_0 is given, there is *no optimization at the first stage*; the transformation equation implicitly determines x_1 in terms of y_1, which is now the stage input parameter, and the constant y_0[1]. Thus we have without maximization

$$x_1 = x_1(y_1), \quad F_1 = F_1(y_1).$$

Proceeding to stage 2 we have

$$f_2 = r_2(y_1, x_2) + F_1(y_1) = \max_{x_2}$$

where $y_1 = t_2^*(y_2, x_2)$; the solution to this parametric maximization problem has the form

$$x_2 = x_2(y_2), \quad F_2 = F_2(y_2).$$

The optimizations at stages 3, 4, ... are analogous. For stage N we get the optimum solution

$$x_N = x_N(y_N), \quad F_N = F_N(y_N).$$

If we knew the final state y_N, we could solve the total problem by going back through the system of stage solutions and transformations; but y_N is unknown. To determine the final state we must *maximize* $F_N(y_N)$ *with respect to* y_N[2,3],

$$F_N(y_N) = \max_{y_N},$$

and the optimal value of y_N now determines the entire system[4]:

$$y_N = y_N \quad \text{(optimal)} \searrow$$

$$\swarrow x_N = x_N(y_N)$$

$$y_{N-1} = t_N^*(y_N, x_N) \searrow$$

$$\swarrow x_{N-1} = x_{N-1}(y_{N-1})$$

This forward recursion procedure for given y_0 is well suited for exploring the effects of making the horizon longer, that is, the dependence of the total return $F_N(y_N)$ on the number of stages (N) in cases where it makes sense to add another stage to the sequence (as in value ite-

---

[1] The result would of course have been the same if we had used the return function in the form (4), i.e., $f_1 = r_1^*(y_1, x_1)$.

[2] This makes up for the missing maximization at stage 1; there are N maximizations in all to be performed just as in the backward procedure.

[3] The maximum condition may have the form $dF_N/dy_N = 0$, or it may be $y_N = 0$ (in case y_N is required to be ≥ 0).

[4] If we wish to keep y_0 as a parameter in the solution instead of substituting the given value, we get at the first stage $x_1 = x_1(y_0, y_1)$, $F_1 = F_1(y_0, y_1)$. y_0 will then automatically be carried over to the next stages, so we end up with $x_N(y_0, y_N)$ and $F_N(y_0, y_N)$.

ration). If forward recursion is not possible (because the transformations cannot be inverted), value iteration is most conveniently carried out by numbering the stages in reverse order as shown in Fig. 36 (which is identical with Fig. 35, only read from right to left).

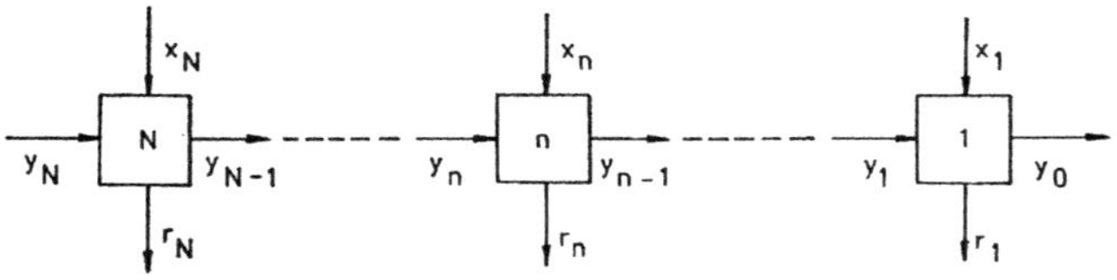

Fig. 36

Having determined the stage optima $x_1(y_1), \ldots, x_N(y_N)$—in that order—we find the solution as follows:

$$y_N = y_N \quad \text{(given)} \searrow$$

$$\swarrow x_N = x_N(y_N)$$

$$y_{N-1} = t_N(y_N, x_N) \searrow$$

$$\swarrow x_{N-1} = x_{N-1}(y_{N-1})$$

which is backward recursion for given initial state, now called y_N.

D. Forward Recursion for Given Final State

For given final state y_N, the forward recursion procedure is symmetrical with backward recursion for given y_0 (section B above); they differ only in the order in which the stages are optimized. For stage 1 we have

$$f_1 = r_1(y_0, x_1) = \max_{x_1}$$

where

$$y_0 = t_1^*(y_1, x_1);$$

the solution has the form

$$x_1 = x_1(y_1), \quad F_1 = F_1(y_1).$$

Proceeding through stages 2, 3, . . . we end up with

$$x_N = x_N(y_N), \quad F_N(y_N).$$

There is a maximization at each stage and the total solution is determined recursively, starting with the given y_N.

E. Backward Recursion for Given Final State

This procedure is symmetrical with forward recursion for given initial state (section C above). The decision function for stage N,

$$f_1 = r_N\,(y_{N-1}, x_N),$$

and the transformation equation

$$y_N = t_N\,(y_{N-1}, x_N)$$

determine x_N as a function of the parameter y_{N-1} for given y_N,

$$x_N = x_N\,(y_{N-1}), \quad F_1 = F_1\,(y_{N-1}),$$

so that there is *no maximization at stage N*. Maximizing f_n for $n = 2, 3, \ldots, N$ we end up with

$$x_1 = x_1\,(y_0), \quad F_N = F_N\,(y_0)$$

where *F_N is to be maximized with respect to the unknown initial state y_0*. (Thus there are N maximizations to be performed in the procedure.) When y_0 has been determined, everything else follows recursively.

F. Given Initial and Final States

When y_0 and y_N are both given, backward and forward recursion are quite symmetrical. The case differs from those dealt with above in that there are *only $N - 1$ maximizations*; there is no optimization at the first step of the computations (stage N or stage 1) and this is not made up for by a final maximization with respect to y_0 or y_N since they are both given. This reflects the fact that the system has one parameter less when both the final and the initial state are given.

Answers to Exercises

Chapter II

1. Substituting $x = 3 - x'$ into the objective function and maximizing subject to $x \geqslant 0$, $x' \geqslant 0$, the same four solutions emerge.

3. The solution is $v_1 = 2$, $v_2 = 3$. The multipliers have the values 5/2 and 3/2.

Chapter III

4. Using the six slack variables as the initial basis we get the optimal solution (which is degenerate) in the third tableau.

5. Replacing (2) by

$$\begin{aligned} x_1 &= u_1 + u_2 \\ 0 &\leqslant u_1 \leqslant 2 \\ 0 &\leqslant u_2 \leqslant 3 \\ f_1{}^* &= 6u_1 + 1u_2 \end{aligned}$$

and solving as indicated, the fourth tableau yields the approximate solution $u_1 = 2$, $u_2 = 1$, $v_1 = 2$, $v_2 = 0$, $f^* = 25$.

6. With an initial basis consisting of the two slack variables and the special variables z_1 and z_4 the fourth tableau gives the (degenerate) solution.

Chapter IV

8. Q_1 is positive definite, the values of the determinants being 26 and 64. Q_2—which is the negative of Q_1—is negative definite (determinant values -26 and 64). Q_3 is neither positive nor negative definite since both determinants are negative (-26 and -17); cf., e.g., $Q_3(1, 1) = -4$, $Q_3(1, 2) = 2$.

9. y_1 will replace x_1 in the basis, resulting in a solution where $u_1 y_1 \neq$ $\neq 0$; similarly for the other three variables.

12. The values of the determinants being—0.25 and $0.25 \cdot 0.75$, the quadratic form in (34) is negative definite.—Assuming the second side condition to be binding we get $x_1 = 640/7$, $x_2 = 200/7$, which is a feasible solution. The multiplier u_2 is positive ($= 190/7$). Hence the solution is optimal.

13. The solution is $x_1 = 3$, $x_2 = 2$, $u_1 = 2$, $u_2 = 0$.

14. The solution is $s_1 = x_1 = 12$, $s_2 = 20$, $x_2 = 24$.

15. For constant prices, the profit function will be linear and it clearly pays to produce $x_1 = 15$ (and $x_2 = 30$); selling less than the quantities produced will reduce sales revenue without reducing the cost of production. This is not so when prices are decreasing functions of the quantities sold because (in the example) the marginal revenue obtained from selling a unit more of the second commodity becomes negative for $s_2 > 20$.

16. The solution is (Tableau VI) $x_1 = 600$, $x_2 = 700$, $x_3 = 800$, $x_4 = 900$, $c = 11{,}800$.

Chapter V

17. df/dy_0 is the marginal increase in total profit for a unit increase in the capacity y_0, i.e., the shadow price of an additional unit of capacity (the maximum amount the firm would pay for another machine hour per period—or the opportunity cost of not using the "last" machine hour, in terms of forgone profit).

Chapter VI

20. The system has one parameter less when both the final and the initial state are given, and therefore requires one optimization less for the determination of the parameters (x_n and y_n).

21. The solutions in the three cases are

	t_1	u	t_2	v	C
(a)	2.6833	2.2361			32.6839
(b)			3	2	32.8800
(c)	1.1305	2.2361	3	1.1574	32.5609

23. Going back through the tables we get:

y_3	x_3	y_2	x_2	y_1	x_1	
6	0	6	3	3	3	(9^0)
6	1	5	2	3	3	(8^0)
6	1	5	3	2	2	(5^0)
6	2	4	1	3	3	(7^0)
6	2	4	3	1	1	(3^0)
6	3	3	0	3	3	(6^0)
6	3	3	1	2	2	(4^0)
6	3	3	2	1	1	(2^0)
6	3	3	3	0	0	(1^0)

26. The problem can be formulated as follows:

$$f = 5x_1 + 11x_2 + 8.5x_3 = \max$$
$$2x_1 + 4x_2 + 3x_3 \leqslant 20$$
$$x_j \geqslant 0 \text{ and integer } \quad (j = 1, 2, 3).$$

27. One unit of each item reduces y_3 by $2 + 4 + 3 = 9$ lbs., x_n now being redefined as the number of units of the nth item in excess of one. Then $y_3 = 11$, whereas y_2 can take the values 11, 8, 5, and 2 (for $x_3 = 0$, 1, 2, and 3). y_1 cannot be greater than 11 and x_1 cannot exceed 5. The first two stage tables are reduced accordingly; in the third table, $y_3 = 20$ is replaced by $y_3 = 11$. There are two optimal solutions:

x_1	x_2	x_3
0	2	1
1	0	3

To get the total number of each item in the knapsack these numbers must be increased by 1.

Chapter VIII

29. The greater profit coefficient is more than offset by the larger probability of breakdown which will reduce profits in future periods—except at the end of the horizon where this consideration no longer counts.

Chapter IX

31. The relevant transition probabilities are in this case

p_{ij}	$j = 1$	$j = 2$
$i = 1$	0.8	0.2
$i = 2$	0.2	0.8

The state probabilities are for the initial state $i = 1$

m	0	1	2	3	...	∞
$\pi_m(1)$	1	0.8	0.68	0.608	...	0.5
$\pi_m(2)$	0	0.2	0.32	0.392	...	0.5

and for $i = 2$

m	0	1	2	3	...	∞
$\pi_m(1)$	0	0.2	0.32	0.392	...	0.5
$\pi_m(2)$	1	0.8	0.68	0.608	...	0.5

where the stationary solution is determined by

$$\pi(1) = 0.8\pi(1) + 0.2\pi(2)$$

$$\pi(2) = 0.2\pi(1) + 0.8\pi(2)$$

[each of which gives $\pi(1) = \pi(2)$] and by the condition that the probabilities must add up to unity. The total expected stage return will be

$$g = \pi(1) \cdot r_1{}^1 + \pi(2) \cdot r_2{}^2 \quad \text{where} \quad r_1{}^1 = 67.4,\ r_2{}^2 = 62.4,$$

i.e., $g = 64.9$.

32. This guess leads to

$$v_1{}^0 = 8.6, \quad v_2{}^0 = 0, \quad g^0 = 65.36$$

$$k^1(1) = 1, \quad k^1(2) = 1$$

$$v_1{}^1 = 9, \quad v_2{}^1 = 0, \quad g^1 = 65.6$$

$$k^2(1) = 1, \quad k^2(2) = 1,$$

so that further iterations are unnecessary.

GPSR Compliance

The European Union's (EU) General Product Safety Regulation (GPSR) is a set of rules that requires consumer products to be safe and our obligations to ensure this.

If you have any concerns about our products, you can contact us on ProductSafety@springernature.com

In case Publisher is established outside the EU, the EU authorized representative is:

Springer Nature Customer Service Center GmbH
Europaplatz 3
69115 Heidelberg, Germany

Batch number: 09661801

Printed by Printforce, the Netherlands